Birds Etc View Of
Dodge 1879 City
Ford Co.
Kan.

Ford Co. Court House
1879

DODGE CITY

UP THROUGH
A CENTURY
IN STORY
AND PICTURES

by Fredric R. Young

Contents

AND ACKNOWLEDGEMENTS

"All of history, so far as it is not supported by contemporary evidence is romance."
[*Samuel Johnson, in Boswell's* Tour to the Hebrides, *1773*]

Is Dodge City's colorful history romance or fact? Did it rightfully deserve to be called, "The wickedest little city in America," or was this the invention of an overimaginative dime novelist?

The search for contemporary evidence of Dodge City's history leads one at last to its newspapers. Kansas newspapers in the 1870's and 1880's were unique in their journalistic style, and Dodge City's were in a class of their own.

To its founders and its pioneer newspaper editors, Dodge City was in the heart of the Far West — geographically and philosophically. In Western tradition these frontier newspapermen set their type with candor, labeling their enemies "sons of bitches" with no apologies. Their use of the vernacular mixed with the Victorian writing style of the period makes entertaining reading.

Criminals were not imprisoned, they were sent to the "regions of the unjust" where they "languished" in the "dog house." Cowboys did not fight, they "closed in deadly combat." The loser of the battle was not run out of town, he "shook the dust of the city from his feet by request." Even if the fight was missed by the reporter it rated a colorful review in the weekly edition: "The slugology racket loomed up like five aces in a 'deck of humps' last Sunday night. Several peacemakers tried to intercede, but were knocked out of time by the festive sluggers. The result was one head worth $700, with several others ranging in value from $250 upwards. The 'unpleasantness' occurred while ye reporter was in his virtuous bed and therefore no reliable particulars are at hand."[1]

A female victim of the "slugology racket" woefully appeared in police court: "Her starboard eye was closed, and a lump like a burnt bisquit ornamented her forehead."[2]

Some descriptions neared poetry: "The merry music of dancing shoes mingling in sweet concord with the plaintiff [sic] strains of heavenly music floated gracefully over the moon-silvered waters of the raging Arkansas."[3] And some poetry beggared description:

> While there's strength in the whisky,
> Or snap in the gin,
> My heart will continue
> To take it all in.[4]

The early Dodge City newspapers are a helpful source of historical information for nothing escaped their editors' notice: "NEWS! — Mr. Harry E. Gryden has a new overcoat."[5] "The first herds of through cattle are expected to arrive about the tenth of May. . . . The festive house fly has thawed out and takes his meals regularly along with the rest of us."[6] Whenever possible this book attempts to tell its story in the words of Dodge City's editors, Dan Frost, Lloyd Shinn, Nick Klaine, and others. Their episodes sound fictional when written in modern prose; taken directly from the early newspaper accounts, their stories lend authenticity to the claim that "Kansas has but one Dodge City,"[7] . . . "a synonym for all that is wild, reckless, and violent; Hell on the Plains."[8]

Many confusions about Dodge City arise from carelessness in dates — failure to remember that the town of 1874 is not that of 1878; Dodge City in 1880 differed greatly in 1887. For this reason episodes are in approximate chronological order. Materials are based on primary sources — diaries, newspapers, and public documents — when possible. You will find some "well-known facts" about Dodge City missing. The truth about its early days is far more violent, exciting, and "romantic" than the fiction.

Three books were used extensively for reference and background. Stanley Vestal's *Queen of the Cowtowns, Dodge City* (1952) is full of inaccuracies and minor distortions, but is still the most entertaining book about Dodge City. Two recent publications are the most accurate. Miller and Snell's *Why the West Was Wild* (1963) is an excellent reference and contains many excerpts from early Dodge City newspapers. Robert R. Dykstra's *The Cattle Towns* (1968) is a social history of Kansas cattle towns. Its highly accurate reconstruction of the social factors at work in Dodge City is revealing and helpful in understanding the "wicked little city."

I am indebted to a great many persons for aid in the preparation of this volume. I am especially indebted to Joseph W. Snell of the Kansas State Historical Society, Topeka, whose interest and enthusiasm helped over the rough spots, and whose knowledge of Dodge City's history is unequalled. Mrs. Opal Harris and Mrs. Jean Sinclair of Boot Hill Museum in Dodge City, and Mrs. Lola Harper went out of their way to furnish information, aid, and encouragement, and to do the difficult and unexciting work entailed in this project. Special thanks are due to Mrs. Betty Braddock whose research of pre-Dodge City history covered an area unfamiliar to me, and to Ray Pierce, my guide through a forest of words, print, and typographic mysteries.

The photographic reproductions were made possible mainly by the Kansas Historical Society and Boot Hill Museum. Kansans are fortunate to have one of the finest state historical societies, headed by Nyle H. Miller, executive director. Dodge City has a fine museum of its own. It is a young, self-supported organization whose research efforts and photograph collection have too often been overshadowed by its more popular museum displays and cowtown variety show. This book would not have been possible without the aid of these two organizations.

Financial support for this project came from Dodge City Centennial, Inc., James A. Williams, president, Ross D. Hogue, treasurer, and Boot Hill Museum, Inc., George R. Henrichs, executive director. I wish also to thank Noel Ary, G. W. Carter, Mrs. Juliet Denious, John Drake, Miss Lois Flanagan and the staff of the Dodge City Public Library, Mrs. Mary Gamble, Victor Hull, Mrs. Leila F. Johnson, James S. Maag, Art Morenus, Mrs. Beatrice McClure, Philip Newman, Mrs. Rossia B. Noland, Mrs. Jane R. Robison and the staff of the Cultural Heritage Center of Dodge City, Mrs. Trella Schulteis, David K. Strate, Boyd L. Strickland, Violet Watson, and Mrs. Donna Whitson. To the many others who assisted unselfishly — forgive my omissions and accept my thanks.

Fredric R. Young
Dodge City, Kansas
March 3, 1972

Chapter I
A BRANCH IN THE TRAIL

Francisco Vasquez de Coronado found no fabulous golden cities on his search north from Mexico across the plains into the heart of the American continent in 1540 and 1541. He did find, according to Juan Jaramillo who kept a journal of that quest, "a country of fine appearance the like of which I have never seen anywhere in our Spain, in Italy, or in any part of France. . . . It is not a hilly country, but has table-lands, plains, and charming rivers with fine waters. It greatly pleased me, and I am of the belief that it will be productive of all sorts of commodities." Across this "pleasing country" roamed millions of native bison or buffalo, darkening the prairies as far as the eye could see. And ever in pursuit of this roaming commissary were the Indians.

Traveling north-northeast by the needle Coronado, his thirty mounted men, six foot soldiers, some attendants, and Father Juan de Padilla, came to a "large stream" (the Arkansas) on St. Peter's and Paul's day in 1541. After crossing to the north bank of the river the Franciscan missionary, Padilla, and the men celebrated Mass on the highest of the hills and named the river in honor of the two saints.

This natural crossing used by buffalo, Indians, Coronado's expedition, and later wagon trains is in Ford County between Fort Dodge and the city of Ford. Since 1944 a crude wooden cross has marked the "highest of the hills" which now are almost a mile north of the meandering river bed. The Coronado bridge spans the river near this crossing.

For more than two centuries Indians continued to roam the plains and hunt the buffalo. A few Spanish and French expeditions found their ways into the heartland, mapping the area and claiming it for their kings. Only bits of southwest history were recorded until 1804 when Baptiste LaLande, a French trader, made a trip with a train of pack mules from Kaskaskia, Illinois, to Santa Fe following the most direct route to the Southwest, the north bank of the Arkansas River. Soon after, Zebulon Pike took the same path to survey the United States acquisition, the Louisiana Purchase.

In 1821 William Becknell and a small party left Franklin, Missouri, with a train of mules laden with merchandise to trade with Indians. It was autumn and the Indians had gone south of the Arkansas. Nearing the present site of LaJunta, Colorado, without having done any business, Becknell turned southward toward

Coronado marched into central and western Kansas in the summer of 1541. These Spanish conquistadores, in their search for the gold of Quivira, were led by an Indian known as "the Turk." Christianity first reached the Dodge City area with this trek into Kansas. A wooden cross (left) has been placed high on the hill overlooking the site of Coronado's Arkansas River crossing, six miles east of Dodge City, to commemorate the religious service held there in 1541.

the headwaters of the Canadian River in search of the Indians. The traders were surprised by a small troop of Mexican soldiers and fully expected to be arrested. But the soldiers told them that Mexico had won its independence from Spain and urged them to take the goods to Santa Fe. A tremendous profit was quickly made with payment in Spanish silver. Becknell returned to Franklin and his report of the venture was so enthusiastic that the next year a caravan of wagons made the trip. News that New Mexico was open to Americans spread like a contagion and a caravan trade opened that was to continue for more than forty years. The Santa Fe Trail was the principal trade route to the Southwest until the coming of the railroad.

Near the present site of Dodge City the trail split. The more commonly used branch continued up the north bank of the Arkansas to Bent's Old Fort, between the present towns of Las Animas and LaJunta, Colorado. From there the trail turned southwest to Trinidad, pulled its way over Raton Pass, and on to Santa Fe.

For those who were willing to risk the dangers and hardships, a shorter route, blazed by Becknell in 1822, crossed the river near Dodge City and struck southwest across the sandhills toward the Cimarron River. Water holes were scarce, fifty or more miles apart, and the ground bore few visible traces of a trail.

4

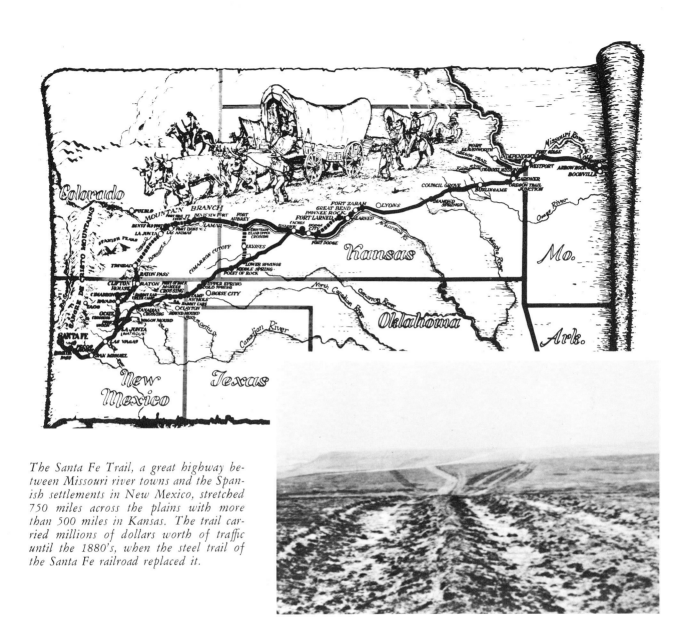

The Santa Fe Trail, a great highway between Missouri river towns and the Spanish settlements in New Mexico, stretched 750 miles across the plains with more than 500 miles in Kansas. The trail carried millions of dollars worth of traffic until the 1880's, when the steel trail of the Santa Fe railroad replaced it.

The ruts of Santa Fe Trail tracks, nine miles west of Dodge City, are the largest continuous stretch of clearly defined tracks along the entire route of the trail. These preserved wagon ruts symbolize the unending American desire to open new frontiers.

Considering that a caravan traveled twenty or fewer miles a day, the hard-pressed animals pulled their loads without water for almost three days. However, to those traveling this route the fear of Indian attacks caused a greater concern than lack of water. At a spring on the Cimarron on May 27, 1831, the mountain man and pathfinder, Jedediah Smith was killed by Indians. His brother Austin Smith wrote home to his father, "Your son Jedediah was killed on the Semerone [sic] the 27th of May on his way to Santa Fe by the Curmanch [sic] Indians, his party was in distress for water, and he had gone alone in search of the above river which he found, when he was attacked by fifteen or twenty of them. . . ." In spite of the hazards the dry route was preferred by many traders because no mountains had to be crossed and the distance was somewhat shorter.

Dedication ceremonies, September 30, 1926, of the granite tablet three miles west of Dodge City, marking the location of the Caches, a famous Santa Fe Trail campsite, and Forts Mann, Mackey, and Atkinson, are shown above. Five of the area's earliest settlers, still living at the time of the dedication, are shown (left to right), H. B. (Ham) Bell, O. A. (Brick) Bond, W. H. Lord, George Reighard, and D. W. (Doc) Barton. The dates of their arrival in southwest Kansas range from 1865 for Reighard, to 1874 for Bell.

Along the Santa Fe Trail, as elsewhere in the West, the Indians at first were more curious than hostile. But as traffic increased, encroachment became more of a threat and small caravans were easy prey. Depredations and retaliations were committed by both sides. Those concerned had long been asking for protection along the western trails and small armed cavalry units sometimes accompanied a train. During the Mexican War the trail became the military road of the West and had to be kept open to supply not only the troops but also the newly acquired American citizens of New Mexico.

In 1847 a fort was established a few miles west of present Dodge City. Garrisoned by a very small force, Fort Mann, named for a master teamster, was primarily a way station for repair of wagons and replacement of animals. The fort was simply four log houses connected by a timber framework, with a diameter of about sixty feet, and walls twenty feet in height. On the northwest was an adobe breastwork for protection from attack and cold winds.

In 1850 Fort Mann was replaced by Fort Atkinson a short distance away. Because it was built of sod this fort was popularly called Fort Sod or Fort Sodom. Monthly mail and passenger service was established the same year between Independence and Santa Fe. Between Fort Leavenworth, Kansas, and Fort Union, New Mexico, the only other military post was Fort Atkinson. Indian Agent Thomas (Brokenhand) Fitzpatrick in 1851 described the fort as "a small insignificant military station, beneath the dignity of the United States, and at the mercy and forebearance of the Indians."

In June, 1853, Indian Agent Fitzpatrick was commissioned to negotiate treaties with the Plains tribes to assure safety to travelers on the trail. On June 20 Fitzpatrick set out from Kansas City, Missouri, for

The monument (above) in Dodge City's Chilton Park honors Major Robert H. Chilton, commander of Fort Atkinson in 1853. This fort, near Dodge City, was the site of a treaty with Plains Indian tribes assuring safety to travelers on the Santa Fe Trail. Major General Grenville Mellen Dodge (left) was born at Danvers, Massachusetts, in 1831. His forces captured Springfield, Missouri, and participated in the battle of Pea Ridge in 1862. In 1863 he had three horses shot from under him, and was wounded while serving in General William T. Sherman's Atlanta campaign. In 1864 Kansas and Utah were merged into his command. As the Civil War was drawing to a close, Major General Dodge, then the commanding officer of the Department of the Missouri, issued an order to Brigadier General James H. Ford to establish a new post, later named Fort Dodge. A few years later, General Dodge, an engineer by profession, gained new fame as the chief builder of the Union Pacific Railroad.

Fort Atkinson with a large wagonload of Indian goods. Comanches, Kiowas, and Apaches began to gather near the fort, waiting for Fitzpatrick and the distribution of goods. By July 16 two hundred eighty lodges of Comanches were on the river nearby. The Kiowa and Apache warriors had gone to fight the Pawnees, but their old men, women, and children were camped on the south bank of the river.

For some reason Fitzpatrick's arrival was delayed until July 25 and the Indians were growing impatient. The councils began on the 26th with some difficulty. Despite the distant and suspicious bearing of the chiefs, the lack of an interpreter, and the inadequacy of sign language for matters of such importance and delicacy, agreement was reached the following day. Distribution of goods and presents was made, and by the end of July the Indians had moved south of the Arkansas leaving the Santa Fe Trail clear. At this time Bvt. Major Robert H. Chilton was in command of the post. Today in Dodge City, north of Comanche Street in Chilton Park, there is a monument to the signing of this treaty.

Fort Atkinson was abandoned in September, 1853, and by October 1, all that remained of Fort Atkinson were "heaps of broken sod leveled to the ground, so that from it the Indians could not ambush mail carriers and other travelers."[1] The legislative council of New Mexico in 1854 asked that Fort Atkinson be re-established to guard against Indian attacks and serve as a repair station. The House Committee on Military Affairs declined the request saying the fort was no longer tenable.

Brigadier General James H. Ford (left), commanding officer of the District of the Upper Arkansas, established a new military post, Fort Dodge, in April of 1865. When new counties were created by the Kansas Legislature in 1867, Ford County was named in his honor. By April of 1865, a crude post of earth dugouts (below) had been fashioned along the north banks of the Arkansas River, and troops had arrived to man the modest fortifications of Fort Dodge. Described as "holes not fit to be dog kennels," they served the post adequately until permanent buildings could be raised.

By 1855 the Santa Fe trade amounted to five million dollars and in 1862 had increased to forty million dollars worth of goods. To subdue the Indians and to make way for white trade and settlement, war on the plains seemed inevitable. The long-proposed chain of military posts along the trail would become a reality.

Major General Grenville M. Dodge, commanding officer of the Department of Missouri, directed a fort to be built near the site of old Fort Atkinson. Brigadier General James H. Ford selected a site between the two fordable crossings of the river, a few miles east of the old fort and of the present Dodge City. In the spring of 1865 the first troops were sheltered in dugouts in the north river bank. Besides carrying out military assignments the soldiers had to quarry stone and chop timber miles from camp for construction of the permanent buildings. Life in these small forts on the plains was harsh and bleak.

Fort Dodge, named for Grenville M. Dodge, was an important supply depot for the southern plains campaigns of the 1860's and '70's. Names familiar in the history of the West were at one time or another associated with Fort Dodge — Sheridan, Sherman, Miles, Hancock, Custer, Little Raven, Dull Knife, and Satanta.

General Winfield S. Hancock's campaign of 1867 set out to "visit" the Plains Indians to investigate Indian "crimes." He attempted, with little success, to bring about order among the troublesome tribes such as the Kiowas. Hancock was impressed by the oratory of the Kiowa chief, Satanta, and presented him with a major general's coat and yellow sash. Shortly after, Satanta and his band of Kiowas drove off seventy-five horses grazing east of the fort. Pursued by men from the fort, the Indians herded the horses across the

8

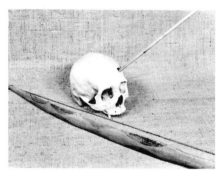

Infantrymen of Company A (top) pose in front of their newly erected barracks at Fort Dodge in 1868. The small boy at far right is the son of the commanding officer, Major Henry E. Douglas. Douglas commanded the fort at a time of troublesome Indian attacks in the area. The skull (left) with a Cheyenne arrow piercing the forehead is allegedly that of a buffalo hunter. It was found on the east slope of Boot Hill in Dodge City. Fort Dodge is seen (right) as a mature post in this picture taken around 1878. The permanent buildings were constructed of limestone and wood. The difficult task of quarrying stone and sawing timber to be hauled to the post for construction and kindling was compounded by the constant threat of Indian attack on work details. The primary task of the post included keeping a watchful eye on the Indian Territory to the south and patrolling the frontier around Dodge City. The small white building in the far right background was the jail that now can be seen on the Boot Hill Museum grounds in Dodge City.

river. Satanta, wearing his general's coat and dress hat with plume, turned, tipped his hat to the troops and disappeared.

During the summer of 1868, Major General Philip H. Sheridan met with little success in controlling several thousand Indian warriors with his troops scattered across the state in various forts. With a change of tactics the General launched campaigns against the Indians in their winter quarters. These attacks proved more successful than any used so far. Fort Dodge was the focal point of these operations in which the Indians were beaten into submission and compelled to live on the reservations allotted them.

General Nelson A. Miles conducted campaigns in 1874 and 1875 using Fort Dodge as a supply post. He moved southward to the Staked Plains of west Texas to initiate the encirclement of the last vestiges of the warring bands of Plains Indians.

The commanding officers of Fort Dodge found it difficult to hire civilians to help with the building, cut the hay, herd the livestock, and perform the other menial tasks not ordinarily required of soldiers.

Gen. William T. Sherman   *Gen. Philip H. Sheridan*   *Gen. Nelson A. Miles*   *Gen. Winfield S. Hancock*

Commanding generals of Indian campaigns of the 1860's and 1870's involving Fort Dodge troops.

Commanding officer's headquarters, Fort Dodge, 1879.

There was little comfort to offer civilians or soldiers at a frontier post like Fort Dodge. To attract civilians and improve the soldiers' lot, the commanding officer at Fort Dodge allowed a sutler's store to be built. This first store was described as "a small, miserable sod building,"² but it was a place where the men could buy merchandise and find diversion. Friendly Indians were sometimes allowed to buy or trade at the store. Because whisky was easily obtained from nearby "whisky ranches," there was no point in barring its sale on the post. The sutler was usually allowed to sell this profitable frontier commodity.

10

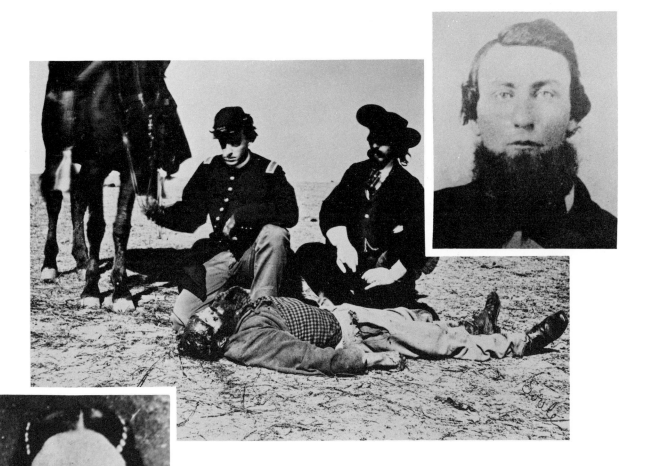

An officer and scout are shown (above) examining the body of a buffalo hunter killed and scalped near Fort Dodge. Loren L. Warren (right above) of Dodge City is believed by some to be the "scalped hunter." Warren was returning to Dodge City with a load of freight in June, 1874. During the night, Indians ran off his stock, and in the morning he started on foot to search for them. He ran across a pony left behind, and started toward Dodge in search of assistance. His scalped body was found about six miles from Dodge City. He left a wife, Sarah (lower left), one daughter, and five sons. Sons Frank and Loren (Lo) bartended, dealt faro and monte, and played in the orchestra at the Long Branch saloon. Frank bought out Luke Short's interest in the Long Branch after Luke and Bat Masterson left Dodge City at the conclusion of the "saloon war" of 1883. Lo was drum major with Dodge City's Cowboy Band on its trip to the inauguration of President Harrison in 1892. Son Albert, born in a prairie schooner approaching Dodge City in 1872, was a head waiter at Dodge City's Delmonico restaurant and an early day Dodge City fire chief.

Thedore Weichselbaum, a Riley County freighter and trader, secured the first contract to supply the Fort Dodge sutler's store in 1866. His brother, Albert, was killed while on a hunting trip with a Fort Dodge cavalry sergeant. Albert Weichselbaum's body was found on a sand bar near the Arkansas River; the sergeant disappeared. A third brother, Samuel, who clerked in the post trader's stores at Forts Larned and Dodge, was a charter signer of the Dodge City Town Company.

Sutler's buildings at Fort Dodge about 1872 are seen in the upper picture. The long stone building was a saloon and billiard hall. The building at its left was Wright and Anthony's sutler's store. A Harper's Weekly sketch (left) shows the interior of the sutler's store in 1867, a commissary for soldiers, settlers, and friendly Indians. A center for card games, music, and billiards — whisky could be purchased at the sutler's saloon by both military and civilian personnel. The use of the saloon by enlisted men was regulated closely; it was sometimes shut down completely when the soldiers "got to the joint" too freely.

From the beginning the lives of the people of Dodge City and Fort Dodge were interwoven. Four of the signers of the Town Company were Army officers at the fort; two were clerks in the sutler's store. Officers and enlisted men shared in the social life of the town, and some mixed in the rowdyism of Front Street. For a time the fort offered the nearest hospital and medical treatment as well as law enforcement. Reputable townspeople were buried in the fort cemetery in preference to the hill overlooking early Dodge City.

In 1872 Robert M. Wright and A. J. Anthony were co-owners of the sutler's store at Fort Dodge. Wright made an overland trip with oxen in 1859, at the age of sixteen, from St. Louis to Denver. Later he worked for the Barlow, Sanderson & Company stage line making tri-weekly runs through Fort Dodge over the Santa Fe Trail. In 1866 he moved to Fort Dodge where he had a contract with the quartermaster for supplying firewood. In 1867 he and A. J. Anthony were appointed post traders at the fort.

Anthony had been an express messenger from Leavenworth, Kansas, to Denver in the early sixties, and had worked alongside young Buffalo Bill Cody. He was conductor and express messenger on the stage line from Lawrence to Osawatomie, Kansas, at the time of Quantrill's guerrilla raid on Lawrence in 1863. From 1863 to 1867 he was express messenger on the Barlow, Sanderson & Company stage line from Kansas City to Santa Fe.

Colonel Richard Irving Dodge assumed the command at Fort Dodge in the summer of 1872. He found on his first tour of the post, a lieutenant of the United States Tenth Cavalry drinking with the enlisted men of his company, an extreme breach of military etiquette. The lieutenant, tipsy and incensed, struck Colonel Dodge, knocking him down. After mounting his horse, the lieutenant rode through the post recreation

Robert M. Wright (left) and A. J. Anthony (right) were partners in ranching west of Fort Dodge and were co-owners of the fort's sutler store in 1872. Both were stage drivers, ranchers, and charter signers of the Dodge City Town Company. Wright, born in Bladensburg, Maryland, in 1840, came west at the age of sixteen. He was a Front Street merchant, dealer in buffalo hides, stockman, Ford County treasurer, mayor of Dodge City, and a representative to the Kansas legislature from Ford County. The city of Wright, Kansas, and Wright Park in Dodge City are named in his honor. Anthony, born in 1830, at Staunton, Virginia, homesteaded one mile west of Dodge City in 1872, and was a partner with Charles Rath and Robert M. Wright in the pioneer Dodge City firm, Chas. Rath & Co., when it was organized in 1872. He was a county commissioner for thirteen years and served for thirty-two years as a trustee of the Presbyterian Church. He lived eighty-nine years, and, unlike some early residents of Dodge City, was known for his temperate habits. He had a forty-year unblemished record of retiring before eight o'clock at night.

room, firing several shots from his revolver through the sutler's store. He was finally subdued by a sharp blow to the head with a billiard cue.

Colonel Dodge was opposed to the sale of whisky on the post. The sutler's bar was closed to enlisted men briefly during the summer of 1872 when the officer of the day discovered that all of the men assigned to escort the mail to Camp Supply were so intoxicated they had difficulty mounting their horses. The post surgeon, Dr. William S. Tremaine, complained to Commander Dodge that quantities of whisky were being smuggled into the hospital, and that he could hardly be expected to nurse soldiers back to health if they were consuming excessive amounts of "firewater."

As the whisky problem became more troublesome within the military reservation, storekeepers Wright and Anthony and their clerks, A. J. Peacock and Herman J. Fringer, became more aware of the need for facilities outside the post where enlisted men could find amusement and relaxation in a freer atmosphere.

As the railroads pushed westward, the deluge of hunters to the plains accomplished what the Army had long advocated — subdue the Indians by exterminating their buffalo. In the Medicine Lodge Treaty of 1867 Indians had been granted the right to hunt north into Kansas as far as the Arkansas River "so long as the buffalo may range thereon, in such numbers to justify the chase." By 1872 the hide men were eyeing the herds in northern Texas and Indian Territory, off limits by treaty to all but Indians. By 1872 the area around Dodge City was becoming a headquarters for the hunters. Two hunters, Wright Mooar and John Webb, went to Fort Dodge to sound out the commandant, Colonel Richard I. Dodge, on the Army's attitude toward white hunters in the Indians' territory. Dodge gave them an open invitation — "Boys, if I were a buffalo hunter, I would hunt where the buffalo are."[3] — thus ending the promised protection of the Indians' hunting grounds.

Fort Dodge was decommissioned in 1882 and is now a state soldiers' home. Two of the original adobe structures of the fort still stand, now veneered with stone. Two buildings built in 1867, whose exteriors have not been altered, are still in use, the commandant's quarters, now the superintendent's home, and an administration building. Five other buildings remaining from the days of military occupancy include the old fort hospital, commissary, and three small stone cottages. The old jail has been removed to the Boot Hill Museum grounds in Dodge City.

Here, near Coronado's crossing place, near the river crossing of the Santa Fe Trail, near the site of three frontier forts, the gathering spot for buffalo hunters, and the surveyors' stakes of the westward moving rails of the Santa Fe railroad, inevitably, a town had to grow.

Chapter II
BUFFALO CITY

The first structure erected on the site of Dodge City was a three-room sod house built by Henry L. Sitler. Sitler, a veteran frontiersman, contracted to supply wood to Fort Dodge from Sawlog and Mulberry Creeks. After surveying the grazing lands near the fort he decided that ranching would be a better business. In 1871 Sitler built his sod house west of the military reservation to oversee his cattle ranch which lay to the north and the west of Fort Dodge. Close to the Santa Fe Trail, it became a stopping place for buffalo hunters and traders. It was located approximately where the present Rock Island depot now stands, just south of the railroad tracks and west of Second Avenue. Sitler kept his ranching operation near Dodge City for many years and operated a brick yard in the city. His bricks with the initials, *H. L. S.* can still be seen on buildings in Dodge City. The Sitler soddie remained the sole landmark on the site of Dodge City until the approaching railroad encouraged a settlement in the area west of Fort Dodge.

Cyrus K. Holliday's dream of building a railroad along the Santa Fe Trail became a reality in November, 1868, when the first ground was broken in Topeka for the construction of the Atchison, Topeka & Santa Fe Railroad across Kansas. By July, 1870, it had been constructed seventy-five miles to Emporia; during 1871, the railroad was completed only seventy-five more miles to Newton; and there it remained until the spring of 1872. The congressional land grant of 1863 had stipulated that the line must be completed within ten years. With less than a year to reach the Colorado line, work started from Newton around May 1, 1871. The road was completed to Hutchinson, June 8; to Great Bend, July 11; it arrived in Dodge City on September 5; and reached the state line on December 28, 1872.[1]

In the spring of 1872, as the steel rails of the new railroad came closer each day, more and more hunters, traders, merchants, and adventurers entered the area west of the military reservation and set up camp in dugouts, tents, and wagons. Whisky and women, guns and groceries, were needs that Fort Dodge could not supply for these new arrivals and for the hundreds of railroad workers expected soon. Colonel Richard I. Dodge, commanding officer at Fort Dodge in 1872, did not favor the sale of whisky on the military reservation, but he realized the difficulty of trying to enforce prohibition within the military reser-

Henry L. Sitler (right) built his sod house (above) on the site of Dodge City in 1871. Used as headquarters for his cattle ranch, it was located near the Santa Fe Trail between Second and Third Avenues, south of the railroad tracks. This picture probably was taken in the summer of 1872, as the railroad approached Dodge City. Note the telegraph pole which would have been just south of the railroad bed. The hill to the right of Sitler's soddie is Boot Hill as it looked about the time the first unfortunate soul died with his boots on and was buried there.

vation boundary. When the civilians at Fort Dodge began talking of starting a settlement west of the reservation boundary, Colonel Dodge approved and helped with the planning.

The solution to Colonel Dodge's problem was anticipated by a twenty-four-year-old Canadian, George M. Hoover, who came to western Kansas in 1871 with his possessions in a sack on his back. Hearing the plans for a new town, he backtracked to eastern Kansas and brought back a wagon loaded with whisky, the merchandise in greatest demand on the frontier. The military reservation boundary extended to the 100th meridian, five miles west of Fort Dodge. Hoover tied a rag to the wheel of his wagon, measured off the five miles, and dropped the tail gate of his wagon. He set up shop on June 17, 1872, at eight o'clock in the morning, about half way between Dodge City's present First and Second Avenues, just south of the railroad grading stakes.[2] In their hastily erected tent, Hoover and his partner, John G. McDonald, piled the sod high enough at each end of a foot-wide board to support a bar and opened for business.

About the same time a buffalo hunter, George W. (Hoodoo) Brown, and his partner, Charley Stewart, hauled lumber from Russell, Kansas, a hundred miles to the north, and built a fourteen foot square building

16

End of the Atchison, Topeka & Santa Fe Railroad track as it appeared between Hutchinson, Kansas, and Dodge City in 1872.

with a dirt floor, south of the railroad right-of-way. The house was operated as a profitable saloon — whisky cost two dollars a gallon and sold for twenty-five cents a drink.[3]

The railroad had passed through Hutchinson, Kansas, 120 miles to the east, and was headed toward Dodge City by the time George M. Hoover set up his tent. Knowing that it was but a matter of months before the tracks would be laid through, the buffalo hunters began piling their dried hides near the surveyor's stakes.

By the time the iron rails had replaced the surveyor's stakes in September, 1872, a busy street south of the tracks was lined with hastily built frame buildings and tents. Daniel Wolf set up and operated a general merchandise store north of the Santa Fe Trail (today's Santa Fe Trail Street). His store was just southeast of H. L. Sitler's sod house and next to Hoover and McDonald's tent saloon. By 1873, when the main businesses had built up north of the tracks, Wolf had pulled up stakes and left.

Just east of Wolf's store was the grocery and general merchandise store of J. B. Edwards and George O. Smith. Edwards, a merchant in Abilene, Kansas, had yearned for a more exciting trade territory. He left Abilene in 1872, and headed west to get a first try at the new settlements growing up ahead of the railroad. Hauling lumber in a wagon from the end of the track at Great Bend, he built his general merchandise store in Dodge City in June, 1872. He and Smith, his partner, sold goods and bought buffalo hides in Dodge City from June to December, 1872, when they moved their store, merchandise, building and all, to the end of the tracks near the state line.[4]

Just east of Smith and Edwards was a dance hall and a row of tents containing a restaurant, a barber shop, and other less savory business establishments. Opposite them, facing south, lying just south of where the railroad tracks were laid, were Cutler and Wiley's large frame building and a blacksmith shop. The firm of Cutler and Wiley was the chief contractor for the railroad grading. Their building was probably used as a company store and warehouse to supply their workmen with groceries, clothing, boots, and tools.

Construction workers and cars on the A. T. & S. F. Railroad west of Dodge City in 1872.

Two of Cutler and Wiley's subcontractors from Sedgwick County, Bat and Ed Masterson, laid four miles of grade through Ford County in 1872, but gained their fame in Dodge City behind badges and six-shooters a few years later.

Herman J. Fringer and A. J. Peacock, clerks at the Fort Dodge sutler's store, began building a drug store north of the tracks in July, 1872, the first frame building on what shortly was to become Dodge City's famous Front Street.[5] Robert M. Wright, rancher, trader, and Fort Dodge sutler, and Charles Rath, Indian trader and buffalo hunter, combined their resources and started building an imposing two-story frame building north of the railroad bed and east of Fringer's drug store. It was headquarters for the sale of general merchandise and outfitting goods, and the shipment of buffalo hides. This firm, known as Charles Rath & Co., did the biggest business in buffalo hides, bones and meat, and was largely the firm that made Dodge City the "buffalo city."

Rath established outposts over the plains where supplies were offered in exchange for buffalo hides. He also hunted buffalo with a train of wagons, sending a wagon off to market as soon as it was filled with hides and meat. He is credited with killing 107 buffalo in one stand. Rath's resourcefulness kept a stream of wagons coming and going to the Dodge City buffalo market. Charles Rath's early success as an Indian trader was not hindered when he chose a Cheyenne squaw as his first wife. He had heard there were two ways of getting on with the Indians — sell them whisky or marry into the tribe. He picked a Cheyenne of the Little Bear Tribe named Maker-of-Roads, a former wife of Kit Carson.[6]

The Town Company completed its formal organization on August 15, 1872. Seeking acquisition under the townsite purchase act of 1872, they first planned a development of 320 acres. The regulations

required that a tract of such size be shared among one hundred to two hundred occupants. The Dodge City promoters decided this to be unrealistic and entered a plat encompassing a modest eighty-seven acres.

The founders of Dodge City, the signers of the Dodge City Town Company charter, were a varied group of frontier speculators. Colonel Richard I. Dodge, commanding officer, William S. Tremaine, post surgeon, and Edward Moale, captain of Company A, Third Infantry, were Fort Dodge officers who recog-

A boxcar used as a temporary depot for a short time after the railroad reached Dodge City, is shown at the top of the page. Below, to the left, is the first Santa Fe depot built in Dodge City in 1873. It was located at the foot of Central Avenue, then called Railroad Avenue. At the right is shown John Bender, conductor on the first Santa Fe train into Dodge City in September, 1872.

This locomotive is shown a mile east of Dodge City in 1879. The shanty town in the background shows examples of the earliest structures built in Dodge City.

nized the investment possibilities of the new town. Major David Taylor, the only other Army officer, was paymaster at Fort Leavenworth. An attorney, Major Taylor was probably in charge of drawing the legal documents for the establishment of the private corporation to be known as the Dodge City Town Company.

The civilian signers who were residents of the area included Robert M. Wright and A. J. Anthony, ranchers and Fort Dodge storekeepers, Henry L. Sitler, rancher, and A. J. Peacock and Herman J. Fringer, sutler store clerks at Fort Dodge. Samuel Weichselbaum was a Riley County trader who had freighted supplies to Fort Dodge and was interested in buying town lots in the new city. Lyman B. Shaw was probably a civilian employee at Fort Dodge or a frontier merchant. The last signer of the founding document was Alexander S. Johnson from Topeka, a land commissioner for the Santa Fe railroad. Johnson, born at the Shawnee Mission and Indian school near Kansas City, was the son of its founder, Rev. Thomas Johnson.

While the enterprising merchants prepared for the coming of the rails, members of the Dodge City Town Company completed their plans and asked A. A. Robinson, chief engineer for the Atchison, Topeka and Santa Fe Railroad to lay out the town. The town-to-be was marked off in a grid pattern north and south of the proposed railroad right-of-way with narrow streets by today's standards, but wide enough to turn around an eight-mule team.

Dodge City was not incorporated until November 2, 1875. Its first three years were without elected city officials. Ford County was not organized until 1873, at which time county officials were elected. The first year of Dodge City's existence was without government or law, and more especially, without law enforcement. In 1925 J. B. Edwards, recalling his frontier experience in the wicked Dodge City of 1872, calmly remarked, "there was no law, no organized law in existence during the period I was there. We needed officers of the law bad enough, God knows! but some way, or somehow, only those died with their boots on [at first] who could well be spared. I assisted to bury a few of the first ones killed there, on Boot Hill."[7]

The Town Company stockholders owned the real estate comprising the city limits of Dodge City. Fifty dollars would buy a choice lot location on Front Street for anyone with cash in hand. For the first

20

Santa Fe Railroad officials stopped at the end of the track west of Larned, Kansas, in 1872, to pose for this photograph.

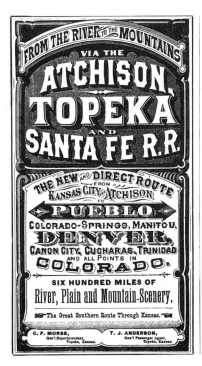

The timetable (above) of the Atchison, Topeka & Santa Fe Railroad schedules a thirty-hour trip from Kansas City to Dodge City in 1876. The 1874 advertisement (left) appeared in Dodge City's earliest newspaper, the Dodge City Messenger.

21

HOOVER & McDONALD,
Wholesale and Retail dealers in Foreign and Domestic
WINES AND LIQUORS,
Also, the Finest brands of CIGARS.
Main Street, Dodge City, Kans.
☞ Orders solicited and promptly filled.
Pure KENTUCKY BOURBONS, a specialty.
A fine assortment of Buffalo ROBES on hand.   feb. 26th, '74.

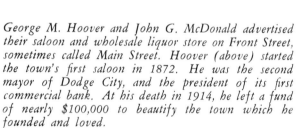

George M. Hoover and John G. McDonald advertised their saloon and wholesale liquor store on Front Street, sometimes called Main Street. Hoover (above) started the town's first saloon in 1872. He was the second mayor of Dodge City, and the president of its first commercial bank. At his death in 1914, he left a fund of nearly $100,000 to beautify the town which he founded and loved.

George W. (Hoodoo) Brown was a soldier in the Union Army, a freighter, Indian scout, buffalo hunter, and saloonkeeper. His saloon was the second permanent structure built in Dodge City. In 1872 he hunted buffalo near Dodge City with Prairie Dog Dave Morrow. Brown continued to hunt buffalo as late as 1885. While operating a road ranch on Crooked Creek, near Meade, Kansas, he shot and killed a man, mistaken for an ambusher, hiding in the brush behind his sod house. Although tried and acquitted for his action, a stigma attached to Brown, a hard-bitten frontiersman, and he gained the dubious reputation of a "gunman."

year to eighteen months, the problems of law enforcement and city services probably were handled by meetings of the Town Company, the members being the principal merchants and saloonkeepers of the new settlement.

The county of Ford, named for Brigadier General James H. Ford who established and laid out Fort Dodge, was created by the Kansas legislature in 1867 in an act providing for the division into counties of all the unorganized part of the state of Kansas west of range line 26 west.[8] The act provided that these counties could be formally organized when they reached a minimum requisite population. Proof of sufficient population was not made until 1873, when on April 5, the governor of Kansas, Thomas A. Osborn, issued his proclamation providing for the organization of Ford County.

Governor Osborn appointed Charles Rath, John G. McDonald, and Daniel Wolf, special county commissioners, and Herman J. Fringer, special county clerk. James Hanrahan, a buffalo hunter and saloonkeeper, was later appointed commissioner in place of Wolf who had left the county. At the first election held June 5, 1873, Charles Rath, F. C. Zimmermann, and A. C. Myers were elected county commissioners.[9]

Myers was a merchant whose "Pioneer Store" south of the tracks sold groceries, liquors, clothing, and outfitting goods, and bought hides, pelts, furs, and buffalo meat, fresh or dried. In 1874 Myers went into

These first buildings were erected in Dodge City in 1872. They were photographed looking west, just south of the railroad tracks. Cutler and Wiley's store is on the right. A tent barber shop is on the left, followed by two frame buildings, a restaurant, and a saloon.

The three buildings in the center background of the top picture are shown here, from left: a dance hall, Smith and Edwards' store, and Daniel Wolf's store. Two loads of buffalo hides are shown in the wagons in front of Smith and Edwards' store.

This sketch of Dodge City is as it appeared in 1872, looking southeast from Boot Hill. The buildings at the right, south of the railroad tracks, are those shown in the two photographs above. Henry L. Sitler's sod house is shown next to the telegraph pole at the far right. The buildings at the left include the Dodge House, Chas. Rath & Co.'s store, Fringer's Drug Store, and the Santa Fe depot.

This photograph was taken around 1873, and looks east along Front Street, north of the railroad tracks. The two buildings at the left are Col. Isaac Young's harness shop and Herman J. Fringer's drug store. The two-story frame building with stairway on the west side is Rath and Wright's store. The Dodge House is at the far end of these buildings, just north of the railroad depot and water tank.

partnership with Fred Leonard, but by 1876, no further references can be found of Myers in Dodge City records. George Reighard, a contemporary of Myers, recalled nearly a half century later, an explanation for Myers' sudden disappearance. Reighard alleged that an ungrateful ex-employee had stolen Myers' only team and wagon. The theft of this equipment, without which he could not carry on his business, was considered by many, a crime worse than murder. According to Reighard, Myers caught the thief, shot him, and left him for dead. This self-styled form of frontier justice turned out to be less than fatal for the thief. He recovered, and Myers left for the cooler climate of Colorado shortly after.[10]

At the first county election in June, 1873, Herman J. Fringer was elected county clerk and clerk of the district court; A. J. Anthony, county treasurer; and T. L. McCarty, Dodge City's first civilian doctor, was given the job of coroner. George B. Cox, proprietor of Dodge City's famous hotel, the Dodge House, was elected probate judge; M. V. Cutler of the railroad contracting firm of Cutler and Wiley was Ford County's first county attorney.[11]

Charles E. Bassett was the first sheriff of Ford County and served the office until 1878 when he was replaced by Bat Masterson. Bassett was the only official law enforcement officer in the county until the city elections of 1875. Little is known of Bassett's early years as a lawman in Ford County, but he must have been an efficient officer. Limited by the state constitution, Bassett could not run for a successive third regular term as sheriff. After Bat Masterson took office as sheriff in 1878 he promptly appointed Bassett as his undersheriff.

At the regular county election held November 4, 1873, A. J. Anthony and A. J. Peacock replaced Myers and Zimmermann as county commissioners; William F. Sweeney was elected county clerk; A. B. Webster, a famous mayor of Dodge City, replaced Anthony as county treasurer; L. D. Henderson replaced Cutler as county attorney; Morris Collar was elected superintendent of public instruction; and John G. McDonald

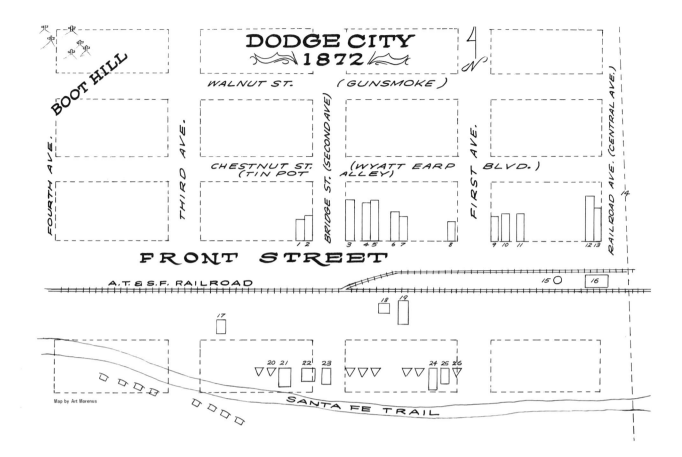

The map above shows locations in Dodge City shortly after its founding in 1872, according to interviews with George M. Hoover in 1903, and J. B. Edwards in 1935. Numbered locations on the map indicate:

1. Isaac Young's harness shop
2. Herman J. Fringer's drug store
3. Rath & Co.'s general store (Charles Rath and Robert M. Wright.)
4. George M. Hoover's and John G. McDonald's wholesale liquor store and saloon
5. F. C. Zimmermann's hardware store
6. Morris Collar's dry goods store
7. A. J. Peacock's saloon
8. P. L. Beatty's and James H. Kelley's saloon
9. A. B. Webster's grocery and dry good store
10. Moses Waters' and James Hanrahan's saloon
11. R. W. Evans' general store
12. George B. Cox's and F. W. Boyd's Dodge House hotel
13. Dodge House saloon and restaurant
14. West boundary line of Fort Dodge Military Reservation
15. Railroad water tank
16. Depot
17. Henry L. Sitler's sod house, the first building on the townsite of Dodge City
18. Blacksmith shop
19. Cutler & Wiley's railroad company store
20. Hoover & McDonald's tent saloon
21. Daniel Wolf's general store
22. George O. Smith's and J. B. Edwards' grocery and general store
23. Dance hall
24. Saloon
25. Restaurant.
26. Barber shop
▽ Tents
⌂ Dugouts

replaced Fringer as clerk of the district court. A. J. Peacock, Dodge City's foremost "saloonist," was elected chairman of the board of county commissioners.[12]

The new town was informally christened, *Buffalo City,* because of the buffalo trade that was building to great proportions. Buffalo City was the name used by some until a post office was applied for in October, 1872. Mail was already being delivered to a Buffalo, Kansas, and the application was denied under that name. The name, *Dodge City,* became a logical choice, not only because of Fort Dodge nearby, named for

25

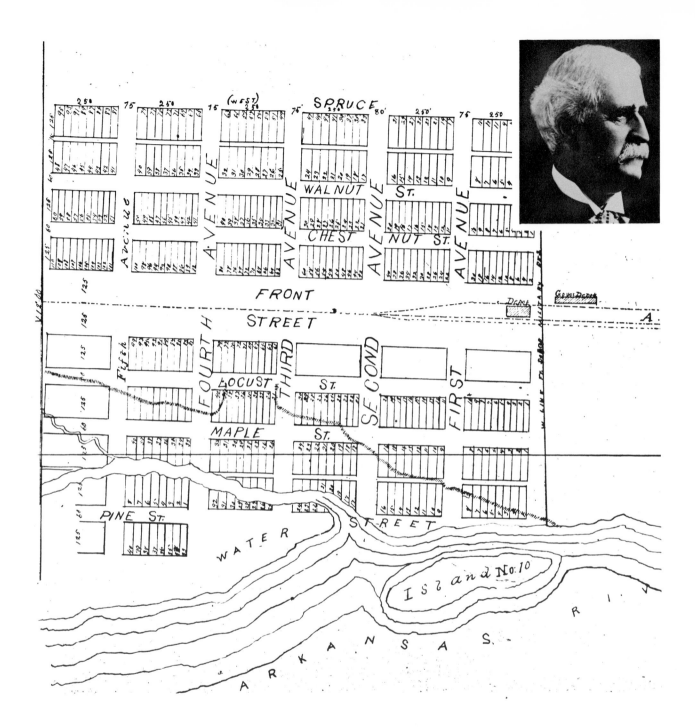

Albert A. Robinson (inset, right above) was a civil engineer and assistant in charge of constructing the Atchison, Topeka & Santa Fe Railroad in 1871. In July of 1872 he supervised the laying out of the original town plat of Dodge City (above). The Town Company advertisement (lower left) appeared in the Dodge City Messenger in 1874. The inducement advertising a "Free Bridge Across the Arkansas River!" was premature. It remained a toll bridge until 1885.

Colonel Richard Irving Dodge was commanding officer at Fort Dodge during the summer of 1872. He participated in the founding of Dodge City, encouraging several of his junior officers to buy town lots, and was a charter member of the Dodge City Town Company. He was replaced as the fort's commander in October, 1873. While at Fort Dodge he was considered by the men of the garrison to be a somewhat inflexible officer who "went by the book." His opposition to the sale of whisky on the military garrison encouraged an early build-up of saloons and dance halls just west of the military reservation boundary. After his personal servant was shot to death and mutilated by drunken gunmen, Colonel Dodge telegraphed the Governor of Kansas and threatened to put Dodge City under martial law. His action became the first force of law and order to come to Dodge City — a year after its founding.

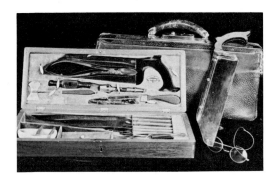

Major Ezra B. Kirk (left), quartermaster at Fort Dodge in 1872, assisted the founders of Dodge City and became the first secretary and treasurer of the Dodge City Town Company.

The surgical instruments (right) are an example of the unsophisticated tools of the medical profession in the 1870's, such as those used by Dr. William S. Tremaine, a charter member of the Town Company, and post surgeon at Fort Dodge. During his services at the fort he performed several hundred amputations, and during the winter of 1872 he removed over seventy fingers and toes from frostbitten soldiers. This experience influenced him to petition the Office of the Surgeon General in Washington for better housing facilities, modern medical equipment, and improved clothing for the fort's frontier soldiers.

Dr. Tremaine assisted Dr. T. L. McCarty at his office on Front Street, and served as secretary and treasurer of the Town Company according to this 1877 Dodge City Times advertisement.

Herman J. Fringer (above) came to Fort Dodge as quarter-master's clerk in 1867. In 1872, he and A. J. Peacock were clerks in the sutler's store at the fort. In June Fringer built a drug store on Front Street. He was appointed county clerk to assist in organizing Ford County in 1873, and was a probate judge and assistant cashier of The Bank of Dodge City in later years. A. J. Peacock, Dodge City's foremost saloonkeeper and colorful character, operated a saloon on Front Street, sometimes called Main Street, in 1872 (right) and continued to cater to the thirst of the buffalo hunter and Texas cowboy until he left Dodge City for Utah Territory in the late 1880's. His saloons, the Billiard Hall, the Saratoga, the Lady Gay, the Nueces, and the Sample Room, catered to a class slightly below the "genteel" customers of his competitors, the Long Branch, the Alamo, the Old House and the Occident.

CHARTER OF THE DODGE CITY TOWN COMPANY
OF FORD COUNTY, STATE OF KANSAS

State of Kansas, County of Ford, s.s.

Be it remembered that on this 15″ day of August 1872, we Henry L. Sitler, Robert M. Wright, A. J. Peacock, A. J. Anthony, Herman J. Fringer, and Lyman B. Shaw, of said County, and Samuel Weichelsbaum, of Riley County, Kansas, Edward Moale of Maryland, Richard I. Dodge of New York, W. S. Tremaine of New York, David Taylor of Leavenworth County, Kansas and Alex S. Johnson of Shawnee County, Kansas, do hereby associate ourselves together as a private Corporation to be known as the Dodge City Town Company, for the purpose of creating a Town to be located in the County of Ford, State of Kansas, and to be designated and known as "Dodge City" — Kansas, the said Town to be situated upon lands, selected and entered under the act of Congress of March 2″ 1869, entitled, "An act for the relief of the inhabitants of Cities and Towns upon the public lands" which lands have been filed upon by our authorized agent under the provisions of the above recited Act of Congress, and for our own use in our corporate capacity, and are described as follows to-wit, The South West Quarter of Section Number Twenty Five (25) less that portion embraced in the Fort Dodge Military Reservation, and Lots numbered one (1) and Two (2) of Section No. Thirty Five (35) with some exception as to military reservation of Fort Dodge, all in Township Twenty Six (26), Range Twenty Five (25) west — lying and being in the County of Ford, State of Kansas, and containing in the aggregate (320) Three Hundred and Twenty acres more or less, where the office of the Company shall be established. That the number of directors shall be (7) seven named as follows

Robert M. Wright,	Fort Dodge, Kansas
Herman J. Fringer,	" "
Henry L. Stitler [sic],	" "
Lyman B. Shaw,	" "
Richard I. Dodge,	New York
W. S. Tremaine,	" "
Edward Moale,	Maryland

That the Company shall be a joint Stock Company with Capital Stock of ($6000) Sixty hundred dollars, divided into 600 Shares at ($10) Ten Dollars each which may be increased as the majority of the Stockholders may decide upon at a regular meeting.

In testimony whereof we hereunto set our hands and affix our seals the day and year above written.

H. L. Sitler	(Seal)	Herman J. Fringer	(Seal)
R. M. Wright	(Seal)	Saml. Weichelsbaum	(Seal)
A. J. Anthony	(Seal)	Edw. Moale	(Seal)
A. J. Peacock	(Seal)	Richard I. Dodge	(Seal)
W. S. Tremaine	(Seal)	Lyman B. Shaw	(Seal)
David Taylor	(Seal)	A. S. Johnson	(Seal)

Major General Grenville M. Dodge, but in honor of Colonel Richard I. Dodge, commanding officer at the fort and a leading member of the Town Company.

When the rails were finally laid into Dodge City in September, 1872, there were thousands of hides to be shipped out. The first freight and passenger trains arrived that month, bringing supplies and carload lots of whisky and beer, and carrying out buffalo hides, meat, and tongues to the eastern markets.

Dodge City quickly acquired a large floating population, and its trade assumed enormous proportions. It was the shipping point for government freight, south into Indian Territory. Supplies were stored in a large government warehouse located on the site of the present Santa Fe depot. The railroad business boomed immediately; a box car served for a short time as the first depot and railroad office.

In November of 1872, a special dispatch to the *Kansas Daily Commonwealth*, Topeka, Kansas, reported: "The buffaloes are moving south and crossing the Arkansas. Twenty miles west of Dodge an immense herd of the creatures, covering an extent of country two miles in width and ten in length were passed by the construction train. Fourteen were run over and killed by the engine. Two hours were consumed by the construction train in endeavoring to get through this herd. Several calves were run over and injured, and the construction men, while in the act of capturing some of them, were charged upon by several hundred

Certificate No. 76 of the Dodge City Town Company for ten shares of capital stock issued to R. W. Evans, December 22, 1884, is reproduced below.

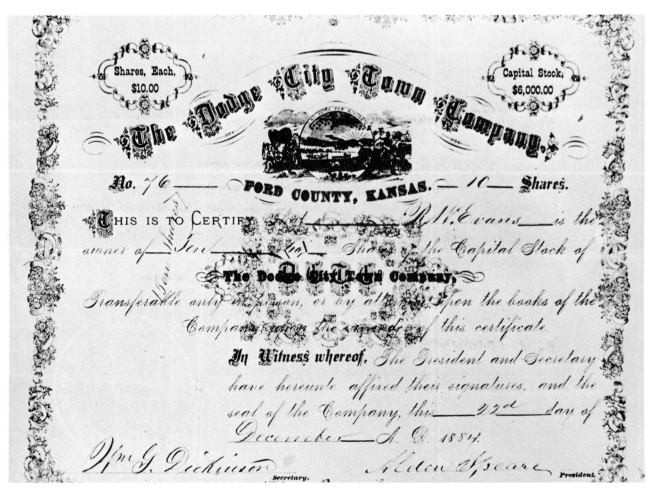

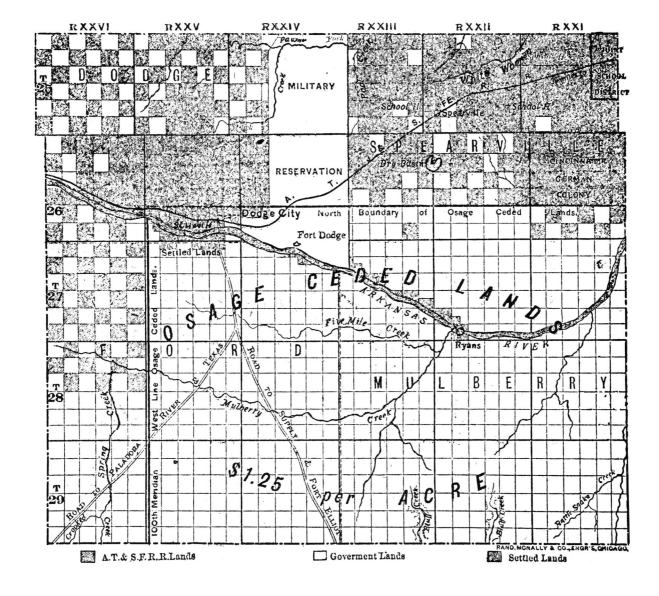

buffalo and barely escaped with their lives. Every ravine is full of hunters, and camp fires can be seen for miles in every direction. The hides and saddles of fourteen hundred buffalo were brought into town today."

In 1872, with a population of around 500, Dodge City was almost entirely supported by the buffalo trade. During the summer of 1872, buffalo hides were bartered freely for goods and supplies in this frontier community where cash was sometimes scarce and credit was unheard of. There were 2,000 buffalo hunters shooting down their prey in western Kansas in 1872 and 1873. They conservatively averaged fifteen animals a day. Their hides brought $1.25 to $3.50 each. With a little luck a good man with rifle could make twenty or thirty dollars a day and be rich in no time. A single hide was worth a week's wages to a laboring man, and hundreds of the Santa Fe construction crews joined the hunt.

During the winter season the preserving and shipping of buffalo meat was nearly as extensive a business as that of caring for the hides. Dodge City soon had several houses for the curing of buffalo hams and preparing them for shipment, in addition to a hide tannery and large warehouses for hide storage. In the

"Curing Hides and Bones" (left), a sketch drawn in Dodge City in October, 1878, by artists, Paul Frenzeny and Jules Tavernier, for Harper's Weekly. This sketch shows the hide yard of Chas. Rath & Co., alongside the railroad, where hides were unloaded, stretched, dried, and baled for shipment to tanneries.

Charles Rath (lower left), an itchy-footed frontiersman, Indian trader, and buffalo hunter, abandoned the comforts of an Ohio home to roam the plains. He bought and sold millions of buffalo hides, and with Robert M. Wright and A. J. Anthony started the firm of Chas. Rath & Co. in Dodge City in 1872. Rath is shown (above) sitting on top of a rick of hides in the Rath & Co. hide yard, which contained as many as fifty thousand green and dried buffalo hides at a time.

Shooting buffalo from a train sometimes became necessary to get through the immense herds roaming freely without regard to the railroad's right of way.

Wagons loaded with buffalo hides were a common sight in Dodge City in the early 1870's. Tanneries and hide dealers sent representatives to Dodge City to deal with hunters on their arrival from the buffalo hunting areas in southwest Kansas and Indian Territory.

Buffalo hides were staked out on the ground to dry. The hides were stretched and pinned flesh side up, where they were left two to five days to dry and harden in the sun.

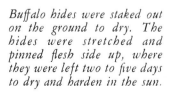

George W. Reighard, frontier freighter, began hunting buffalo south of Dodge City in 1872. As the grass grew greener south of the Arkansas River, Reighard said he could see "the whole country to where sky and earth merged in a purplish haze covered with one mass of buffaloes." He claimed that the "sound of buffaloes on the march could be heard a mile and more away like the roll of distant thunder."

Prairie Dog Dave Morrow, a part-time Dodge City lawman and friend of Bat Masterson, gained a niche in buffalo hunting history as the killer of the legendary white buffalo. Morrow's buffalo was stuffed and exhibited by Robert M. Wright throughout the Midwest until moths and the ravages of time destroyed the albino curiosity. Morrow and Reighard traded their buffalo hides with dealers such as A. C. Myers, whose "Pioneer Store" south of the railroad tracks was advertised in the Dodge City Messenger (left).

years of 1872, 1873, and 1874, over 850,000 buffalo hides were shipped from Dodge City. In 1873, over a million and a half pounds of buffalo meat left Dodge City, and during the winter of the same year, fifty carloads of buffalo tongues were shipped east.[13]

David (Prairie Dog Dave) Morrow, one of Dodge City's early day buffalo hunters, was a rebellious, eccentric, and adventurous offspring of a prominent eastern family; he was an uncle of Dwight Morrow, former U. S. Ambassador to Mexico, and great-uncle to Mrs. Charles A. Lindbergh. He acquired his western title in Hays City, while selling prairie dogs to passing trainloads of tourists. Prairie Dog Dave hunted buffalo near Dodge City, beginning like many others by supplying military forts with meat. He is credited with killing a white buffalo, a shaggy albino beast, which was sold to Robert M. Wright for $1,000.[14]

Another buffalo hunter, George W. Reighard, a resident of Dodge City for sixty-four years, was a Pennsylvania veteran of the Civil War. He entered the army at sixteen, fought in the battles of Spotsylvania and Cold Harbor, where he was wounded. He came to Hays City in 1869, and was employed as a U. S. Government teamster, delivering freight in trains of thirty six-mule teams to Fort Dodge, Camp Supply, and Fort Sill. In a month-long trip south of Fort Dodge, with a team and wagon and three skinners, he killed a few more than 3,000 buffalo. His biggest kill was made into a stand of over a thousand buffalo that had come to a creek to drink their fill, and strolled out onto the prairie to rest. He told of shooting steadily for an hour and a half, alternating guns as they heated up. From ninety-one shots fired from his two fifty caliber Sharps rifles he killed seventy-nine animals.

Henry H. Raymond grew up in Illinois with Bat Masterson and his brothers, Jim and Ed. He arrived in Dodge City on November 16, 1872, where he joined the Mastersons who had arrived earlier as part of the crew building the railroad. Shortly after, the four left for buffalo hunting grounds. They stoically endured the biting cold and loneliness, but were successful in killing and butchering as many as twenty buffalo a day. Raymond kept a day-by-day diary in which can be found his activities as a buffalo hunter and as an early day Dodge City resident.

Thomas C. Nixon, another Dodge City buffalo hunter, hunted with five two-horse teams and fifteen men. About thirty-five miles southeast of Dodge City at the head of Rattlesnake Creek he killed 3,200 buffalo in thirty-five days. He claims to have killed 120 in forty minutes using two guns. When one got too hot he threw the breach block down, ran a wet rag through it and took the other gun until it got too hot. Nixon served as assistant marshal of Dodge City from 1881 to July 21, 1884, when he was shot and killed by Mysterious Dave Mather, another Dodge City lawman.

Orlando A. (Brick) Bond, a twenty-three-year-old redhead, left Minnesota in 1871 for a job supplying beef and buffalo meat to the steel gangs laying rails from Newton, Kansas, to LaJunta, Colorado. He came to Dodge City in the spring of 1872, outfitted as a buffalo hunter, and in the months of November and December, 1874, tallied 6,183 head. In another sixty-day period Bond took five wagons deep into the Panhandle of Texas and, keeping five skinners busy, brought back 5,855 hides. After the herds thinned, Bond joined with a fellow buffalo hunter, Tom Nixon, and operated a dance hall and saloon during Dodge's lusty cowtown period. After the enforcement of prohibition, Bond joined with Mayor A. B. Webster to found the Palace Drug Company, still in existence in Dodge City.

An artist's romanticized version of a buffalo skinner is shown at the left. Such Dodge City skinners as Dirty Ike and Stinker Jim probably were not as handsome and dashing as the frontiersman pictured here. It was common to kill so many buffalo in one stand during winter (below) that it was impossible to skin all the animals before they froze. The animals left unskinned in wintertime were sometimes skinned later after thawing. These hides smelled nearly as bad as the skinners who brought them in. The slang expression, "a stinker," was first used in Dodge City to refer to those unscrupulous hunters who brought in these worthless hides.

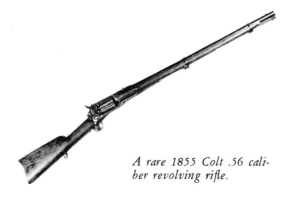

*A rare 1855 Colt .56 cali-
ber revolving rifle.*

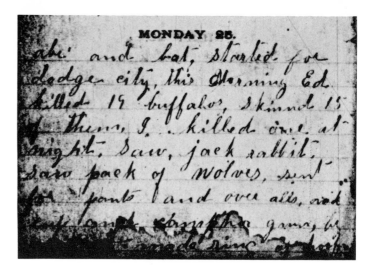

*Henry H. Raymond (left) arrived in Dodge City in November, 1872,
where, according to his diary, he journeyed from Illinois to meet Bat and
Ed Masterson who had a grading subcontract with the Santa Fe Railroad.
Raymond's buffalo hunting and other Dodge City activities were "care-
lessly jotted down . . . to recall incidents of the times" in a diary (above).
When lacking ink, Raymond mixed gunpowder with water to make his
daily entries.*

EXCERPTS FROM
HENRY H. RAYMOND'S DIARY (above)

Nov. Monday 25. 1872. Abe [Mahew] and Bat
[Masterson] started for Dodge City this morning.
Ed [Masterson] killed 19 buffalos. Skinned 15 of
them. I killed one at night. Saw jack rabbit. Saw
pack of wolves. Sent for pants and over alls, and
cup and camphor gum, by Bat. made ring of hoof.

Feb. Monday 24. 1873. . . . went down to town,
called at Shermans [Tom Sherman's dance hall]
heard die fraulins mach gantz slicht aussprechin die
Lill and die Nell [the girls speak quite openly about
Lill and Nell] Ed [Masterson] in town at night.
[Tom] Nixons outfit came in. all in town at night.

March. Tuesday 4. 1873. beautiful day. down
in town Bill Brooks got shot at with needle gun the
ball passing through two barrels of watter lodging in
outside iron hoop. Jerdon [Jake? Jordan] shot at
him. I was down town most all day. Pat [Baker]
and Bat [Masterson] went to hunt the horses. Soldier got beat over the head with boot and $5 taken
from him in town.

March. Thursday 13. 1873. Tom Sherman shot
[Charles?] Burns last night. Nice day. . . . I took
pitcher of milk to Lill Thompson [dance hall girl] at
night. heard nice music at Kelly's [Beatty & Kelley's
saloon and restaurant on Front Street]. Italians played
harp and vio. . . .

March. Thursday 20. 1873. bailed & loaded
hydes. piled some. loaded some bones. worked all
day for [Charles] Rath. hauled two loads corn from
car. hat veil wein getrunk [drank much wine]. nice
day. Recd. $5.00 of Rath. in dance house at night.
splendid music. got sup at restaurant. nice day.

June. Tuesday 24. 1873. . . . got 17 buffalo, 10
in one stand and 7 in another. killed another bull
and some one else skined him. cloudy and thunder-
ing but not much rain.

August. Tuesday 5. 1873. went out south 5 miles
did not see any buffalo. came in to camp. Bat [Mas-
terson] shot and hit kiote [coyote] on run. I got
some ripe grapes around spring. got hackberry stick
split it and made gun stick. made one for Bat.

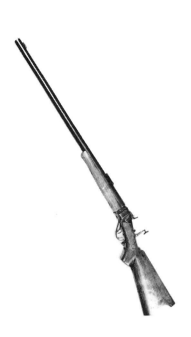

Orlando A. (Brick) Bond (right) was a freighter and buffalo hunter for the first twelve years of Dodge City's history. Bond set many records for large kills of buffalo. He owned a saloon and dance hall with his partner, Thomas C. Nixon, and later started a drug company with ex-Mayor A. B. Webster. Nixon (left), a Dodge City buffalo hunter, blacksmith, rancher, policeman, and saloonkeeper, set similar buffalo hunting records. In 1884 he was shot and killed by Mysterious Dave Mather. In the center, above, is shown a Sharps .50 caliber buffalo rifle, widely used on the frontier.

Brick Bond and other hunters, more famous for other reasons, such as William F. (Buffalo Bill) Cody, Wyatt Earp, Bat Masterson, and William M. Tilghman, little realized that in less than a decade the seemingly unending supply of buffalo, the Indian's commissary, would be exhausted. Bond recalled with regret the passing of not only the buffalo, but the antelope, deer, wild turkey, wild pigeon, curlue, plover, and prairie chicken. Long before his death in 1927, he became a strong advocate for strict game laws. In later years he related that he had been lured west by United States Government pamphlets advertising the profits of buffalo hunting as a means of depriving Indians of their meat and forcing their surrender.

During the three years of 1872, 1873, and 1874, in western Kansas and south into Texas, over three million buffalo were slain, changing the face of the plains with dramatic suddenness. All of the bigger herds had been destroyed, leaving vast pastures empty except for the rotting carcasses and whitened skeletons.

The last traces of the vanishing herds — their bleaching bones — remained a source of ready cash for twenty more years for the destitute homesteader or freighter returning home with empty wagons. The *Ford County Globe* of June 24, 1879, reported: "O. A. Bond arrived in the city from the south yesterday with about 25 tons of buffalo bones"; and as late as September 7, 1880, announced: "Mr. Thomas Nixon, in charge of the freighting train of Charles Rath, arrived in the city loaded to the guards with buffalo bones." The bones poured into Dodge City to be shipped as far east as Wilmington, Delaware. The best were used for combs, knife handles, and other utensils; the next best were ground into dust for use in sugar refining; and the refuse were ground into meal for fertilizer.

In less than ten years the buffalo were gone, and "Nimrod, the mighty hunter," busied himself with the bones of his nearly extinct quarry.

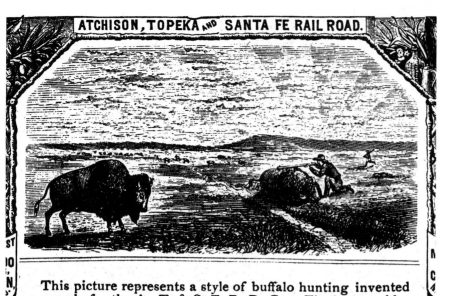

ATCHISON, TOPEKA AND SANTA FE RAIL ROAD.

This picture represents a style of buffalo hunting invented expressly for the A., T. & S. F. R. R. Co. The hunter rides to the bloody field on a tame buffalo, hired for the purpose. On arriving at the location of the herd, the tame buffalo, actuated by sordid and mercenary considerations, lies down on his east side, the hunter lies down behind him and discharges his weapon at the herd. Notice the look of calm resignation on the face of the stricken buffalo, and the sad smile playing around his horns. He is inclined "to get his back up" about it, but his spine has been bored so full of flute holes that he will soon change his tune. He concludes to die, and as he has no property to leave the rest of the herd they go off and leave him. This style of hunting is only practiced under the authority of this Company.

The satirical insert at the left, from an 1876 A. T. & S. F. Railroad timetable, probably was taken for gospel truth by some tenderfeet crossing the great Plains. The buffalo's bleached remains were used by eastern companies for fertilizer, buttons, and sugar refining. The advertisement (below) was posted in the town of Cimarron, twenty miles west of Dodge City, in the 1880's. Thousands of tons of buffalo bones scattered over the Southwest were hauled into Dodge City and piled alongside the railroad (below left) where the ghoulish heaps sometimes startled passersby.

BONES WANTED

We are undertaking to buy a car load of Bones and will pay $8.00 a ton cash delivered at my shop in Cimarron. Will also pay market price for light and heavy Junk such as scrap iron, metals, rubber, etc. :   :

JOHN W. SALLEE

Chapter III
A WICKED LITTLE TOWN

The first ten years in Dodge City were the years that built the wild and wicked reputation that Dodge City has held since its unholy beginning over a century ago.

During these first ten years visitors to "the front" spread the word that established Dodge City as the "wickedest little city in America." Dodge City's legend began to grow early in its history. The following newspaper accounts were written in the years 1877 to 1881 describing the "Bibulous Babylon of the Frontier."

"Dodge has many characteristics which prevent its being classed as a town of strictly moral ideas and principles, . . . fast men and fast women are around by the score, seeking whom they may devour, . . . and many is the Texas cowboy who can testify as to their ability . . ." [*Corpus Christi* (Tex.) *Gazette*] "Dodge is the Deadwood of Kansas; her incorporate limits are the rendezvous of all the unemployed scallawagism in seven States; her principal business is polygamy without the sanction of religion; her code of morals is the honor of thieves, and decency she knows not." [*Hays* (Kan.) *Sentinel*] "Dodge City. A Den Of Thieves And Cut Throats — The Whole Town In League To Rob The Unwary Stranger." [*Yates Center* (Kan.) *News*]

"She awakes from her slumbers about 11 a.m.; takes her sugar and lemon at 12 m., a square meal at 1 p.m., commences biz at 2 o'clock, gets lively at 4, and at 10 p.m. it is hip — hip — hurrah! 'till 5 o'clock in the morning. . . . nineteen saloons. No little 10x12s, but 75 to 100 feet long, glittering with paint and mirrors, . . ." [*Kansas City Times*]

"Gambling ranges from a game of five-cent chuck-a-luck to a thousand dollar poker-pot." [*Corpus Christi Gazette*] "Dodge is a fast town, . . . The employment of many citizens is gambling, her virtue is prostitution and her beverage is whisky. She is a merry town, and the only visible means of support of a great number of her citizens is jocularity. Here rowdyism has taken its most aggravated form, . . . Seventeen saloons furnish inspiration, and many people become inspired — not to say drunk. Every facility is afforded for the exercise of conviviality, and no restriction is placed on licentiousness." [*Hays Sentinel*]

"More than occasionally some dark-eyed virago or some brazen-faced blonde, . . . will saunter in among the roughs of the gambling-houses and saloons, entering with inexplicable zest into the disgusting sport, breathing the immoral atmosphere with a gusto . . . Dance houses are ranged along at convenient distances . . . Here you see the greatest abandon. Nice men with white neckties, the cattle dealer with his good clothes, the sport with his well-turned fingers, smooth tongue and artistically twisted moustache, and last but not least the cow-boy, booted and spurred as he comes from the trail, his hard earnings in his pocket, all join in the wild revel; . . ." [*Corpus Christi Gazette*] "The town is full of prostitutes and every other house is a brothel. . . . the street is brilliantly lighted and thronged with gaudily dressed women, and men whose garb betokens the cow-boy; from many saloons proceeds rolicking strains of music . . . the dance halls are crowded with lewd women and rough men who plunge into the intimacies of the dance with a reckless abandon and inflamed drink, make the night hideous with their boisterous revelrie [sic] and so through the night it goes." [*Hays Sentinel*]

"Dodge City is a wicked little town . . . the Texas cattle drovers . . . loiter and dissipate sometime for months, and share the boughten dalliances of fallen women." [*Washington Evening Star*] "Here may be seen the 'cow boy' after his long drive of many miles, with his pockets filled to bursting with silver dollar pieces, wending his way in the evening, to some of the 'dance halls,' of which there are three in the city, there to engage in the merry dance with the drunken frail ones, to the drunken music of a third-class violin and bass fiddle, until suddenly the unsuspecting 'cow boy' finds himself without money, which is nothing remarkable, as each 'set' of ten minutes duration, costs 75 cents. He, in his rage and chagrin at spending his money too foolishly, generally produces and flourishes a revolver with the evident intention of having satisfaction, which he is generally able to procure in the calaboose." [*Sterling* (Rice Co., Kan.) *Gazette*]

". . . the famous Dodge City, at the time [1873] a perfect paradise for gamblers, cut throats and 'girls' . . . Every one in town, nearly, sold whisky, or kept restaurant, perhaps both. . . . Dodge was the frontier town. . . . they were a 'jolly set of boys' there. They carried a pair of Colt's revolvers in their belts, wore their pants in their boots, and when they died generally did so 'with their boots on.' It wasn't safe in those times to call a man a liar, or intimate that his reputation for honesty was none of the best — unless you were 'spoiling for a fight.' In those days 'Boot Hill' was founded, and the way it grew was astonishing to new-comers and terrifying to 'tender feet.' " [*North Topeka Times*]

"Dodge boasts of two burying spots, one for the tainted, whose very souls were steeped in immorality, and who have generally died with their boots on. 'Boot Hill' is the somewhat singular title applied to the burial place of the class just mentioned." [*Corpus Christi Gazette*] "On a lonely side hill near by this modern Sodom there are twenty-eight tolerably new graves, and all but three of the occupants are reported to have 'died with their boots on' — victims to the sweet music of the pistol or the pleasant toyings of the bowie knife. Bullwackers, cat guards, dance girls, saloonists, gamblers, and border ruffians have given Dodge a most unenviable reputation." [*Troy* (N. Y.) *Budget*] "Mr. L. [T. W. Ludwig, a visitor from Pennsylvania in 1877] says that Dodge City has a very hard name in the east, and that 'Boot Hill,' our graveyard, is considered almost as great a curiosity as the grave of Shakespeare. Mr. L. selected some small pebbles from 'Boot Hill,' and will carry them home . . . as a constant reminder of the renowned graveyard of the far west." [*Dodge City Times*]

"The money spent foolishly in the 'Famous City' in one week would be sufficient to keep the poor of the county the entire winter. . . . We think if those who spend their money in riotous living, would let up for about a week on oyster suppers, saloons, gambling halls and 'bed houses' and . . . devote the amount to the poor, they would feel exceedingly better in so doing." [*Spearville* (Kan.) *News*]

"Even the Mayor of the city indulges in the giddy dance with the girls and with his cigar in one corner of his mouth and his hat tilted to one side, he makes a charming looking officer." [*Corpus Christi Gazette*] "The mayor is a flannel mouthed Irishman and keeps a saloon and gambling house which he attends to in person. The city marshal and assistant are gamblers and each keep a 'woman' — as does the mayor also. The marshal and assistant for their services (as city officials) receive one hundred dollars per month, each. The sheriff owns a saloon and the deputy sheriff is a bar tender in a saloon. . . . The ex-chairman of the Board of County Commissioners runs a saloon and dance hall, where the unwary are enticed, made drunk and robbed. Six men were knocked down and robbed one night last week. . . . If any of your readers anticipate immigrating to Kansas, advise them to shun Dodge City as they would the yellow fever, measles, smallpox and seven year itch combined, as I think they would all be preferable in a civilized country to residence in this town.

"My opinion of this place is pretty much the same as that of a certain Santa Fe conductor. A drunken Texas cowboy boarded his train east of here and when he called 'tickets' Texas responded 'hint got none.' 'Where are you going?' 'Goin to — hic — hell.' 'All right, give me fifty cents and get off at Dodge.' " [*Oskaloosa* (Iowa) *Herald*]

Is it any wonder that a young man, known only to the pages of history as "Herbert," wrote his father a post card, dated May 7, 1877, while camped fifteen miles east of Dodge City, and mailed at the city of Lakin, Kansas, west of the "infamous hell-hole" which recited in part as follows: "Dear Father: — As I've a little time I'll drop you a card, so you can see we are all well and headed West. Have laid over here to wait for a larger crowd, so as to be perfectly safe going through Dodge. There are nine teams now and will be three more in the morning, so we will be safe anyway. . . ."[1]

Dodge City's reputation took on this shade of barbarism in its earliest days because it was populated largely by hunters, freighters, soldiers, and border ruffians, men who lived by their own standards of the frontier. The emptiness, loneliness, and solemnity of the great plains where "one could see the sky under a horse's belly," did not oppress these men. Most were of old North European stock, hard-drinking, hard-fighting warriors and wanderers, gamblers, and explorers. They loved the plains, the receding horizons, the loneliness, the short grass, sand, and silence. The buffalo hunter found on these plains a region where he might do impromptu battle and ride away to fight some other day. In Dodge City he found a trading and shipping center for his buffalo hides and a place where he could test his antidotes for weary days and lonely nights.

A hunter's gun was his most important possession and a good gunsmith was a much sought after man in Dodge City. Frederick C. Zimmermann, born in Prussia, Saxony, left his native land to evade service in the Prussian army. At the age of twenty-six he was foreman for a famous gunsmith in Paris, having charge of forty workmen. He came to New York in 1863, working at his trade in several eastern states. He started his business in Dodge City in July, 1872. Out of a tent stocked with firearms and ammunition, he built up an extensive hardware business and became one of Dodge City's most successful merchants.

His advertisements in the local newspapers announced: "The latest improved Winchester Rifles which shoot seventy grains of powder, for sale by F. C. Zimmermann. . . . the mammoth establishment of F. C. Zimmermann, . . . carries the largest stock of hardware, and the best selected assortment of fire-arms, ammunition, and gun fixtures, in Western Kansas. Here you can buy at eastern prices, pistols, rifles and shotguns of every caliber. . . . pistol-belts or holsters, saddle-bags, . . . Here you can have your pistols and guns repaired promptly and with satisfaction. . . . The opinion and conclusion of buffalo hunters and frontiersmen in our State and Territories concerning the 'future gun' has been satisfactorily settled upon the Freund improved Sharp's Rifle, which is to-day the favorite of those that chase the game and fight the Indians, . . . For the Freund's improved Sharp's Rifle is the strongest, simplest, and most perfect, consequently the most reliable arm manufactured in the world, and for military service it cannot be excelled. F. C. Zimmermann, Practical Gunsmith for 31 years."

By the fall of 1872, almost three blocks of frame, false-front buildings had been built up on the north side of the railroad tracks. These buildings on the north side of Front Street, facing the tracks, became Dodge City's center of trade for the next thirty years. West of Second Avenue was Col. Isaac Young's

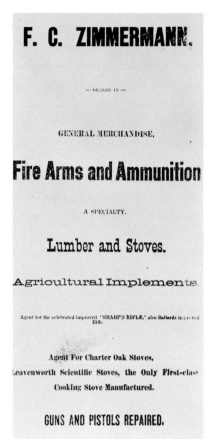

F. C. ZIMMERMANN,

— DEALER IN —

GENERAL MERCHANDISE,

Fire Arms and Ammunition

A SPECIALTY.

Lumber and Stoves.

Agricultural Implements.

Agent for the celebrated improved "SHARP'S RIFLE," also Ballards improved Rifle.

Agent For Charter Oak Stoves,
Leavenworth Scientific Stoves, the Only First-class
Cooking Stove Manufactured.

GUNS AND PISTOLS REPAIRED.

Frederick C. Zimmermann (left), a Prussian emigrant, learned the gunsmith trade at age twenty-six in Paris. Arriving in the United States eight years later, he practiced his trade in New York and Connecticut, then Laramie, Wyoming, and Kit Carson, Colorado. Zimmermann arrived in Dodge City from Kit Carson in September, 1872, and opened his business in a tent. His wife and two babies arrived shortly after. His store on Front Street was the source of firearms and ammunition (center above) for the hunters and cowboys of Dodge City's early history. Zimmermann (right) was an expert gunsmith whose services were in much demand. He was, however, an ardent foe of the gambling and saloon element in Dodge City's cattle town days. A pioneer merchant, his gunsmith trade grew into a substantial hardware and lumber business. Before his death in 1888 he was a gentleman farmer who experimented with shade trees, planted orchards and vineyards, and demonstrated the successful growth of alfalfa in Ford County.

harness and saddle shop and Herman J. Fringer's drug store on the corner. Fringer's building served as Dodge City's first post office and the office of Dodge City's first "doc," T. L. McCarty. It was still standing and in use as a hardware store thirty years later.

On the east corner of Second Avenue, then known as Bridge Street, was Chas. Rath & Co., general merchandise. In the same block from west to east were Hoover & McDonald's wholesale liquor store and saloon, Morris Collar's clothing store, F. C. Zimmermann's hardware store, A. J. Peacock's Billiard Hall saloon, later known as the Saratoga, and at the east end of the block on the corner of First Avenue was P. L. Beatty's and James H. Kelley's saloon and restaurant. This building, sometimes known as the Alhambra saloon, was moved in from Hays, Kansas, in the early summer of 1872.

On the east corner of First Avenue, at the west end of the next block, was A. B. Webster's dry goods and clothing store, later converted to the Old House saloon. Next door was Moses Waters' and James

The bewhiskered Frederick C. Zimmermann stands in front of his Front Street store (right) around 1873 or 1874. Holding Zimmermann's hand is Arthur, his son, killed by a wild horse on the Zimmermann homestead in 1886. Next to Arthur sits Zimmermann's wife, Matilda, and in the buggy is his daughter Clarissa. The interior of the Zimmermann hardware store is pictured below as it appeared shortly before the owner's death in 1888.

Hanrahan's Occident saloon, later owned by Henry Sturm; next, R. W. Evans' grocery store, and at the east end of the block on the corner of Central Avenue, then known as Railroad Avenue, was the famous Dodge City Hotel or Dodge House. Originally the Essington Hotel, it became the Dodge House shortly after its erection. It was located directly north, across Front Street, from the Santa Fe depot. The proprietors were George B. (Deacon) Cox and F. W. Boyd. The hotel housed a restaurant, a saloon, and a billiard hall.

During the first ten years of Front Street's business history, as businesses changed and moved to new locations, Young's harness shop became L. A. Logan's saddlery; Chas. Rath & Co., rebuilt in brick in 1876, later became Wright, Beverley & Co., one of Dodge City's largest general merchandise stores in the 1870's and '80's; the Alamo saloon, next door, became Dr. T. L. McCarty's City Drug Store; F. C. Zimmermann enlarged his store into the old City Drug Store location; Morris Collar's clothing store became, under new and various ownerships, a barber shop, a dry goods establishment, the Lone Star saloon and restaurant, and finally the Delmonico restaurant; the Saratoga saloon was converted to Hadder and Draper's Mercantile company west location; Jacob Collar built up a general merchandise store east of the Saratoga which became known as the Blue Front Store, the first store to offer coffins and undertaker's goods; Beatty & Kelley's old

Buffalo hunters, soldiers, merchants, and gamblers pose on Front Street in 1873 (above) — from the left: Hoover & McDonald's liquor store, Zimmermann's hardware store, Dr. McCarty's drug store, Morris Collar's clothing store, and A. J. Peacock's billiard hall and saloon, "the Place for Sporting on the Green." The woman sitting on the beer keg in front of Hoover & McDonald's saloon is Mollie Whitecamp, alias Dutch Jake. Her reputation as a sporting woman was enhanced by her habits of smoking big cigars and swearing like a bullwhacker. In pictures below, Front Street (upper right) was a bustling center of business as the first cattle herds began to arrive in 1875. From right to left, the three small buildings are Beatty & Kelley's saloon, barbershop, and restaurant. The two-story building is Jacob Collar's store — general merchandise, furniture, coffins, and undertaker's goods. Next is the Saratoga saloon, John Tyler's Tonsorial Parlor, McCarty's drug store, Zimmermann's hardware store, the new location of Morris Collar's dry goods and clothing store, Hoover's saloon and wholesale liquor store, the Long Branch saloon, Alamo saloon, and Chas. Rath & Co. general merchandise. Following left, across Second Avenue, can be seen Herman J. Fringer's drug store. A closer view (bottom left) of five businesses in the same block of Front Street shows, from left to right, the general outfitting store of Charles Rath and Robert M. Wright, the narrow quarters of the Alamo saloon, the Long Branch saloon with steer head mounted in front, Hoover's wholesale liquor store, and Collar's dry goods. The Front Street replica (below right) built in 1958, is a reproduction of some of these buildings as they appeared in 1875.

44

saloon building became a meat market; their buildings east of the saloon, a barber shop and restaurant, were moved off in 1879. A large two-story frame building, thirty by eighty feet, was constructed to house their restaurant, saloon, and barber shop on the first floor; the second floor was constructed as a theater and meeting hall. This building became known as Kelley's Opera House and the Opera House saloon.

George H. Tepe started his Pioneer boot and shoe shop in a narrow room between the Old House saloon and the Occident saloon; shortly after, this space became the quarters of three different tailors who came to Dodge City in the 1870's. The first two were murdered; the third was frightened away when he discovered the fate of his predecessors. East of the Occident saloon was the Old Stand Meat Market of Charles S. Hungerford; R. W. Evans' grocery store became the east location of the Hadder & Draper general merchandise store, known as the Red Front Store; east of Hadder & Draper was a bakery and John Mueller's boot and shoe shop. Mueller kept six employees busy cutting, sewing, and ornamenting boots. He became a wealthy merchant in a short time selling boots to the cowboys at eight to eighteen dollars a pair. The Dodge House finished out the three main blocks of Front Street and remained the largest hotel in the area for over twenty years.

South of the railroad tracks, opposite this row of Front Street businesses, were grocery stores, outfitting and supply houses and numerous dance halls and saloons, all of a short-lived variety. A traveler passing through Dodge City in September of 1872, remarked, "Saturday evening we reached Dodge, or Buffalo City, as it is called, a small town on the Atchison, Topeka and Santa Fe Railroad, five miles west of Fort Dodge. The 'city' consists of about a dozen frame houses and about two dozen tents, besides a few adobe houses. The town contains several stores, a gunsmith's establishment and barber shop. Nearly every building has out the sign, in large letters, 'Saloon.' The road is being pushed along with surprising rapidity and is now running trains fifteen miles west of the town."[2]

Mrs. Calvina Anthony, wife of A. J. Anthony and daughter of a Presbyterian minister, came to Dodge City from St. Louis in 1872 and wrote in her diary: "Just before our marriage the town of Dodge City was started, on what might be called the borders of Sahara. Very few families had yet shown the courage to locate in this frontier town. The morning I arrived I looked around in vain for a woman's face, and did not see one until I was taken into the Dodge House and introduced to the landlady. We sat down to our breakfast with a great crowd of long haired hunters, with their buckskin suits and pistols. All was excitement and trading. A man stood by the door as they went out and collected a dollar from each one for their meal."[3]

During the first year of Dodge City's existence, even though the Town Company had organized, the still unincorporated city had no elected or appointed officials; the county government was not yet organized, and consequently there were no courts, jails, or official law enforcement nearby. Through June of 1873 there were seventeen killings in Dodge City according to various area newspaper accounts. George M. Hoover recalled in 1903 that he remembered of no less than fifteen men killed in Dodge City during the winter of 1872 and spring of 1873, all buried on Boot Hill.[4] Some claim even more died with their boots on that first year, but at any rate, the homicide rate for a frontier settlement of 300 population was exceedingly high.

Dodge City's Boot Hill found its way into frontier legend during the first three years of Dodge City's existence. It became a catch word for any graveyard of the unknown, unsung, and friendless renegades and mavericks of the Western frontier. In 1872 the hill was a bold, treeless bluff protruding southward into the broad bottoms of the Arkansas River, made of gypsum, rock, clay, and sand, covered with buffalo grass, and decorated with clumps of soapweed and prickly pear, about half a mile north of the river. The highest point near the town, about 700 feet from Front Street and Second Avenue, it was a convenient spot for burials.

County Attorney Mike Sutton recalled in 1880 that a man was shot a few hundred yards from the top of the hill in 1872. His body lay nearly all day without anyone to care for it, when toward evening a grave was dug on the hill, becoming the first, to be followed by twenty-five or thirty others until the hill was dotted with little mounds.[5] The hill became known as Boot Hill by the citizens of Dodge City in the early 1870's because most of its tenants died with their boots on.

George M. Hoover recalled in 1903 that the first burial on Boot Hill was in September of 1872. A negro, Black Jack, was shot through the head in front of Beatty & Kelley's saloon and restaurant by a gambler known as Denver. Robert M. Wright recalled the same incident in 1913, but claimed the name of the murdered party was Tex.[6]

The first known recorded killing in Dodge City, according to Kansas newspapers, was in September, 1872. A desperado named Jack Reynolds who had been threatening employees of the western division of the A. T. & S. F. Railroad "was forever quieted at Dodge City . . . by a track layer, who put six balls through him before he could say scat."

In November, 1872, J. M. Essington, owner of the Essington Hotel, was "while drunk and in a fuss, shot and killed instantly by the cook." The hotel's name was changed soon after to the Dodge House by the new owners, George B. Cox and F. W. Boyd.

The Newton *Kansan* reported that four men were killed during the week of December 3 to 9, 1872. No particulars were given.

Jack L. Bridges, an early day buffalo hunter, was a deputy United States marshal at Hays City from 1868 to 1876, and is believed by some to have been an acting marshal in Dodge City in 1872 or 1873. Few records can be found to substantiate this fact. He did return to Dodge City, however, and served as city marshal from 1882 to 1884.

In December of 1872, Billy (Bully) Brooks, former marshal of Newton, Kansas, shot it out with the Santa Fe yardmaster over a girl named "Captain" Drew. Brooks may have been acting as a lawman in Dodge City at the time, possibly having been hired privately by Dodge City merchants. Five days after the shooting a saloonkeeper was shot and killed by an unknown person. The blame was placed on Brooks, but nothing was proved. In March of 1873 Brooks was shot at by a buffalo hunter. Bully ducked behind the barrels of water placed at intervals along Front Street for fire protection. The ball from the hunter's rifle passed through two barrels of water and lodged in the outside iron hoop before reaching Brooks. It was evidently not the first close call for Brooks in Dodge City. He left Dodge City soon after, and in July of 1874, was arrested with an alleged gang of mule thieves in Sumner County, Kansas, and hanged by a party of vigilantes.

Dodge City's privately hired "lawmen" were not up to the job and in February of 1873, a "vigilance committee" was organized. They started things off with a bang by killing two men in one of the dance halls and running five others out of town. In March of 1873 members of the vigilantes, including James Hanrahan of the Occident Saloon and John (Scotty) Scott of Peacock's Billiard saloon, saddled up in pursuit of a buffalo hunter named McGill who had been shooting up the town. Just outside of town, "he opened fire on the party with his needle gun. They responded; and the result was, he was brought into town riddled with bullets."[7]

By June of 1873 the "vigilance committee" had attracted undesirable members until they outnumbered the men who had formed the committee originally for the public good. On the night of June 3, 1873, several members of the committee who had been imbibing freely, seized the wagon and team of an industrious negro, William Taylor, a personal servant of Colonel Richard I. Dodge. When the orderly ran out to stop the men who were driving off with the wagon and mules, they shot one of his mules. When Taylor objected to this, several of them, Scotty in particular, opened fire, fatally wounding the negro. He was taken to Herman J. Fringer's drug store, and while Fringer was dressing the wounds, the drunken mob entered the drug store, drove off Fringer, dragged Taylor to the street, and finished him off with a dozen more shots.

Boot Hill might have looked like this, 1872-1878.

The police court warrant at the upper left, signed by Marshal L. E. Deger, was for the arrest of Alice Chambers, a dance hall "queen." Her offense was brawling with "one Miss Howe — alias Dutch Kate." Alice, who died in May, 1878, was the last person buried on Boot Hill and the only woman known to have been buried there. To the right is pictured William L. (Billy or Bully) Brooks, a stage coach driver and marshal of Newton, Kansas, in 1872. He was implicated in two killings in Dodge City in December, 1872, and is believed to have served as a privately hired lawman there in 1873. He was captured as one of a gang of mule thieves in Sumner County in July, 1874, and hanged by vigilantes.

This burial service for ex-Mayor Alonzo B. Webster was photographed at Prairie Grove Cemetery in April, 1887. Prairie Grove was Dodge City's first official graveyard, a private cemetery northeast of town. Prior to its existence in 1878, citizens with means were buried at Fort Dodge; those with none were buried on Boot Hill. The twenty-odd mounds and wooden markers in the foreground, outside the wooden fence of the cemetery, are the graves which were removed from Boot Hill by the county coroner in 1879.

John W. Straughn, a lieutenant colonel with the Indiana Volunteers during the Civil War, was an early citizen of Dodge City, a deputy sheriff, the county jailer, and county coroner in the 1870's and 1880's. Colonel Straughn became associated with a group of Dodge City speculators who organized "The Dodge City Mining Company" in 1881. Straughn conducted mining operations for the company in Colorado several years. While in Denver, Colonel Straughn posed with his mining gear for the picture at the lower right, which was enlarged to life size, painted, and displayed at the Chicago World's Fair in 1893. It was used as a model for the statue (right) placed on top of the old Mining Exchange building in Denver.

Colonel Dodge, the fort commander, was outraged. He telegraphed the Governor and was given permission, since there were no proper civil law enforcement authorities in the area, to make arrests. One member of the vigilantes, Bill Hicks, who bragged of his part in the murder, was taken into custody and later convicted. The other accused member of the mob, John Scott, hid in the icebox in Peacock's saloon and during the night was helped to escape.

In July of 1873 a cattle herder attempted to bring a prostitute into the Dodge House. When the bartender refused her admittance, he was shot and killed. The cattle herder was in turn shot and killed by another party.

And so went the killings as more fresh mounds of earth dotted the sides of Boot Hill.

Five years later, as the city was booming with the Texas cattle trade, the land covered with these unmarked graves became too valuable to reserve exclusively for the "motley crowd of sinners" buried there. The Town Company sold the "old burying ground west of the city, known as Boot Hill," to Herman J. Fringer and Samuel Marshall who were planning to sell off lots for residences. The Dodge City *Times* reported on May 4, 1878, "No more burying on 'boot hill.' The Town Company have forbidden it." The next day, however, the last interment was made. On a Sunday morning, May 5, 1878, Miss Alice Chambers, former owner of an unsuccessful dance hall and saloon, died from natural causes. Possessed of no money and few friends, she was laid to rest somewhere on the hill.

Alice was one of Dodge City's fallen frails to whom fate had been more than fickle. In October, 1876, she was attended for an unknown ailment by Dr. Samuel Galland. In January, 1877, the impatient doctor filed suit against Alice for payment of $15.75 for medical services. The case was appealed and while in continuance in the District Court of Ford County, the disdaining editor of the Dodge City *Times* had this to say about unlucky Alice: "On Wednesday a gust of wind removed seven dollars out of the stocking of Alice Chambers as she was walking up Front Street. After a six hours search, participated in by all the tramps in town, one dollar was recovered. We had supposed that the Kansas wind was of a higher order, and did not stoop to such larceny. The thing is now settled, that under some circumstances even the wind can be found feeling around in by and forbidden paths."

The case of Galland vs. Chambers was finally tried by jury after a year's delay. Alice's peers, all male, awarded Dr. Galland the generous sum of $2.00 for his troubles. In June, either Alice's physical or financial health worsened to the point that she dissolved her partnership with Susie Foster in the operation of a dance hall and saloon. Shortly thereafter Susie was taken to court by a disgruntled musician who had been serenading the evening's festivities for several months without pay.

In July, 1877, Assistant Marshal Ed Masterson arrested Alice, who "with force and arms, did make an offence by fighting with one Miss Howe — alias Dutch Kate — within the corporate limits of the City of Dodge City." The testimony of saloonkeeper, A. J. Peacock, and Marshal Masterson was evidently more convincing than that of Charles Ronan, Alice's friend and one of Dodge City's notorious gamblers. For this disturbance Alice was fined $3.00 and costs of $12.90. Marshal Masterson pocketed $2.00 of the costs for making the arrest and probably felt he earned it.

In August, Alice appeared in D. M. Frost's police court to answer Dr. T. L. McCarty's and Dr. W. S. Tremaine's suit for recovery of $30.20 owed them for medical services. To avoid attachment of her modest home on Gunsmoke Street (then called Walnut Street), she deeded the property to her friend, Charles Ronan. Eight months later she ceased from troubling and was laid to rest, the last burial on Boot Hill and the only woman known to have been buried there.

Up until now the cemetery at Fort Dodge was used for the burial of those in Dodge City whose families or friends could make the proper arrangements. In May of 1878, the same time the Town Company had ordered the abandonment of Boot Hill as a burial site, several of the town's leading citizens made plans for a proper cemetery. Dr. Tremaine, Robert M. Wright, P. L. Beatty, James H. Kelley, and Samuel

Marshall put up enough capital to buy five acres of ground for use as a private cemetery. It was located about one-half mile northeast of the business center of town. The new burial place, known as Prairie Grove Cemetery, was surrounded with a wooden fence and laid out in lots and walks. Single graves were sold for $5.00 each, and family lots, twenty feet square, were $25.00 each, to "Anyone wanting a decent place in which to hide his bones . . ."[8]

It was January of 1879 before the bodies in Boot Hill were disinterred and removed to Prairie Grove Cemetery. John W. Straughn, a deputy sheriff, coroner, and county jailor, was engaged to move the bodies. Straughn had purposely delayed his grisly job from the putrifying heat of summer to a colder time of year, even though the frozen ground in January made the job go slower. The *Ford County Globe* reported on the completion of Straughn's efforts: "The skeletons removed from the graves on Boot Hill were found to be in a fine state of preservation, and even the rude box coffins were as sound as when placed in the ground. . . . Col. Straughn, the coroner, who removed them, says they were as fine a collection of the extinct human race as ever handled. Some were resting quietly with their boots on, while others made more pretensions to style, having had their boots taken off and placed under their heads for a pillow. Only a few of them could be recognized as all the head-boards, if there ever were any, had long since wasted away, and nothing remained to denote where their bodies lay but little mounds of clay. They are now all resting side by side, like one happy family, at the lower end of Prairie Grove Cemetery. . . . The enchanting click of the festive revolver they no longer hear."

The January 28, 1879, issue of the *Ford County Globe,* announced: "The body of Alice Chambers was removed last week from its former resting place to the Prairie Grove Cemetery." Burials on Boot Hill ended, but its legend was just beginning to grow.

During the first two decades after the Civil War in Texas, the immense tracts of open range, covered with luxuriant grass, encouraged the breeding of cattle. The cattle were driven north on the Chisholm Trail to Abilene in 1867, but as the farmers' frontier advanced westward, the railheads shifted south to Newton and Wichita and west to Ellsworth. A branch of the Chisholm Trail, sometimes called the Eastern Trail, forked into Dodge City. The Western Trail came north through Dodge City to its railhead at Ogallala, Nebraska, on the Union Pacific Railroad. By 1880 Dodge City had replaced Ogallala as the railhead of the Western Trail.

As the buffalo hunters' campfires died away and the Indian submitted to confinement on reservations to avoid starvation, the Texas drovers were heading their longhorns up the trails from as far south as the Nueces River in Texas. The drive from Texas to Kansas came to be known as "going up the trail," for the cattle really made permanent, deep-cut trails across the otherwise trackless hills and plains of the long way. One old cowboy who rode up the Western Trail in 1884 described it as a "chocolate brown and brick red ribbon that wound up over the hills and down to the rivers and creek bottoms and was fifty to a hundred feet in width, cut into the prairie sod a foot or more in depth by the hooves of the longhorn cattle."[9]

Not all of the cattle reaching Dodge City were shipped east by rail. Many were driven on to northern and western destinations for sale to meat packers, mining areas, Army posts, Indian reservations, and railroad construction gangs. Young steers were driven on to fatten on the grasses of Montana or Wyoming.

In spite of the fact that some buffalo hunters had voiced opinions that the buffalo would not be cleared from the plains in less than a hundred years, four years of intensive hunting caused a noticeable decline in hide and meat shipments. By 1874 the enterprising merchants of Dodge City were becoming aware of the tremendous potential that was being thrown in their laps by the westward turn of the cattle trails. The Santa Fe railroad built a small stock yard that winter, and by 1875 Dodge City was a regular shipping point for Texas cattle. Dodge City's cattle shipments were second only to Wichita in 1876. In 1877 the Chisholm Trail to Wichita was choked off by rural settlement and new quarantine legislation, and Dodge City became

The longhorn herds of the 1870's ranged from 2,500 to 3,000 head and were ideal for long drives.
These animals could travel nearly as far as a camel without water, and once arrived at the lush grass south
of Dodge City, they would fatten in good shape for market in a few weeks. It was possible
to fatten a longhorn from a lean 800 pounds to a fat 1,200 pounds in a few months.

A Texas longhorn (Bos Texanus) was a hard, wiry animal fitted for travel and for self-preservation.
It was a descendant of Spanish cattle brought to Santa Domingo by Columbus.

These real cowboys (below) pose on a roundup in 1884.

Heading "up the trail to Dodge" with 3,000 head of longhorns, sometimes at twenty-four hour stretches in the saddle, caused "frequent hankerings for the chuckwagon." When anyone complained about the chuck, he had to do the cooking. One cowboy broke open a biscuit and said, "They are burnt on the bottom and top and raw in the middle and salty as hell, but shore fine! Just the way I like'm." Lower right is a tin "safe" used to store the wagon cook's supplies of coffee, beans, baking powder, flour, rice and dried fruit.

Herds of longhorns grazing south of the railroad tracks were a common sight in Dodge City from 1875 to 1885.

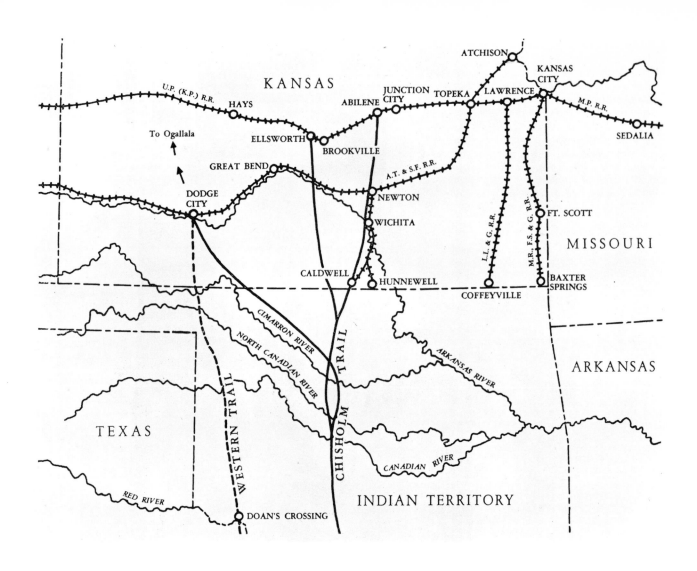

Kansas railheads and Texas cattle trails, 1867 to 1885.

the Cowboy Capital. The Santa Fe railroad built a new and larger stockyard in Dodge City, and its citizens prepared for a lively trade with the Texas cattlemen.

In June 1877, as the first cattle shipments were leaving Texas, Dodge City's promoters bragged: "The grass is remarkably fine, the water plenty, drinks two for a quarter and no grangers. These facts make Dodge City THE cattle point."[10] By the end of the year, Dodge City had left its Santa Fe competitors far behind, having shipped over a quarter of the Santa Fe's total shipments.

A Texas trail drive was a serious operation. As many as 3,000 cattle were collected in south Texas and consigned by the owners to the care of a trail boss for delivery at a railhead which might be 1,500 miles or more away. Ten to twelve hands handled the herd, along with a cook and a wrangler to care for the remuda, a herd of a hundred or more saddle horses. The cowboys spent fourteen to sixteen hours a day in the saddle — a hard, lonely, and monotonous routine for thirty dollars a month and board. They "punched" the cattle along the Western Trail some ten to twelve miles a day from south Texas to the rip-snorting village of Fort Griffin, then on to Doan's Store on the Red River to refill the chuckwagon with frijoles, bacon, and dried fruit. They crossed Indian Territory leaving a few beeves with the Indians to endure a safe crossing, then across the Canadian River and the hot dry sands of the Cimarron, finally to wash away the dust and lubricate parched throats, in the bars of Dodge City.

52

In the spring of 1877, as the merchants of Dodge City prepared for the coming of the cattle drives, the Dodge City *Times* advertised reduced prices for whisky and cigars, and announced: "Accommodations for a large influx of people are being made by the hotels and restaurants, and with a view to the adage of 'live and let live.' . . . The agents of the A. T. & S. F. road at this point are gentlemen of integrity . . . The stock yards are commodious and capable of accommodating a large number of cattle. . . . A general effort is being made to make Dodge City an attractive point for the Texas cattle dealers, and our united citizens send forth their greeting to our Texas neighbors inviting their presence to our community, . . ."

The adage of "live and let live" was a necessary business philosophy for trade with the Texans. Dodge City merchants knew that the newly arrived cowboys and cattlemen expected the company of women, plenty of whisky, and a chance to lay a few bets at the faro and monte tables. "Shooting up the town just for fun" was also a Texas cowboy's privilege if he was man enough to try.

Dodge City businessmen knew the likes and dislikes of the men who followed the dusty, dangerous trails, and knew that most Texans shied away from anything that betrayed a Yankee background. To draw the Texas trade, the saloonkeepers of Dodge City picked appropriate names for their watering places — the Alamo, the Alhambra, the Nueces, and the Lone Star. The stores made special efforts to hire employees who could "talk the lingo." Chas. Rath & Co. hired Henry M. Beverley, a popular Texan and former cattle drover, and Sam Samuels who spoke fluent Spanish. After Charles Rath and Robert M. Wright dissolved partnership in the fall of 1877, Wright took Beverley into full partnership and changed the name of his firm to Wright, Beverley & Co. A reporter remarked in 1878 that "Judge Beverley has sold a few goods this week — perhaps eight or ten thousand dollars worth. The Texas drovers seem [to] think a heap of the 'Old Jedge.' "[11] "Wright, Beverley & Co's store was a perfect bee-hive last Tuesday, . . . About thirty Mexican customers dropped in at the same time and purchased goods to the amount of seven or eight hundred dollars. The Mexicans look upon Sam Samuels as their Moses in this strange land."[12] Wright's firm sent a Texan out to meet the incoming herds and solicit their trade, a common practice for large cattle mercantile houses.

Dodge City was ten years old before its first bank, the Bank of Dodge City, was organized. The financial needs of the cattle buyers and sellers during the turbulent cattle town years were met by mercantile houses such as Wright, Beverley & Co. and Hadder & Draper Mercantile Co. While hundreds of thousands of dollars changed hands, these outfitting stores and general merchandise dealers carried on a banking service in connection with their commercial trade. They accepted deposits of large sums and allowed the cattlemen to draw on their accounts as needed. Robert M. Wright recalled that his store's remittances to banks in Leavenworth were frequently as high as $50,000. Hadder & Draper made a point of hiring personnel that had been trained in eastern Kansas financial institutions.

The land south of the Arkansas River at Dodge City in the 1870's was largely U. S. Government land, still unsettled. The homesteaders stayed mostly north of the river, leaving the rolling plains south of the river open for grazing. The Texans camped on the prairie south of town and grazed their herds until ready for shipping east on the railroad or driving on farther north or west. A visitor to Dodge City in 1877 reported: "Standing on top of the new and handsome court house, a lovely prairie landscape was here spread out before me. Five miles to the southeast nestled Fort Dodge, then as far as the eye could reach for miles up the river and past the city, the bright green velvety carpet was dotted by thousands of long horns which have in the last few days arrived after months of travel, some of them from beyond the Rio Grande."[13]

In July, 1877, a reporter from the Kansas City *Times* announced that "Dodge City, Kansas, has become the great bovine market of the world, the number of buyers from afar being unprecedented large this year, giving an impetus to the cattle trade that cannot but speedily show its fruits. The wonderful rank growth of grasses and an abundance of water this season has brought the conditions of the stock to the very highest

Frederick C. Zimmermann stands in front of his hardware store on Front Street in 1876, above. The building partially seen at far right was John Tyler's Tonsorial Parlor, later the location of the Lone Star saloon and the Delmonico restaurant and hotel.

When drovers of Texas cattle began to arrive in 1875, tired and dusty after three months in the saddle, the "Tonsorial Parlor" or barber shop was the first place they visited. Dieter and Lemley opened their shop in 1876, conveniently located next door to

Centennial Barber Shop !

DIETER & LEMLEY, Proprietors.

SHAVING, SHAMPOOING

AND HAIRCUTTIG DONE IN THE
LATEST FASHION.

First door east of Beatty & Kelley's Restaurant, Dodge City, Kansas.   10

Beatty & Kelley's restaurant and saloon on Front Street. George Dieter advertised himself as "the eminent tonsorial artist of the Arkansas valley," who "gives a clean shave, trims hair in the latest fashion and with exquisite taste, according to the rules of the tonsorial art."

Front Street is seen above around 1880, looking east from the corner of Third Avenue.

This was Front Street between First and Second Avenues around 1883. At left is the York, Parker, Draper Mercantile Company, formerly the Saratoga saloon. The furniture store is the successor to Jacob Collar's furniture business, supplier of coffins and undertaker's goods. The small building at the right, is Beatty & Kelley's Alhambra saloon, later rebuilt into a two-story building, known as the Junction saloon, where the disastrous fire of 1885 started.

 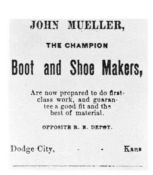

JOHN MUELLER,

THE CHAMPION

Boot and Shoe Makers,

Are now prepared to do first-class work, and guarantee a good fit and the best of material.

OPPOSITE R. R. DEPOT.

Dodge City, - - Kans

Dodge City Market.	
Corrected weekly by York, Hadder & Draper.	
Flour, per cwt........	$2 00 a 2 80
Corn meal, per cwt	1 50
Oats. per bush	40
Corn, per bush	45
Hides—Buffalo per lb..	3½ a 4½c
Wolf	75 a 1 75
Coyotes	50c
Skunks	10 a 15c
Chickens, dressed, per lb	10c
Turkeys	12½c
Potatoes, per bush.....	90c
Apples, dried, per lb...	8 a 10c
Peaches, dried, per lb..	12½c
Bacon..............	10½c
Hams	14 a 15c
Lard	12 a 14c
Beef	8 a 10c
Butter..............	20c
Eggs, per doz	15c
Salt, per bbl	3 50
Coffee—Java..........	30c
Rio	22½c
Tea, per lb...........	50 a 100
Sugar	11 a 14c
Syrup per gal	75 a 1 00
Coal Oil............	40c
Coal, per ton........	8 00 a 10 00

John Mueller (left above), a successful bootmaker in Ellsworth, followed the cattle trade to Dodge City in 1874. His successful boot shop west of the Dodge House, on Front Sreet, was identified with a large boot-shaped sign. In 1880 Mueller sold out and turned his full attention to a growing herd of livestock, identified with a boot-shaped brand. Weekly market quotations (right) were furnished by York, Hadder & Draper Mercantile Co. in a September, 1878, issue of the Ford County Globe.

The view of Front Street above, around 1880, is looking east from the corner brick building of Wright, Beverley & Co. at Second Avenue. Robert M. Wright rebuilt his store in brick in 1876, changing the name of his business from Chas. Rath & Co. to Wright, Beverley & Co. a year later. The Long Branch saloon can be seen two doors to the right. The sign nailed to the city well in the foreground reads, "The Carrying of Fire Arms Strictly Prohibited." This order was difficult to enforce, and not always taken seriously. Robert M. Wright (lower right), an early resident and founder of Dodge City, built his general merchandise store into a retail trade of $250,000 annually with a branch store at Fort Griffin, Texas. In addition to sheep dip (below) his store catered "to the wants of their immense Texas trade, the jingling spur, the carved ivory handled 'Colt,' or the suit of velveteen, and the many other Texas 'necessaries' you here find by the gross or cord."

Wright, Beverley & Co.,

DEALERS IN

General Merchandise,

DODGE CITY, KANSAS.

AND MANUFACTURERS' AGENTS FOR

LADD'S CELEBRATED SHEEP DIP.

The only certain cure for Scab and its Prevention. It Destroys Vermin and Increases the Growth of Wool. The cheapest, most safe and effective remedy known. Non-Poisonous. Orders Promptly Filled.

Wright, Beverley & Co., "Headquarters for Cattlemen and Drovers" on the corner of Second Avenue and Front Street, is shown above around 1883. Two doors to the right stands the popular Long Branch saloon. The man standing in front of the hitching rack is believed to be Henry M. Beverley. Born in Virginia, raised in Kentucky, "Judge" Beverley fought with Texas troops of the Confederate forces, then followed the cattle trade from Texas to Abilene, then Ellsworth, and finally, Dodge City.

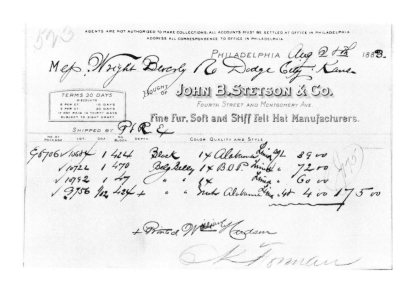

The invoices at the left from Wright, Beverley & Co. accounts show 1883 billings for saddles ordered from a Denver manufacturer, and cowboy headgear ordered from John B. Stetson & Co.

57

The Dodge House was the principal hostelry from 1872 to 1883. Owned and operated by F. W. Boyd and George B. (Deacon) Cox, it contained thirty-eight rooms, a restaurant, bar, and billiard hall, and could accommodate up to ninety persons. Cox (right below with wife Annie and daughter Clara Bell) was a member of the Fourth Georgia Volunteer Infantry during the Civil War. He drifted to Kansas, ran a hotel in Larned for a short time, and came to Dodge City in the fall of 1872. Deacon Cox kept an old Jersey cow that was often borrowed by trail men, taken to the south side of the Arkansas River, and used to pilot herds across.

The Western House or Great Western hotel was the chief competitor of the Dodge House. Owned and operated by Dr. Samuel Galland, it was located south of the railroad tracks.

The Western House offered plainer fare than the Dodge House, but served venison, buffalo humps, and other wild game, specialities of Mrs. Galland (left). Dr. Galland (right) was a controversial member of the cattle town community. A friend of Luke Short during the saloon war of 1883, he also was a Prohibitionist, who proudly advertised, "No liquor on the premises." The Great Western hotel (center above) located on Trail Street between First and Second Avenue is seen here in the 1890's after a snow. At the right is a tub and chair from the "bath" of that time.

Hamilton B. (Ham) Bell (upper left) was born in Pleasant Valley, Maryland, in 1853. He came to Dodge City in 1874 from Great Bend, Kansas, and entered into the livery business. His large stable, shown above, built in 1885, was known as the Elephant Livery Stable. It was a rendezvous where freighters could leave their expensive equipment and turn their mules and horses into the big corral. As many as fifty men made their beds in the hayloft at night during the cattle season. The Elephant stable served as an undertaking establishment where Ham Bell kept the first hearse in Dodge City. Bell served as a deputy United States marshal at various periods from 1880 to 1885 and as sheriff of Ford County from 1888 to 1892.

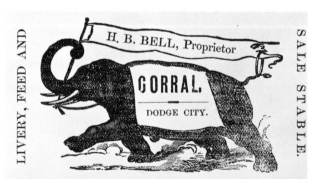

A United States weather observatory was started in Dodge City in September, 1874, housed in the Dodge House hotel. Later, it was moved to the building (left) at the corner of Second Avenue and Gunsmoke (Walnut) Street. Called the United States Signal Station, it recorded the first weather statistics of Ford County.

Philander Gillette Reynolds, better known as P. G., came to Dodge City in 1875. Born in Elmira, New York, in 1827, Reynolds established his first stage line in Lawrence, Kansas, in 1856. He and son George (above) ran the Dodge City and Panhandle Stage line carrying U. S. mail, freight, and passengers into Indian Territory and south to Fort Elliott, Texas. His 1878 newspaper advertisement (right) proudly announced a forty-hour connection between Dodge City and Fort Elliott, a distance of 200 miles via Camp Supply.

Covered wagons heading west were once a familiar sight on the streets of Dodge City. These wagons are headed west on what then was Chestnut Street.

Mule trains below are leaving the warehouse of York, Parker, Draper Mercantile Company in Dodge City. The railhead at Dodge was the center for supplying the vast country of the Indian Territory, Panhandle of Texas, and western Kansas. Millions of pounds of supplies were transferred from the railroad at Dodge City to the mule and cattle trains bound for the forts and cattle camps south and west of the "frontier Babylon."

standard, the ruling prices showing a corresponding improvement. There are now upwards of one hundred thousand head of cattle in the immediate vicinity of Dodge City, and some of the herds run high into the thousands. There is a single herd numbering forty thousand, another of twenty-one thousand, another of seventeen thousand, and several of five thousand or thereabouts. On Saturday no less than twenty-five thousand head were sold. The Texas drive to Dodge this year will run close to two hundred thousand head."

In May, 1878, Nicholas B. (Deacon) Klaine waxed eloquently in the pages of his newspaper, the Dodge City *Times:*

PREPARING FOR THE CATTLE TRADE.

In this delectable city of the plains the winter of discontent is made glorious by the return of the cattle trade. With the countless herds come the hordes of bipeds. Weeks and months before, through the blasts of winter and the gentle zephers of spring, has impecuniosity longed for the opening of the cattle trade, in which Dodge City outshines all enmity and rivalry.

This "cattle village" and far-famed "wicked city" is decked in gorgeous attire in preparation for the long horn. Like the sweet harbinger of spring, the boot black came, he of white and he of black. Next the barber "with his lather and shave." Too, with all that go to make up the busy throng of life's faithful fever, come the Mary Magdalenes, "selling their souls to whoever'll buy." There is "high, low, jack and the game," all adding to the great expectation so important an event brings about.

The merchants and the "hardware" dealer has filled his store and renovated his "palace." There are goods in profusion in warehouse and on shelves; the best markets were sought, and goods are in store and to arrive. Necessarily, there is great ado, for soon the vast plains will be covered with the long horn — and the "wicked city" is the source from which the great army of herder and driver is fed.

DODGE CITY 1878-1882

The following legend identifies sites numbered on the map of Dodge City, 1878-1882, on the opposite page.

1. Hospital
2. Union Church
3. Court House
4. First school house
5. U. S. Signal Service office
6. Dodge City Times newspaper office
7. Wright House hotel
8. Ford County Globe newspaper office
9. Odd Fellows Hall
10. Henry Sturm's ice house
11. Dodge House livery stables
12. Blacksmith and wagon shop
13. Saddle and harness shop
14. Dr. T. L. McCarty's drug store and post office (Herman J. Fringer's drug store and post office from 1872 to 1881)
15. Wright, Beverley & Co. general merchandise
16. Alamo saloon
17. Long Branch saloon
18. Hoover's wholesale liquors and saloon
19. Zimmermann's hardware
20. Lone Star saloon
21. York, Hadder & Draper Mercantile Company (Saratoga saloon from 1876 to 1878)
22. Jacob Collar's dry goods, furniture, coffins, and undertaker's goods
23. Alhambra saloon
24. Centennial barber shop from 1876 to 1879
25. Beatty & Kelley's restaurant from 1872 to 1879
24 & 25. Kelley's Opera House from 1879 to 1898
26. Old House saloon
27. Boot shop; tailor shop
28. Occident saloon
29. Butcher shop
30. York, Hadder & Draper (east store)
31. Bakery
32. Mueller's boot and shoe shop
33. Dodge House hotel, billiard hall, and saloon
34. Railroad water tank and depot
35. City offices and jail
36. Ham Bell's livery stable
37. Varieties dance hall
38. Lady Gay dance hall and saloon (Comique theater)
39. Great Western hotel

Residences:
40. Chalk Beeson
41. Bat Masterson — Annie Ladue
42. Alice Chambers — Charles Ronan
43. Henry L. Sitler
44. W. H. Harris
45. Sarah Warren
46. Mollie Whitecamp (Dutch Jake)
47. Dog Kelley (scene of Dora Hand killing)

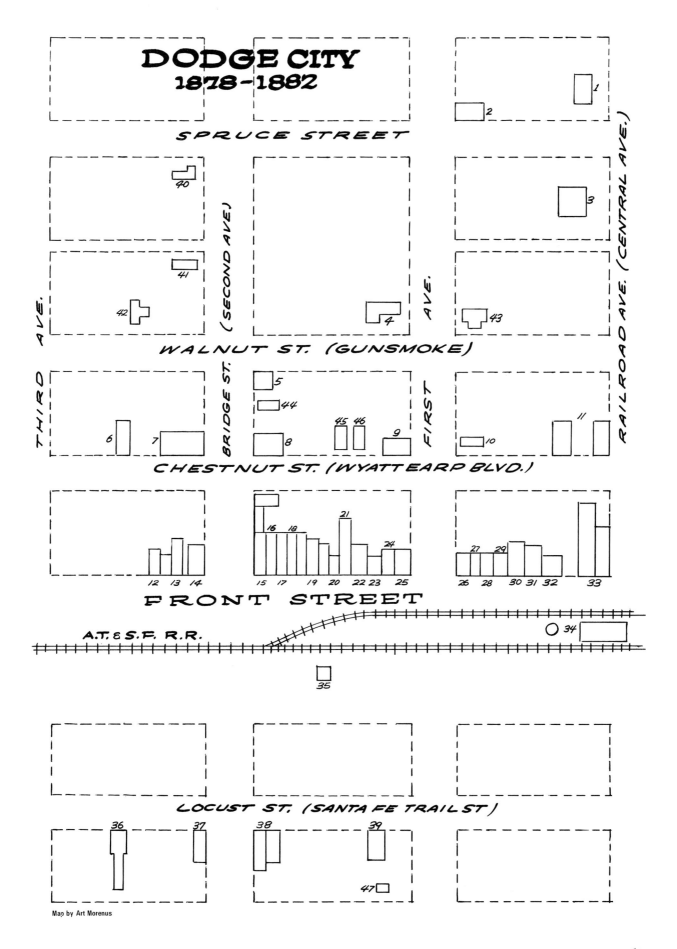

DODGE CITY
1878-1882

SPRUCE STREET

WALNUT ST. (GUNSMOKE)

CHESTNUT ST. (WYATT EARP BLVD.)

FRONT STREET

A.T. & S.F. R.R.

LOCUST ST. (SANTA FE TRAIL ST.)

THIRD AVE.

(SECOND AVE.)

BRIDGE ST.

FIRST AVE.

RAILROAD AVE. (CENTRAL AVE.)

Map by Art Morenus

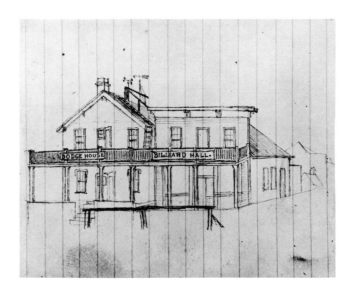

The sketch of the Dodge House above was made by Ado Hunnius on April 26, 1876. Carl Junius Adolph Hunnius was a thirty-four-year-old surveyor who kept a diary with drawings of his experiences in Dodge City from April to June, 1876. He shows the U. S. Signal Station's weather observing instruments on the roof.

A view of the Dodge House (below), looking west from the railroad depot in May, 1879, shows John Mueller's boot shop, Mary Goudy's bakery, Samuel Marshall's land office, York, Hadder & Draper Mercantile Co., C. S. Hungerford's meat market, and the Occident and Old House saloons at the west end of the block. Just west of First Avenue can be seen James H. Kelley's new two-story Opera House under construction.

The season promises to be a remarkable one. The drive is reported to be larger, and the first herd will probably reach this point within a couple of weeks. There has been no undue preparation, and the earlier season has stimulated activity to the greatest measure of expectation.

As many as 1,500 of Klaine's "bipeds" — cowboys, owners, and buyers, invaded the environs of Dodge City during the cattle months from June through September, in both 1877 and 1878, doubling the population.

The herds of longhorn grazing south of the railroad tracks became so numerous that soon trains were impeded in much the same way that the buffalo blocked the engines' paths five years earlier. As a train came down from the west one evening in June, 1877, its progress was retarded by the herds of cattle grazing near the track. While a bunch of frightened steers were attempting to cross in front of the engine, two of them fell into the trestle work of a bridge and had to be dragged out by the horns before the train could proceed.

"Standing out on the extreme border of civilization, like an oasis in the desert, or like a light house off a rocky coast, is 'the beautiful, bibulous Babylon of the frontier' — Dodge City," so stated the newspaper editor of a neighboring town in 1878.[14] Dodge City's reputation as a bibulous Babylon started early. One of its earliest saloons, Tom Sherman's, was a simple frame building with a canvas roof, south of the railroad tracks, north of the Santa Fe Trail. Sherman was a lame, oversized killer who opened his saloon shortly after Dodge City's founding. By the time he had left Dodge City in 1875, his saloon was legend. A cowboy ballad grew up on the trails from Texas, sung to the tune of an old Irish song, "The Unfortunate Rake." Today the ballad is known as "The Cowboy's Lament," the commonest version beginning, "As I walked out in the streets of Laredo." One version, however begins, "As I walked through Tom Sherman's barroom." Another version of the same ballad concludes, "And take me to Boot Hill and cover me with roses, I'm just a young cowboy and I know I done wrong."[15]

Dodge City's saloons numbered sixteen in 1877, its population less than 1,000. Names of Dodge City's saloons, painted in large letters to catch the eye of thirsty cowboys in from the range, ring in the ear like the clink of glass mugs on beer taps and the smash of empty glasses against varnished mahogany — the Alamo, the Long Branch, the Billiard Hall, the Alhambra, the Saratoga, the Occident, the Nueces, the Crystal Palace, the Lone Star, the Old House, the Hub, the Sample Room, the Oasis, the Junction, the Green Front, the South Side, the Congress Hall, the Stock Exchange, and the St. James. Some saloons, disdaining pretensions to style, were known only by their proprietors, good men and true, whose reputations were the only advertising needed — Hoover's, Peacock's, Beatty & Kelley's, Sturm's. Some were bars run in connection with hotels, dance halls, and theaters — the Dodge House, the Lady Gay, the Varieties, the Comique, and the Opera House.

The saloons of Dodge City ranged from one-room shanties with dirt floors and backroom bordellos, to thirty by one hundred foot wooden buildings with painted interiors, fancily carved mahogany bars, mirrors, and paintings. The better saloons on Front Street were narrow buildings divided into two or three separate rooms, the front room for drinking, the back rooms for billiards and gambling. The dance halls and saloons south of the railroad tracks had elevated stages, a cleared area for dancing, and a simple bar; the back rooms of some were divided off into cribs for private pleasures.

Chalk Beeson and his partner, W. H. Harris, bought out A. J. Peacock's Billiard Hall saloon in 1876 and opened it out anew as the Saratoga. Beeson's Saratoga in the east half of the block on Front Street between First and Second Avenues, was a class above Peacock's and became known for its music and attractive surroundings. In 1878 Beeson and Harris sold the Saratoga and bought the Long Branch saloon, six doors west. The Long Branch, with its five piece orchestra, became the town's fanciest gathering place, the most popular for cattlemen and gamblers. Beeson's musical abilities on violin were abetted by four other musicians, second violin, trombone, cornet, and piano. The Long Branch allowed no dancing. It offered Dodge City's "champion milkpunch mixer," Adam Jackson, who had moved west on Front Street with Beeson and Harris from the Saratoga to the Long Branch. The front room contained a bar, a billiard table, a coal stove, and a corner reserved for the orchestra; in the back was a private gambling room and a room where drunks were locked up. "Getting to the joint" or "crooking the arm" was a hallowed tradition among rangers and cattlemen, but "wearing calluses on the elbow" often resulted in "sleeping it off" in the back room of the Long Branch.

The Alamo saloon was a narrow eighteen foot dram shop squeezed between R. M. Wright's bustling mercantile firm on the corner of Front Street and Second Avenue and the Long Branch saloon one door east. It started as a service to the customers of Wright's firm, a handy place to imbibe after outfitting the crew from Texas for the last leg of the trail or the trip back home. Its proprietors changed frequently; in 1877 the Alamo was presided over by Henry V. Cook, "a reformed Quaker from New York, . . . it is hinted that the manner in which he concocts a toddy (every genuine cattle man drinks toddy) increases the value of a Texas steer about $2.75."[16]

In 1880 the United States census listed twenty saloonkeepers among a population of 1,087 in the "beautiful, bibulous Babylon of the frontier." One of its early Front Street saloons, the Occident, originally was owned by Moses Waters and James Hanrahan, later by Henry Sturm, who built up a wholesale trade to compete with the profitable business of George M. Hoover. These advertisements appeared in Dodge City newspapers from 1874 to 1877.

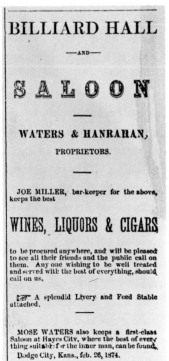

Chalkley M. Beeson (left), born in Salem, Ohio, came to Dodge City in 1875 from Colorado, where he was employed as a stage driver. He came to collect a debt, stayed on, and purchased the Long Branch saloon property in 1878 from Robert M. Wright. Beeson owned the Long Branch site until 1918, but sold his interest in the business operation to Luke Short in 1883, to devote full time to stock raising and music interests. Beeson's musical background helped make the Long Branch the most popular saloon in Dodge City where a six- to eight-piece orchestra played to the delight of thirsty cowboys and cattlemen.

William H. Harris (right) joined Chalk Beeson in partnership as owner and operator of the Saratoga saloon shortly after Beeson's arrival in Dodge City. Beeson furnished musical entertainment; Harris managed the gambling and liquor sales. In 1878 Beeson and Harris sold the Saratoga and moved to Beeson's new property, the Long Branch. W. H. Harris remained an operator of the Long Branch until 1883. He joined Chalk Beeson in stock raising, became vice president of the Bank of Dodge City, and served as city treasurer.

LONG BRANCH SALOON.

DRAKE & WARREN, Proprietors.

WINES,
LIQUORS,
& CIGARS.

Also Billiard Parlor &
a Club Room.

GENERAL HEADQUARTERS OF STOCKMEN.

THE OLD RELIABLE

LONG BRANCH SALOON

—AND—

BILLIARD PARLOR.

The reputation of this house for good goods will be maintained by

Drake & Warren, Proprietors.

These saloon advertisements from the Dodge City Democrat *and* Ford County Globe *show Roy Drake and Frank Warren as successors to Luke Short and W. H. Harris, operators of the Long Branch.*

The highball gambling device (above) was used in the Long Branch saloon according to Frank Warren, at one time a part owner and dealer there. This painting (center above), "The Cowboy's Dream," is one of several that adorned the Long Branch and accounted for its designation as an "art gallery," a term humorously applied after the passage of Kansas prohibition law. The clock shown above ticked away the wee hours in the Long Branch and witnessed the killings there of Deputy U.S. Marshal Harry McCarty and freighter Levi Richardson. P. L. Beatty and James H. Kelley advertised their restaurant on Front Street (far right). Their saloon next door, the Alhambra, was the hangout of Dog Kelley's political Gang where one of his bartenders, Jacob Schaefer (right), world billiards champion, first learned his mastery of the cue.

BEATTY & KELLEY,

PROPRIETORS OF THE

Dodge City Restaurant.

—

Best Restaurant in the City.

MEALS AT ALL HOURS.

The interior view (above) of the St. James saloon and billiard hall was taken shortly before the St. James burned in the Front Street fire of 1885. The St. James was the successor to Culver and Romero's saloon and billiard hall. The picture below, taken in the 1890's shows the interior of Baeder and Laubner's saloon on Front Street.

These saloons in Dodge City witnessed an excitement and festive spirit that rivaled New York's Tenderloin and the Barbary Coast of San Francisco. Mayor Webster's Old House was a competitor of the Long Branch that brought about the saloon war of 1883. M. S. Culver's and Casimero Romero's saloon and billiard parlor opened in George Hoover's building on Front Street when he moved his wholesale liquor store and saloon in 1884. The Oasis was operated by Dodge's famous marshal, Bill Tilghman, south of the "dead-line" where the legal restriction against carrying firearms was less strictly adhered to. Brick Bond's and Tom Nixon's saloon was in the old Lady Gay dance hall building, the location of Dodge City's most notorious after-dark activities. Nat Haywood, bartender at the Congress Hall saloon, was a former policeman who resigned shortly after his experience with drunken cowboys south of the tracks that resulted in the killing of Marshal Ed Masterson.

George M. Hoover's saloon and wholesale liquor store was one door east of the Long Branch. Hoover's was a simple bar run in connection with his wholesale trade which extended south into Indian Territory and the Texas Panhandle. He allowed no dancing, no gambling except occasional games of cribbage, and kept a strict business-like house. His bartender, George T. Hinkle, defeated Bat Masterson for Sheriff of Ford County in the bitter election of November, 1879. Cigars were a necessity in the cowtown atmosphere of Dodge City. In 1877 George M. Hoover received upwards of five thousand fresh cigars in one week's shipment.

Henry Sturm's Occident saloon, formerly owned by James Hanrahan and Moses Waters, was a block east of Hoover's on Front Street. Sturm, a prominent member of the German community in Dodge City, also ran a wholesale liquor business in connection with his saloon, and ran a strict house. Sturm specialized in expensive wines and liquors. Not all the liquor of the legendary West would "draw blisters on a raw-hide boot." He bragged in his newspaper advertisements, that Henry Sturm's was the place to wet your whistle "or get a pint, keg or barrel of the very best, old irish, hot scotch, six year old hand made sour mash Kentucky copper distilled bourbon or old Holland gin; or, . . . try some of Henry Sturm's Rhine wine sent him all the way from Alsace by his father-in-law Mr. F. Dorsheimer, and top it off with some of Best's Milwaukee beer and a Monogram cigar and the chances are that you 'will not go home till morning.' "[17] Sturm also kept a lunch counter advertising such delicacies as Limburger cheese. A jokester went into the saloon, took a seat, threw his feet on the table, and called for a glass of beer, a sandwich, and some Limburger cheese, which was promptly placed on the table beside his feet. He called to the proprietor and told him that the cheese was of no account, as he could not smell it, whereupon the proprietor replied, "Damn it, take your feet down and give the cheese a chance."[18]

The soldiers at Fort Dodge did not mix well with Texas cowboys and were not welcomed in all Dodge City's saloons. Beeson's Saratoga and Long Branch, and Sturm's Occident were three of the town's more strictly run saloons where soldiers could drink without fear of attracting the brawling element.

Beer was a popular drink and was kept cool during the summer cattle trading months in large warehouses filled with straw and blocks of ice cut from the Arkansas River during the winter months. When the heat of summer depleted the ice supply, carloads of ice were brought in from the mountains of Colorado.

The better saloons and bars such as the Occident, Dodge House, Beatty & Kelley's, Long Branch, Alamo, and Old House, had billiard tables. Jacob Schaefer, Sr., a world champion billiard player, first learned his skill from the gambler, Charles Ronan, in Beatty & Kelley's saloon on Front Street in the 1870's. Schaefer won his first billiard championship in 1879, and soon became hailed as "The Wizard" because of his fine cue markmanship. Schaefer won his last match against Willie Hoppe in 1908 after thirty years as master of the cue.

The quantity of alcoholic beverage consumed in Dodge City during the cattle trade of the 1870's and 1880's is impossible to estimate accurately. Suffice it to repeat the comments of the editor of the Dodge City *Times* in 1878: "We don't suppose we can form an estimate of the quantity of whisky drank in Dodge City by the number of whisky barrels lying around loose. Morris Collar purchased one hundred empty whisky barrels, the supposed number of barrels emptied during the year up to this date. But it would be safe to say one hundred more have been disposed of, leaving the supposed number of barrels of whisky consumed in Dodge City in eight months at 200 barrels, or 300 barrels for one year. We don't know whether there is any credit in making this statement, and whether it reflects any credit or not, it reflects that the Bibulous Babylon keeps up its credit on a commercial commodity. The curious can estimate the number of drinks in 300 barrels of whisky."

"Getting to the booze joint" was at the heart of most of the trouble and violence during the cattle period. Many of Dodge City's citizens and visitors were good hearted, like the Irishman, James H. Kelley.

"But when full of booze . . . [he] got on the warpath and made trouble . . ."[19] Kelley, a partner in the Beatty & Kelley restaurant and saloon, was an early mayor of Dodge City and a leader in Dodge City politics during the cattle years. One day, while under the influence, he went hunting buffalo with Ed and Bat Masterson. While in a drunken state he mounted his horse, Calamity, and rode off with his greyhounds after buffalo. Calamity stumbled in a prairie dog hole and Kelley fell. Bat went for a wagon and hauled Kelley back to Dodge City, where before sobering up he made his will. His injuries did not prove nearly as fatal as he imagined in his drunken stupor.

Joe Mason, a Dodge City assistant marshal, brought a pet bear back from Fort Supply in 1880 and gave it to Kelley, the town's mayor. Kelley raised the bear from a cub, and "Paddy-the-Bear" became a prominent character around Front Street. Most of the time he was kept chained in the back yard of Kelley's restaurant where he was much admired by the children. By the time the bear was full grown he became the victim of many practical jokes. The pranksters around town loved to slip Paddy a drink of whisky from time to time. Paddy enjoyed the free drinks, but the teasing that followed made Paddy constantly on the lookout for hiding places. One day while Paddy was seeking escape from his tormentors, a visiting salesman happened to finish one of Dodge City's hardest drinking bouts ever endured by any man without fatal results. He sought a room at the Dodge House to rest his bemuddled brain, and settling down, he viewed the revolution of walls, ceiling, and furniture, interwoven with imaginary chains of boa constrictors, before finally falling into a deep drunken sleep.

Next morning while the salesman was balancing between a state of "busthead" and delirium tremens in a corner room on the lower floor of the Dodge House, Paddy-the-Bear spied the open window leading to this room and pounced upon it. He entered his new retreat, looked about the room, then crawled beneath the bed. It was a tight squeeze, and as the bear laid in his close, warm quarters he breathed heavily; as he breathed the booze-saturated occupant gently rose and fell with the movement of the bed.

About this time a terrible headache had brought the spifflicated carouser back again to a state of semi-consciousness, and with it came once more the awful fear that he was to be the victim of delirium tremens. He worked himself into a panic and was about to cry out, when he noticed for the first time that the bed was gently, but surely, rising and falling. He was so scared that his voice would not come, the terror almost crowding the whisky out of his system — the bed rising and falling. He could stand it no longer. He reached to a table, and grasping a tumbler, threw it under the bed with a crash, not knowing what he was doing.

The tumbler struck poor Paddy squarely between the eyes and the brute, suddenly frightened, forgot that he was in close quarters. Bringing his powerful muscles to play, he rose quickly to a full standing posture, bearing the terrified drunk aloft so that when he fell forward his hands dropped to the floor at the outer side of the bed. His face came into a position where his eyes looked directly under the wrecked bed. He gazed into two glowing balls of fire made by the eyes of the beast under the mattress looking out from darkness.

At this time the Dodge House was the largest hotel in western Kansas and was filled with cattle-men, boarders, and commercial travelers, most of whom, including several ladies, were in the dining room at breakfast. The apartment where Paddy lay frightened under the bed was partitioned off of one corner of the dining room. After a long look into the balls of fire beneath the bed and a remembrance of horrible accounts of the delirium tremens, the terror stricken boarder, scantily attired, burst through the door of his room and landed among the astonished guests at the breakfast table. As he broke through the door, and at each leap toward the middle of the room, he roared at the top of his voice, "boys, I've got 'em! By God, I've got 'em!"[20]

Teasing and whisky turned Paddy into an outlaw, and she was made into Christmas meat in December, 1883. The Dodge City *Democrat* eloquently recorded Paddy's obituary: "Paddy is Dead. Yes, as frequently observed by our religious contemporary [Deacon Klaine, editor of the *Democrat's* competitor, the *Times*], 'civilization is advancing, and slowly but surely the early landmarks of Dodge City barbarism are passing away.' 'Paddy' was a bear, (and we presume that the half of her that this morning remains at Olive & Scearcy's [butchers] unsold, is still bear.) She was captured while a cub of a bearess, by a dismounted cavalryman, was educated at Camp Supply by a negro corporal, and was owned by an Irishman; this, we presume accounts for her incongruous cognomen, Paddy being a female. Her early education was not neglected; the loss of an eye and the caving in of a couple of ribs attest the thorough displin[e] of the corporal's training. Her early escapades, her appetite for lawyers and shoemakers, her love of the 'bloods' and 'velvet gowns,' and her adventures while attempting to play chambermaid at the Dodge House will be remembered affectionately and otherwise as evidence of her female frailties and follies. But Paddy is gone! Her spirit has taken its flight, perhaps to the dusky woods and mountainous recesses of her ancestors; the canine friends of her cubhood have gone before her, most of them, no doubt, by way of the sausage machine. The boys who in days of yore petted and fondled her, now stand silently gazing on her well rounded buttox, licking their chops in anticipation of bear steak at twenty-five cents per pound, and envying the fellow to whom she, by will no doubt, left her overcoat. In life she was a prominent member of the gang [Kelley's political clique], in death she held her own. She weighed more than the city Mayor, was a better solo bass singer than the Police Judge, was as moral as the biblical Joseph and sold for more money, and could drink more whisky than her biographer. Requiscat in pace."

One of the barbarisms that particularly annoyed the pious editor of the *Times* was prostitution — a subject that many Dodge City historians have seen fit to overlook. During Dodge City's history as "the end of the trail," the colorful euphemisms used in her newspapers for prostitutes showed much imagination — *demi monde, fallen frails, soiled doves, daughters of sin, fast women, fast girls, occupants of bed houses, doves of the roost, cyprians.*

Dodge City "girls" were housed in dugouts and frame houses on various byways of the town. One such house was known as the "Parlour House" and was closed down in 1879 by Justice of the Peace Henry V. Cook, the reformed Quaker from New York and proprietor of the Alamo saloon. The reason for Justice Cook's drastic action is unknown, but the *Globe* coyly reported that his decree resulted in the house being "closed for repairs."

Most of Dodge City's soiled doves were housed in the dance halls south of the tracks. Most of the higher class saloons north of the tracks did not allow women to solicit within their swinging doors. There were two or three dance houses operating in Dodge City during the height of the cattle trade — long frame buildings, with a dance hall and bar in front and rooms in the rear. The hall was nightly used for dancing, well supplied with scarlet ladies who belonged to the house and solicited the male visitors. Hamilton B. (Ham) Bell testified by affidavit in a court proceedings in Leavenworth, Kansas, that he knew a cook who with her husband, fourteen-year-old daughter, and two small children, lived in the rear of a dance hall on Locust Street (now Santa Fe Trail Street); that the "rooms in the rear were occupied, both during the dancing hours and after, and both day and night by . . . women for the purpose of prostitution;" that the young daughter "carried on prostitution like the other women, and with her mother's knowledge she danced and drank as the rest . . .;" that she "helped to keep the family with the money she earned by prostitution; and that her mother instructed and encouraged her to do so. And that, after the family left this house . . . was an inmate of other houses . . ."[21]

One tender female of dance house fame, Miss Minnie Lee, knocked over a coal oil lamp in her back room crib and set the Lone Star dance hall on fire. Dodge City's Fire Company, gentlemen all, hearing the new fire bell ringing, "came dashing to the engine house from every direction, some wearing clothes a la bed room and totally disregarding all toilet formalities. They reached the burning building just in time.

. . . Poor Minnie Lee was sitting on a doorstep giving vent to sobs of the most violent nature over the loss of her wardrobe, towels, &c. But the experienced firemen made short work of it, . . . [the fire] was soon extinguished and a huge conflagration averted."[22]

Dodge City's "doves" were a fighting breed of shady ladies according to the Dodge City *Times* of June, 1877: "A Battle of the Beauties. . . . Josie Armstrong . . . a very pink of feminine symetry and grace . . . fell to pulling hair and kicking shins . . . Just as the combat deepened and the prospect for two bald-headed maidens was bright, the irrepressible Joe Mason [a policeman] . . . sallied in and restored the peace and dignity of the city." The *Times* reported three months later that "several of the fast girls were slightly slugged this week." In January, 1879, the *Ford County Globe* announced: "Scarlet Sluggers. A desperate fight occured at the boarding house of Mrs. W., on 'Tin-Pot Alley,' [Chestnut Street, now named Gunsmoke Street] last Tuesday evening, between two of the most fascinating doves of the roost. . . . Tufts of hair, calico, snuff and gravel flew like fur in a cat fight, and before we could distinguish how the battle waned a chunk of dislocated leg grazed our ear and a cheer from the small boys announced that a battle was lost and won. The crowd separated as the vanquished virgin was carried to her parlors by two 'soups.' A disjointed nose, two or three internal bruises, a chawed ear and a missing eye were the only scars we could see."

In July, 1877, one of Dodge City's fightingest frails, "Miss Frankie Bell, who wears the belt for superiority in point of muscular ability, heaped epithets upon the unoffending head of Mr. [Wyatt] Earp to such an extent as to provoke a slap from the ex-officer [recently resigned as assistant marshal], besides creating a disturbance of the quiet and dignity of the city, for which she received a night's lodging in the dog house [city jail]."[23]

A week later, "Miss Frankie Bell called to administer a horse whipping [to the editor of the *Times* who printed the above]." Three weeks later, "Miss Frankie Bell and one of her associates were deposited in the dog house." And finally on the following week, "Frankie Bell made an oath before Judge Frost, not to indulge in spirits fermenti until next Christmas. Then wont she make Rome howl."[24]

In 1879 a visitor reported that there were fourteen saloons, two dance halls, and forty-seven prostitutes in Dodge City, a frontier village of 700 inhabitants.[25] He may have exaggerated slightly, but there was never a shortage in those days. When business was slow in Dodge City, the girls were transported to Fort Dodge, where they were slipped into the fort quietly in the darkness to join in the festivities. On March 9, 1879, the Dodge City *Times* published the following notice: "No heavy wagons or wagons containing prostitutes are allowed to be driven through the Fort Dodge garrison."

In 1878 the city council passed an ordinance calling for fines to be collected from all persons engaged in gambling and prostitution. The ordinary revenues were not adequate to support a police force large enough to control the explosive mixture of soldier and cowboy, merchant and gambler, prostitute and saloonkeeper. The *Times* reported that "Where the carrion is there you will find the buzzard," feeling that eradication of the "buzzard" was not a question, but that "the class who entail this additional expense should meet it with their own contributions, and thus afford themselves protection under the wings of the law. . . . The fines are extended to the houses of ill-fame and those who inhabit them. The frail humanity will respond to the demand of the depleted city exchecquer, remembering that the wages of sin is death. The 'girls' will feel that they are not answering to the Great Tribunal, though their temporal care is under the brawny arms of a big policeman, who is sworn to protect the peace and dignity of the city." "On with the dance."

A visitor from Pueblo, Colorado, remarked in 1878, that "the average Texas cow man gambles, and to supply this want almost, if not every saloon in the city, has one or more gambling tables. Faro, monte, and the other usual games are dealt openly, and most of the saloons have a private room for the votaries of draw poker."[26]

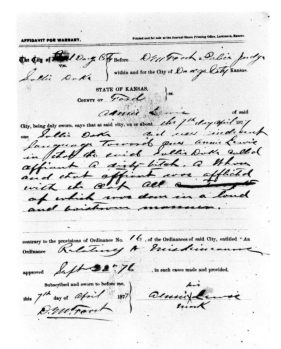

1884

Lillian Handie.

Handie's Park,

Cor. Hickory & Bridge Streets,   DODGE CITY, KS.

Prostitutes flourished in Dodge City from 1872 until their customers — the frontier hunters, soldiers, and cowboys — decreased in number, sending them elsewhere to practice their profession. The scarlet ladies of Dodge City were a quarrelsome and boisterous lot. The affidavit (left) issued in Dan Frost's police court recites as follows: "Annie Lewis of said City, being duly sworn, says that at said city, on or about the 7th day [of] April 1877 one Sallie Doke did use indecent language toward one Annie Lewis in that the said Sallie Doke called affiant a dirty-bitch, a whore and that affiant was afflicted with the clap all of which was done in a loud and boisterous manner, contrary to the provisions of Ordinance No. 16, of the Ordinances of said City, entitled 'An Ordinance Relating to Misdemeanors approved Sept. 22' '76, in such cases made and provided. (Signed) Annie (her X mark) Lewis." Another "document," the calling card (upper right) discreetly advertised the wares of Lillian Handie, one of Dodge City's doves of the roost, whose "Park" was located on the corner of Hickory Street and Second Avenue, then called Bridge Street, in 1884.

This Dodge City soiled dove of the 1880's is identified only by her nickname, Squirrel Tooth Alice. Apparently Alice acquired her sobriquet from her fondness for squirrels, since no rodent-like dental deformities can be detected in these pictures. She married a surveyor working for the Eureka Canal Company on its irrigation ditch north of Dodge City.

The drawing (left) shows a typical cattle town dance hall of the 1870's. The actual photograph (above) taken in 1878 is the interior of Ham Bell's Varieties, a Dodge City dance hall. Clearly shown, from front to back, are the bar, ice chest, monte and faro tables, six couples preparing to "indulge in the giddy dance," and at the far end of the room, a small, raised platform where three musicians are seated.

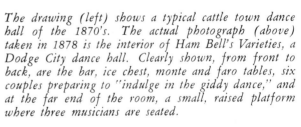

Dodge City's demimonde included Big Emma (left), Sadie Ratzell (center), and Doc Holliday's buxom beauty, Katherine (Big Nose Kate) Elder (right).

Thomas Carney, a wealthy Leavenworth merchant, Governor of Kansas from 1863 to 1864, appeared in Dodge City in 1877 allegedly as a hide and bone buyer for a firm in St. Louis. The ex-Governor "decoy[ed] three of our business men into a social game of poker," thinking the unsophisticated citizens of Dodge were an easy mark. His opponents turned out to be three of Dodge City's most notorious gamblers who fleeced the poor Governor. Carney left town hurriedly minus cash, watch, chain, and cuff links. The winning hand, portrayed below with actual Long Branch playing cards, was four aces over four kings and the joker. Alas! Governor Carney mistook the irregular shaped joker for an ace.

As the cattle arrived from the south in 1878, the *Globe* facetiously remarked, "Just 403,901 (?) gamblers (large and small fry) are already in Dodge, prepared to help themselves to the pickings this summer." Observers of Dodge City at that time guessed at the amount of money in circulation and the general business conditions of the community by the number of gamblers in town and games in progress during the early morning hours along Front Street.

"The faro banks seem to be doing a good business in Dodge City at present, being nightly patronized by gentlemen who flash up considerable 'swag.' " — a common announcement in Dodge City newspapers during the spring of the cattle years. Because of its intricate props and elaborate betting conventions, faro or farobank, once the most popular game of chance in Dodge City, is no longer widely played in the United States. A few faro tables, with their green cloths, dealing boxes, dealers, casekeepers, and lookouts or cashiers, can still be found in Reno and Las Vegas, today. In the 1870's and 1880's, saloons in Dodge City, as elsewhere in the West, advertised that faro was offered with a sign outside bearing the likeness of a tiger. Playing against the faro bank came to be known as "bucking the tiger." "Coppering the bet" and "calling the turn" is faro terminology that has also become part of our language.

Hazard or chuck-a-luck was a popular dice game — sometimes called bird cage, because of the cage shaped like an hour glass in which three dice were placed. Draw poker, which needs no explanation today, was second only to faro as the most popular early morning past time of Texas cowboys.

Robert Gilmore, alias Bobby Gill, was Dodge City's most colorful gambler. Bobby was the instigator of many quarrels and street fights and was considered by many to be "not a law-abiding, peaceful citizen."

76

He was asked to leave Dodge City several times — once a collection was taken up to pay his train fare out of town. Bobby was known around town as "a noted character of the paste-board fraternity," but his unequaled gift of gab and ability to ingratiate himself with the right people kept the scales of justice from weighing too heavily against him.

Bobby's poker game with his fellow "paste-board manipulators" and a former governor of Kansas is a classic story told on the pages of the Dodge City *Times* in March, 1877:

EX-GOV. CARNEY GOES BROKE ON A POKER GAME IN DODGE.

The once famous political boss of the State, ex-Gov. Thos. Carney, of Leavenworth, had arrived on the 6 o'clock train. . . . [He informed] some of our business men that his operations in Dodge City were buying hides and bones for a St. Louis firm. It seems from later developments that the Governor's real business in Dodge City was to entice our unsophisticated denizens into the national game of draw poker, and fleece them of their loose cash . . . the talk he made about the hide and bone business being merely a blind to cover up his real design.

The Governor's reputation and dignified bearing soon enabled him to decoy three of our business men into a social game of poker, 'just to kill time, you know.' Gov. Carney's intended victims were Col. [Charles] Norton, wholesale dealer and general financial operator; Hon. Robert Gilmore, and Chas. Ronan, Esquire [three of Dodge City's well-known gamblers]. The game proceeded merrily and festively for a time, until, under the bracing influence of exhilerating refreshments, the stakes were increased, and the players soon became excitedly interested.

At last the Governor held what he supposed to be an invincible hand. It consisted of four kings and the cuter, or 'imperial trump' [the joker], which the Governor very reasonably supposed to be the ace of spades. The old man tried to repress his delight and appear unconcerned when Col. Norton tossed a $100 bill into the pot; but he saw the bet and went a hundred better. Norton didn't weaken, as the Governor feared he would, but nonchalantly raised the old gent with what he supposed was a fabulous bluff. Governor Carney's eyes glistened with joy as he saw the pile of treasure which would soon be all his own, loom up before his vision, and he hastened to see the Colonel and add the remainder of his funds, his elegant gold watch and chain. Norton was still with the game, and the Governor finally stripped himself of all remaining valuables, when it became necessary for him to 'show up' his hand.

A breathless silence pervaded the room as Gov. Carney spread his four kings on the table with his left hand, and affectionately encircled the glittering heap of gold, silver, greenbacks and precious stones, with his right arm, preparatory to raking in the spoils. But at that moment a sight met the old Governor's gaze which caused his eyes to dilate with terror, a fearful tremor to seize his frame, and his vitals to almost freeze with horror. Right in front of Col. Norton were spread four genuine and perfectly formed aces, and the hideous reality that four aces laid over four kings and a 'cuter' gradually forced itself upon the mind of our illustrious hide and bone merchant. Slowly and reluctantly he uncoiled his arm from around the sparkling treasure; the bright, joyous look faded from his eyes, leaving them gloomy and cadaverous; with a weary, almost painful effort he arose from the table, and, dragging his feet over the floor like balls of lead, he left the room, sadly, tearfully and tremulously muttering, 'I forgot about the cuter.'

The next eastward bound freight train carried an old man, without shirt studs or other ornament, apparently bowed down by overwhelming grief, and the conductor hadn't the heart to throw him overboard. Gov. Carney is not buying bones and hides in this city any more.

Another popular card game was monte or Spanish monte, sometimes called monte bank. This game with its Spanish origins was familiar to south Texans and is not to be confused with a notorious confidence game of Mexican origins — three card monte — also played in Dodge City.

Confidence men were attracted to Dodge City because of the town's liberal attitude toward gambling. There was little objection to "square games," but as "show case games" increased, there was an appeal to the city police officers to "set down on" these "barefaced robbing concerns." "Keep them away from our town, they create more bad blood among both cattle men and citizens than anything else," pleaded a crusading Dodge City newspaper, the *Ford County Globe*. The term "show case game" came from a confidence racket that consisted of setting up a glass show case on the wooden sidewalks of Front Street to entice the unsuspecting granger or youthful laborer to buy fake jewelry displayed under the glass case. In addition to selling fake baubles, the operator would engage his victim in such rackets as three card monte or the pea and shell ruse.

The editor of the *Ford County Globe* conducted a campaign in the fall of 1878 to rid the community of these dishonest operations: "Our Community's Curse. . . . show-case games and robbing devices practiced in our city during the summer upon emigrants and parties coming to Ford County seeking for homes as well as business locations, . . . No less than a dozen men are engaged in this sort of work in our city, . . . land agent, is their pet scheme, knowing that the unsuspecting stranger can be more readily caught on land than most anything else — dice, three-card monte, the great Kentucky Lottery scheme, . . . They pretend to be business men among us . . . don't go to Dodge City or you will be relieved of your cash! I was robbed by a business man, a land agent. This is the reputation we get abroad just because we tolerate these thieves in our city. . . ." The editor's fervor failed to arouse too much excitement among the officers of the law, who probably felt disgust for anyone gullible enough to fall for the brazen schemes practiced by these confidence men.

As the cattle season began again in the spring of 1879, the *Ford County Globe* vividly described the gambling scene in Dodge City:

THE FESTIVE GAMBOLIER.

As strangers begin to congregate in the city, attracted by the approaching cattle trade, the gambler comes also; and he is more numerous this year than ever before. Already the city begins to boom, and at early candle light crowds congregate at the principle saloons, some to gamble, some to drink, and others to see what they can see. The old professional takes off his coat, arranges it on the back of his chair, and sits down in front of the faro table with as much of an air of business and composure as a bookkeeper commencing his daily labor. He bets his 'system' without variation, and his countenance remains calm and immovable whether he wins or loses.

The other class of gamblers are men who have other means of earning money, but who think they are just as liable to win as those more familiar with the game. They stand around the table until they think they see a card that is lucky, and immediately deposit their spare change on that card, and excitedly await developments. It is only a matter of time when their money is gone and they are left with their hands in their empty pockets, staring vacantly at the board.

Then there is a class of young men who bet just because they think it looks smart — boys who are not half decently dressed and who only have a few half dollars in their pockets.

During the last two weeks considerable money had changed hands, mostly between old professionals, some winning and others losing, and the signs seem to indicate that gambling will be indulged in to a greater extent this year than last.

Prize fights as a form of gambling and entertainment were common in the early days of Dodge City. The Dodge City *Times* recorded a bloody one in June, 1877:

On last Tuesday morning the champion prize fight of Dodge City was indulged in by Messrs. Nelson Whitman and the noted Red Hanley, familiarly known as 'the red bird from the South.' An indefinite rumor had been circulated in sporting circles that a fight was to take place, but the time and place was known only to a select few. The sport took place in front of the Saratoga [saloon on Front Street], at the silent hour of 4:30 a.m. when the city police were retiring after the dance hall revelry had subsided, and the belles who reign there were off duty. Promptly at the appointed time the two candidates for championship were at the joint. Col. Norton acted as rounder up and whipper-in for both fighters, while Bobby Gill ably performed the arduous task of healing and handling and sponging off. Norton called 'time,' and the ball opened with some fine hits from the shoulder. Whitman was the favorite in the pools, but Red made a brilliant effort to win the champion belt. During the forty-seventh round Red Hanley implored Norton to take Nelson off for a little while till he could have time to put his right eye back where it belonged, set his jaw bone and have the ragged edge trimmed off his ears where they had been chewed the worst. This was against the rules of the ring, so Norton declined, encouraging him to bear it as well as he could and squeal when he got enough. About the sixty-first round Red squealed unmistakably, and Whitman was declared winner. The only injuries sustained by the loser in this fight were two ears chewed off, one eye bursted and the other disabled, right cheek bone caved in, bridge of the nose broken, seven teeth knocked out, one jaw bone mashed, one side of the tongue chewed off, and several other unimportant fractures and bruises. Red retires from the ring in disgust.

During the winter months of the 1870's and '80's, when times were dull, Dodge City's Luke McGlue outdid himself with hoaxes, pranks, and practical jokes, providing entertainment for his fraternity of frontiersmen. Luke McGlue was a fictitious character invented by Dodge City jokesters. He was Dodge City's nineteenth century Kilroy, on whom all practical jokes, hoaxes, and pranks were blamed — a western Kansas Til Eulenspiegel. The settlers and frontiersmen of Dodge City, like doctors, lawyers, fraternity members, and gangsters, laid down the severe conditions whereby an outsider became a member of the group. The samples of an obnoxious cigar drummer from St. Joseph, Missouri, were stolen in March 1877, and passed around to the "boys." When the tenderfoot salesman discovered his cigars in the mouth of nearly every grinning fellow on Front Street, he began asking who had done such an inconsiderate thing as steal his cigars and pass them about. "Luke McGlue," was the answer given by all.

The Reverend O. W. Wright's prized pony mysteriously disappeared in June, 1877, whereupon "The minister would not be comforted and for a time completely abandoned himself to paroxysms of grief."[27] A deputy sheriff, in on the joke, reported to Reverend Wright that the thief had been captured, and it was up to the minister to decide whether the criminal should be shot or hanged. After some anxious moments struggling with his conscience, the good Reverend discovered that the culprit was none other than Luke McGlue. Reverend Wright's laughter and good-natured submission to this prank ensured the return of the pony and the admiration of Luke's band of merry men. Hoaxes of this type were common in Dodge City throughout its early history, and were more than a form of adolescent horseplay. They were a simple means for testing the relationships between men in the common struggle of frontier existence.

A favorite practical joke, common to many Western frontier communities, was known by its practitioners in Dodge City as "The Indian Act." Mr. Elias Cahn of the House of Cahn & Co., clothiers of Kansas City, arrived in Dodge City in April, 1877, to sell clothing. Mr. Cahn made the mistake of bragging to his customers of his bravery. Mayor Kelley and two of his friends induced Mr. Cahn to join them in a hunting party. Chalk Beeson and six others borrowed Indian costumes brought back to Dodge City after the Battle of Adobe Walls in 1874. The Indian garments were donned by the seven Luke McGlues, and with faces hideously painted, they started in a roundabout way to intercept Mr. Cahn and the hunting party. As word spread through town the population began to turn out. Roofs of houses, old freight wagons, and telegraph poles were quickly covered with anxious spectators; mothers with young babies and decrepit old men could be seen rushing up Boot Hill to view the upcoming "massacre."

When the party of hunters had traveled about four miles they were suddenly startled by a fiendish Indian war whoop, and on looking up the hill on one side, they saw the "bloodthirsty devils" riding furiously toward them. Mr. Cahn, although armed with a murderous revolver carefully loaded with blank cartridges, decided very promptly that discretion was the better part of valor. He turned his fiery steed toward Dodge City, applied whip and spur without restraint, dodging the shots "fired" by his pursuers. The firing increased, but Mr. Cahn's head dodged faster, and he arrived safely within a mile of the city, when firing ceased, and he began to think he was saved. However, it soon occurred to his mind that the city must be besieged, as the hilltops were crowded with people and an excited populace filled the streets. When Mr. Cahn discovered the trick, he joined another group of practical jokesters and warmly saluted the return of the "hunters" and "Indians" with a volley of rotten eggs.

Five months later, the perpetration of "The Indian Act" backfired. P. L. Beatty of Beatty & Kelley's saloon and restaurant rode out with a newcomer to look at the numerous herds of cattle and breathe the country air. A few miles west of the city the "Indians" made their appearance in fantastic array. Beatty advised his guest to run for his life. The Indians, yelling hideously, pressed close behind as the victim rode toward town, losing his hat on the way. Finally the idea of riding into town bareheaded, pursued by Indians was more humiliation than he could bear. He turned his horse to the foe and rode back after his hat. As the "scalpers" came near, the "tenderfoot" drew out a gun of dangerous proportions, and fired into the dusky brigade, sadly disarranging their plans. They were pursued into town by the "greenhorn" where they were greeted by hoots and yells.

The practical joke sometimes went to extremes that were not appreciated nor accepted by the recipient. Miss Susy Haden, a dance hall girl, had been "casting her beautiful eyes and fond and loving glances at Dodge City's modest but susceptible gambler, Bobby Gill." "The rich, creamy complexion, dreamy black eyes, and glossy, raven ringlets" of the "fair enchantress" were too much for Bobby. A little after midnight, in March, 1877, "the report was circulated among the boys that Robert was basking in the enervating luxury of Susy's presence, and a party of convivial spirits, repaired to [her] home, with mischievous designs to ruthlessly drag the gentle Bobby from the genial glow of the balmy smiles of his lady love — just for fun!" The modest editor of the Dodge City *Times* reported that when "the boys" arrived at Miss Haden's room and entered unannounced, they discovered that Bobby "and Susy were occupying positions relative to each other of such a delicate nature as to entirely prohibit us from describing in these chaste and virtuous columns."

Bobby was "dragged from the downy couch," and when he protested, he was "banged and bluffed around." Susy was so unappreciative toward the Luke McGlue crowd, that she made a complaint against one of Bobby's tormentors who was arrested and fined ten dollars and costs. The charge was "carrying deadly weapons, in the city limits."

All the entertainment in the cattle town of Dodge City was not of such informal nature. Amateur benefits and entertainments as well as traveling legitimate theater performances were held at improvised theaters in the county court house and the dining room of the Dodge House. In April, 1877, a new dance hall, the Lady Gay, was opened south of the railroad tracks, on the southeast corner of Trail Street and Second Avenue. A platform decorated with bunting was built up for the orchestra, and a bar was installed at the other end of the hall. The proprietors were Bat Masterson's brother, Jim, and Ben Springer. The following year Springer booked vaudeville performers to entertain in a simple theater added to the dance hall. Ben Springer's Theater Comique opened on July 4, 1878. The Comique (pronounced Comic-Cue by most of its customers) gave a free "blow out" on opening night. The feature performers were Eddie Foy and Jimmie Thompson, direct from a four-week engagement at a Kansas City concert hall. The *Ford County Globe* commented that "Foy and Thompson, at the Comique, 'lay over' anything we had ever seen in the Ethiopian line." Their specialty was black-face and Irish comedy.

Foy's first impression of Dodge City was dust — heat, wind, and flat prairie — "but above all dust!" While approaching Dodge City, Foy sighted from his train window a twenty-five foot high, one hundred foot long, pile of buffalo bones. He recalled hearing his partner, Thompson remark "that they might be killing people in Dodge faster than they could bury them." The one train a day from the east was an important event in Dodge City, and the whole town turned out to greet it. Ben Springer met Foy and began introducing him around the crowd. One introduction Foy remembered vividly for many years was to "a trim, good-looking young man with a pleasant face and carefully barbared mustache, well-tailored clothes, hat with a rakish tilt and two big silver-mounted, ivory-handled pistols in a heavy belt" — Ford County's sheriff, Bat Masterson.[28]

Foy described Dodge City as "an ugly but fascinating little town . . . one broad street running nearly east and west, with most of the buildings on the north side . . . a sprinkling of buildings on the south side

Eddie Foy, actor and vaudeville player, started his career as a singer and comedian in cattle and mining town theaters (above) in 1878. He and his partner, Jim Thompson, played in Dodge's Comique theater from July to September of 1878 and 1879, and became known by their cowboy audiences as the "pets of Dodge City."

This picture (below) of Eddie Foy, his wife, and the "seven little Foys" was autographed in 1906 and sent to Chalk Beeson, a fellow musician and owner of the Long Branch saloon at the time of Foy's triumph in Dodge City.

Foy (above and below), who was an eccentric comedian with many mannerisms, played in musical comedy until 1913, and then went into vaudeville accompanied by his seven children.

of the street, too, fronting on the track, among which was Ben Springer's." The Comique show began at eight o'clock and continued long after midnight. After the show there was dancing until four in the morning or daybreak. At the far end of the hall, opposite the stage, near the bar, tables were set up with gambling devices. Around the room like a mezzanine, ran a row of boxes, where patrons could sit and drink and watch the show.

The programs were varied each night at the Comique. Female performers were popular — such as Miss Belle Lamont, "the queen of song." Miss Lamont performed with Foy in his comedy routines and excelled in such snappy repartee as follows: "Said he: 'Belle, you are my dearest duck.' Said she: 'Foy, you are trying to stuff me.' " Fannie Garrettson, another favorite at the Comique, brought tears to the eyes of the drovers with such songs as "Killarney," "The Flower of Kildare," and "Home Sweet Home."

Foy and Thompson made such a hit in Dodge City their first summer of 1878, that a benefit performance was held in their honor, at which they were described as "the pets of Dodge City." In September the Comique closed its doors as the cattle trade slacked off, and Foy, Thompson, and a female performer, Bessie Bell, left for Leadville, Colorado, to fulfill their next engagement. Foy's popularity in Dodge City brought him back again during the summer of 1879. His good humour and comic talent, so popular with the frontier community of Dodge City, carried him on to vaudeville stardom a few years later.

The competition of Ben Springer's Comique was a dance hall owned by his brother-in-law, Ham Bell. It was located across the street, west of the Lady Gay. In 1878 Bell rebuilt the hall and christened it the Variety Theater. Better known as the Varieties, it had the distinction of being one of the first houses of entertainment in Dodge City to present the Can-Can. The *Ford County Globe* described it thusly: "For two nights the Dodge City Varieties have successfully presented the extravagant Can-Can to large and appreciative audiences. . . . The Can-Can was new to many . . . . The Can-Can does not deprave the moral taste of average Dodgeites or rangers . . . . The Varieties will be crowded tonight. Take a front seat, baldy, or you can-cannot see it — so well." Ham Bell's Varieties ran only one season; the Can-Can failed to draw the crowds away from the more popular Comique and Lady Gay.

Christmas was celebrated in Dodge City as in every Western frontier community. A highlight of Christmas night, 1878, was a masquerade ball given by the "Dodge City Social Club" at the Dodge House. "Champagne and wine flowed freely, but not to excess, and a merrier Christmas night was never enjoyed in Dodge." Among the names of Dodge City's "social elite" at the ball were "W. B. [Bat] Masterson and Miss Brown."[29]

The first Fourth of July celebration in Ford County was held in 1877, a year late for the centennial celebration of the nation's founding. The celebration was sponsored by the Dodge City Fire Company, a volunteer group of young men who were more noted for social activities than fire-fighting. At two o'clock in the afternoon the Fire Company, in uniform, marched around town, headed by a fife and drum and followed by every small boy in town. Tents were erected on a race course southwest of town. Ice cream and harder refreshments were sold by the firemen. Racehorses belonging to P. L. Beatty and James H. Kelley, saloonkeepers, and Fred Singer and Joe Mason, policemen, were entered in a 500-yard race, won by Singer's five-year-old sorrel. Three pony races were held with Ham Bell's pony, Lon, winning the first. The afternoon's activities concluded with a foot race and a wheelbarrow race. The evening's ball, with music furnished by Chalk Beeson's orchestra, broke up early for Dodge City — at two o'clock in the morning — ending the Fourth's festivities.

The highlight of early Dodge City celebrations was a Spanish bull fight held on the fourth and fifth of July, 1884, one of the first of its kind to be staged in the Southwest since Spanish rule. Alonzo B. Webster, former mayor, conceived the original notion that the "Glorious Fourth" should be recognized in Dodge City by holding a contest of matadors and ferocious Texas bulls. "Where is there another town in the country that would have the nerve to get up a genuine Spanish bull fight on American soil?" commented a visiting correspondent from the New York *Herald.*

Dodge City was soon to see the end of its lusty frontier atmosphere. The cattle trade was slowing. Ford County's farm population was increasing, and Texas stock raisers were finding it more difficult to negotiate rights of way to the railhead at Dodge City. The market price of beef was hitting bottom. The businessmen of Dodge City were eager to revive the trail head prosperity of past years. The seamy side of the Frontier Babylon would soon be covered with the mantle of respectability. The Cowboy Capital was determined to "get to the joint" one more time before the preachers and prohibitionists closed her down.

The Dodge City Driving Park and Fair Grounds Association was organized. In less than three months, the president, Ham Bell, and the members of the association raised $10,000. They purchased from A. J. Anthony a forty-acre tract southwest of town and built a half-mile track and seating for 3,500 spectators.

Publicity for the event spread naturally, aided by Dodge City's reputation as a "wild and wicked town of the West." The New York *Herald* correspondent started off with a press agent's typical blow-up: "There are few towns like Dodge. Here the people rule to suit themselves. . . . Prohibition . . . is not the law of Dodge. Saloons, gambling rooms and dance halls run with perfect freedom and their proprietors are the leading men of the town. The audacity of the town is wonderful. Bull fights are to be given on the 'glorious Fourth'. . . . Dodge has its own laws, and these laws are rigidly inforced — an example that many an eastern city might emulate. In the gambling rooms one will see thousands of dollars lying loose on the tables not in use, . . . Yet that money is safer than it would be in the hands of some New York brokers. Money is plentiful here, and consequently every one is extravagant. One pays fifteen cents for a glass of lager beer and for other things in like proportion. The cowboy spends his money recklessly. He is a jovial careless fellow bent on having a big time regardless of expense. He will make way with the wages of a half year in a few weeks, and then go back to his herds for another six months."

D. W. (Doc) Barton, said to be the first man to drive a herd of cattle from Texas to Dodge City, was appointed to round up the bulls. Seven out of ten spectators at the fight would be cattle men, connoisseurs of bull ferocity. Barton fine-combed the prairies south of Dodge City and brought in twelve of the ugliest customers he could find. The frothy bulls were dubbed with appropriate names: Ringtailed Snorter, Iron Gall, Klu Klux, Sheriff, Rustler, Loco Jim, Eat-Em-Up-Richard, Cowboy Killer, Lone Star, Long Branch, and Opera. Opera might sound tame to an uninitiated visitor, but it stood for the Opera House saloon, a competitor of the Long Branch. The twelfth bull was named Doc, in honor of its owner, Doc Barton. Each of the Texas bulls were guaranteed to be "all the time as mad as they can get."

Aware of no statutes that specifically forbid bull fights, Webster contacted an acquaintance, W. K. Moore, a Scotchman practicing law in Paso Del Norte, Mexico. The wiley Scot rounded up five "genuine" matadors and brought them to Dodge City for the big event. They were Captain Gregorio Gallardo, a tailor from Chihuahua; Evarista A. Rivas, superintendent of public works for the State of Chihuahua; Marcus Moyor, a musician from Huejuequillo; Juan Herrera, a musician from Aldama; and Rodrigo Rivas, an artist from Chihuahua.

When Moore arrived with his weekend warriors, he found it necessary to play down the bloody aspects of the forthcoming contest, calling it an "athletic exhibition." The president of the American Society for the Prevention of Cruelty to Animals telegraphed: "In the name of humanity I appeal to you to prevent the contemplated bull fight at Dodge City this day. Let not American soil be polluted by such atrocities." Playing down any possible cruelty to the bulls, Moore did not fail to mention, however, that "it is not unlikely that the fights . . . will result fatally to some of the matadors." This comment failed to arouse any response from the A. S. P. C. A. The newspaper of one of Dodge City's jealous eastern neighbors called the bull fight "a wicked scheme concocted by the denizens of that intemperate village to draw in a big crowd of tender feet."

These four Mexican bull fighters from Chihuahua posed just prior to their encounter with Texas longhorns in the 1884 bull fight at Dodge City. The bull fight was carried out in the bloody ritual of a true Spanish bull ring and was a huge success with the Texas cowboys gathered in Dodge City on July Fourth. The scarf, carried by one of the matadors, now hangs in the Boot Hill Museum in Dodge City.

By noon on the Fourth, Dodge City was jammed with cattlemen, cowboys, and curious spectators. The hitching rails on Front Street were lined with cow ponies as the grand parade proceeded to the arena west of town. Webster and Moore led the procession, followed by dignitaries and the "Cow-Boy Cornet Band." Then came the bullfighters in their scarlet jackets, blue tunics, green sashes, red and yellow knee breeches, white stockings, and dainty slippers, carrying their two-edged Spanish blades and banderillas.

The correspondent for a St. Louis newspaper reported: "At 2:45 the audience commenced filing into the amphitheater, at least one-third of them being women and children. As some of the ladies of this town are not remarkable for sanctity, a dividing line was carefully drawn by a Deputy Sheriff detailed for that purpose. . . . the cowboy's ambition seemed to be to get a big fat girl and a high seat at the same time." Profane and pious, fat girls and thin, were joined by Texans who had seen bull fights south of the border, and cowboys who didn't know a picador from a pissant. All the town's population who could afford a ticket were there in the hundred degree temperature to witness a true Spanish bull fight. They were not disappointed.

This newspaper's front page, sponsored by the hotels, saloons, and merchants of Dodge City, advertised the unique event of 1884 described as a "contest of matadors and ferocious Texas bulls." The arena, racecourse, and grandstand, shown below, were built especially for the Spanish bull fight, a highlight of Dodge City's cattle town history.

The cowboy band sounded the grand entry; the matadors and picadors, four afoot and one mounted, entered and circled the arena; the bulls were barbed and infuriated; the matadors made their passes; the pics with their colored streamers hung from the backs of the bulls; the chief matador, Gallardo, drew cheers from the crowd as his escapes grew narrower as the last bull charged his tormentor; finally, *Death in the Afternoon* came to Dodge City as Gallardo drew his 150-year-old Toledo sword and dispatched it into a vital spot at the last possible instant of the bull's charge.

"Thus," reported the *Ford County Globe,* "ended the first day's bull fight in Dodge City, and for all we know the first fight on American soil. The second day's fighting, with the exception of the killing of the last animal in the ring, was more interesting than the first. . . . The matadors showed to the people of America what bull fighting really was. No one could see it and go away saying that it was not a genuine bull fight."

Dodge City had lost none of its virility; the frontier spirit still lived; it still claimed to be "the leading sporting town between the Missouri river and the mountains." A few days after the fight, a newspaper sixty miles up the Santa Fe line, reported: "Quite a number of our boys visited Dodge last week to see the bull fight. Some of them returned looking as though they had had a personal encounter with the animals."

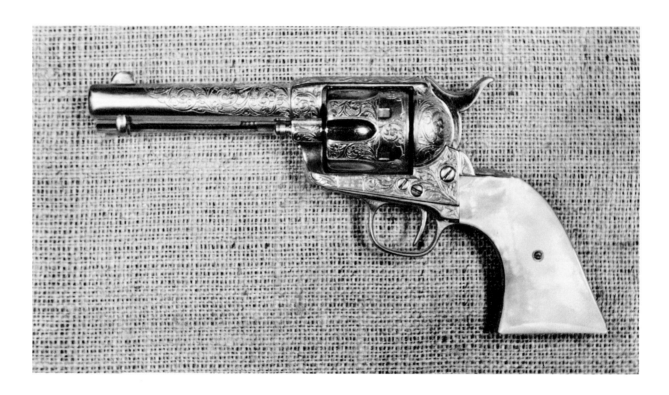

"Peacemaker" is one of the many names given the Colt .45 ("C" engraving Frontier Model).

Chapter IV
THE FESTIVE REVOLVER

Many visitors to Dodge City in its heyday had personal encounters that were not soon forgotten. Forty years later one old timer recalled his four-month trip in 1884, from Castroville, Texas, to Dodge City with 450 head of horses. "We camped with our herd about six miles south of Dodge City, on Mulberry Creek. The first thing we did when we arrived there was to go to town, get a shave and haircut, and tighten our belts by a few good strong drinks."[1]

Another Texas trail driver recalled: "In 1882 I went up the trail to Dodge City, Kansas, . . . We went the western trail and had all sorts of exciting experiences on the trip, thunderstorms, swollen streams, stampedes, Indians, long dry drives, wild animals, loss of sleep, and a frequent hankering for the chuck wagon when kept in the saddle for twenty-four hours or longer. We delivered the cattle at Dodge City, and there I met many of my old friends from Texas. As soon as I could get loose from the herd I took a bath in the river, went to a barber shop and got my face beautified, put on some new clothes, and went forth to see the sights in the toughest town on the map — and I saw 'em."[2]

Dodge City, "the toughest town on the map," needed tough men to keep order and to prevent the vigilante killings of its buffalo hunting days. Wyatt Earp arrived in Dodge City from Wichita in May, 1876. On May 24, a Wichita newspaper reported: "Wyatt Earp has been put on the police force at Dodge City." Earp first served as deputy marshal in Dodge City under Marshal Larry Deger. A month later the Ford County District Court records show Wyatt Earp and Bat Masterson to be deputy sheriffs serving under Ed O. Hougue, under sheriff, and Charlie Bassett, sheriff.

Dodge City's peace officers fell into several classes — city, township, county, and federal officers. The city police force was headed by a marshal, sometimes known as chief marshal. In Dodge City the term "police chief" was not used until the 1900's. The marshal was appointed by the mayor and city council. The marshal in turn appointed his assistant and policemen as they were needed.

The position of assistant marshal, sometimes called deputy marshal, was an important one in Dodge City during its ten years as the Cowboy Capital. The marshal was sometimes a political appointee. The assistant marshal was usually picked for his ability to uphold the law and keep the peace. He often drew the same salary as the marshal. Often the chief marshal and assistant marshal were both called "marshal."

The marshal, assistant marshal, and policemen were responsible for law enforcement only within the corporate limits of the city. It fell to the chief county law enforcement officer, the sheriff, to enforce the law outside the city limits, within Ford County, and within all of the unorganized counties to the south and west which were attached to Ford County for judicial purposes.

The sheriff was elected to his position every other year in November. After serving two full consecutive elected terms, or a total of four years, an individual was not allowed to succeed himself to the office of sheriff. The sheriff appointed an under sheriff to act as his assistant. Deputy sheriffs were appointed as they were needed for the work required.

During the violent years of Dodge City's cattle trade it was common practice for the sheriff to appoint city peace officers as deputy sheriffs, and for the marshal to appoint county officers as special policemen. There was very little distinction made when apprehending criminals as to the proper jurisdiction of the arresting parties.

The two surviving 1876 issues of the Dodge City *Times* do not list Under Sheriff Hougue or Deputy Sheriff Masterson. The only law officers listed in the official directory of these newspapers are Lawrence E. Deger, marshal; Wyatt Earp, deputy marshal; and Charles E. Bassett, sheriff. The *Times* was first published in May, 1876, but no issues earlier than October 14, 1876, are known to be in existence.

It is probable that the listing of Earp as deputy marshal in 1876 implied that the importance of his job was as great as that of the marshal's and sheriff's, or that the name of Wyatt Earp was deemed important enough to demand recognition in the official listing of city and county officers. Wyatt undoubtedly had brought a reputation with him, even though the nature and truthfulness of this reputation has been questioned by some historians.

It is both possible and probable that Earp was appointed deputy marshal in May, 1876, shortly after arriving, and that he served as deputy sheriff along with Bat while carrying out his principal duties as deputy marshal. Shortly before his death in 1929, Earp claimed that his brother, Morgan, and Bat Masterson served with him as deputy sheriffs under Charlie Bassett. Morgan's name appears in the District Court files of Ford County as a deputy sheriff in June and July, 1876, along with Wyatt's and Bat's.

Charlie Bassett's under sheriff, Edward O. Hougue, was a French immigrant. He was a former policeman, marshal, and chief of police in Ellsworth in 1872 and 1873. He came to Dodge City in 1874 or 1875 to serve as a deputy sheriff and under sheriff. In July, 1876, he was arrested by Wyatt Earp for "fighting and disturbing the peace," and left Dodge City in 1876 or 1877. He died in Wyoming Territory shortly after.

Charles E. (Senator) Bassett was the first sheriff of Ford County, taking office after a special election, June 5, 1873. Up until 1876 little is known about Bassett's activities as a lawman in and around Dodge City. As more and more unorganized counties became attached to Ford County for judicial purposes, his job took him farther from Dodge City. As his duties increased he appointed deputies among whom were the legendary lawmen, Wyatt Earp and Bat Masterson.

Lawrence E. (Larry) Deger lent dignity to the office of city marshal and backed it up with the authority of weight — 250 to 300 pounds of it. A blond, blue-eyed, sandy moustached freighter, he came to southwest Kansas in November, 1868, as a wagon boss for Lt. Col. George A. Custer. He provisioned at Fort Hays and Fort Dodge during Custer's winter Indian campaigns on the Washita River and later came to Dodge City. He probably was appointed the first marshal in Dodge City after its incorporation in November, 1875.

The city of Dodge City was incorporated as a city of the third class in the chambers of District Court Judge Samuel R. Peters on November 2, 1875. Its first election was held December 1, 1875. P. L. Beatty, partner of James H. Kelley, was selected first mayor of the town. Beatty served until the following April when George M. Hoover was chosen mayor in the first regular election.

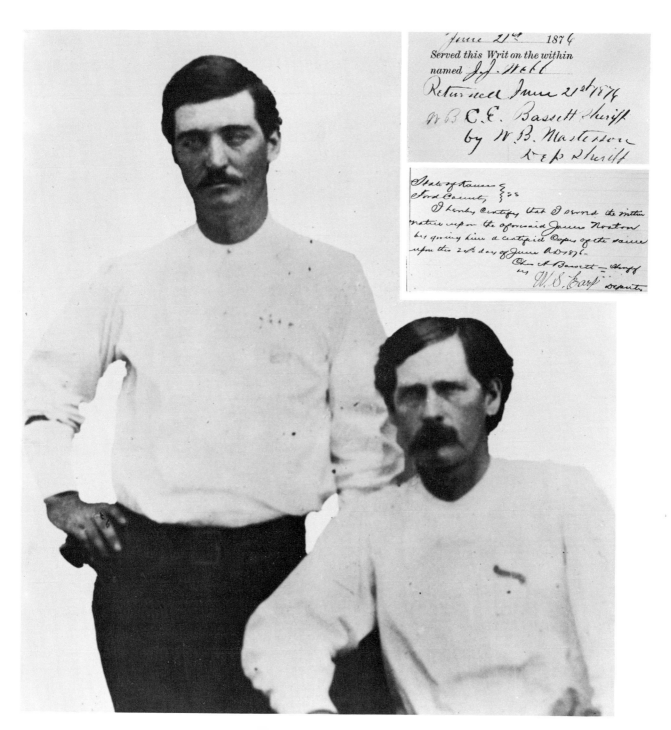

This photograph, taken in 1876, is reproduced from a tintype made by an itinerant photographer in Dodge City. It shows Bat Masterson, twenty-three years old (standing) and Wyatt Earp at age twenty-eight. Earp and Masterson were friends and fellow deputy sheriffs of Ford County at the time. The signatures of Earp and Masterson (above) from documents in the district court of Ford County show them to be deputies serving under Sheriff Charles A. Bassett in June, 1876. At that time, in addition to his duties as deputy sheriff of Ford County, Earp also held the office of assistant marshal of Dodge City. This picture of Masterson and Earp is shown here with the kind permission of Miss Carolyn Lake, daughter of Stuart N. Lake. Stuart Lake obtained the tintype from Wyatt Earp while preparing the biography, Wyatt Earp, Frontier Marshal, *a book that has stirred the imagination of Western fans since its publication in 1931.*

Charles E. Bassett (above), the first sheriff of Ford County, 1876 to 1878, recruited the help of deputies Wyatt Earp, Morgan Earp, Bat Masterson, and others in 1876 when the Texas cattle herds began arriving in great numbers with their thirsty cowboys.

Wyatt Earp, assistant marshal, signed this complaint against Under Sheriff Ed Hougue [Hogue] in July, 1876, for "fighting and disturbing the peace and quiet of the City of Dodge City..." Hougue, a former marshal of Ellsworth, left Dodge shortly after. The Remington .44 caliber Model 1874 Army revolver (right) is similar to the gun used by the gambler, Cock-eyed Frank Loving, killer of mule-skinner Levi Richardson.

Lawrence E. Deger was Dodge City's first marshal after incorporation as a third class city in 1875. A real heavyweight, 250 to 300 pounds, he later served as mayor, and was a key figure in the saloon war of 1883.

Joseph W. Mason, former Army scout, Dodge City policeman, and Long Branch bartender, was especially admired by the "ladies."

Morgan Earp, Wyatt's younger brother, served as a deputy sheriff in Dodge City in 1876. He was assassinated in 1882 by Earp's enemies in Tombstone after the O. K. Corral fight.

This Winchester Model 1873 repeating rifle and Frontier Model 1872 Colt single action revolver were both chambered for a .44-40 cartridge which could be used interchangeably in both hand gun or shoulder arm.

An unknown artist's drawing shows the first city jail, built of two-by-sixes, with peep holes, laid flat and spiked together with iron rods at each end. A second story was built on top in 1876 to house the city clerk's office and police court.

This sketch, made by Ado Hunnius on June 29, 1876, looking to the northeast, shows the calaboose and city offices. From left, Hunnius shows wagons loaded with buffalo hides, A. B. Webster's dry goods store, Moses Waters' Occident saloon, and the Dodge House where Hunnius said he found bedbugs and watered milk. Continuing to the right of the jail he shows a blacksmith's shop, the railroad water tank and windmill, government freight depot, and Santa Fe railroad depot.

James H. (Dog) Kelley (above), mayor and saloonkeeper, and Charles S. Hungerford, butcher, were hunting companions. The dog is one of many owned by Kelley that earned him his nickname. One of Mayor Kelley's deer hunting parties with Hungerford, bartender Adam Jackson, newspaperman Lloyd Shinn, and six others, was reported in an 1877 edition of the Times: *"They rode fifty miles, let a deer escape (Hungerford's fault) crossed and recrossed the river seven times, chased a herd of antelope four miles, caught 00, struck a skunk's nest, killed 8 and came home highly perfumed."*

Wyatt Earp's biographer, Stuart Lake, wrote that Earp left Dodge City with his brother, Morgan, during Hoover's term as mayor, in September, 1876. Lake further stated that the two Earp brothers went to Deadwood, South Dakota, but the Dodge City *Times* still listed Wyatt as deputy marshal on March 24, 1877. Nothing more is known concerning Earp's activities in Dodge City until July, 1877.

James H. (Dog) Kelley succeeded George Hoover as mayor of Dodge City in April, 1877, and was re-elected to the office until 1881. A former Confederate soldier, Kelley served with Custer's Seventh Cavalry at Fort Hays, employed as a scout. Included in his duties were caring for Custer's horses and his pack of greyhounds. Kelley brought some of General Custer's dogs with him when he arrived at Fort Dodge in 1872.

Jim Kelley loved to hunt and race his greyhounds and quickly became known as Dog Kelley. He left Fort Dodge in the summer of 1872 and decided to settle in the newly organizing Dodge City. With P. L.

Beatty, his partner, he moved a frame building from Hays City to the corner of Front Street and First Avenue, the site of Kelley's saloon, restaurant, and opera house for twenty-six years.

During his four terms as mayor Dog Kelley was the acknowledged head of the city's political establishment, known as the "Gang." His support came from the old frontier element — buffalo hunters, freighters, ex-soldiers, border characters, and the saloonkeepers and gamblers devoted to the Texas cattle trade.

When after his election in 1877, Kelley re-appointed Larry Deger as marshal, the Dodge City *Times* commented: "It is thought by many that a change would be made in this branch of the government . . ." This remark confirmed suspicion of a break that was to take place later in July between Mayor Kelley and Marshal Deger.

In May, 1877, Dodge City began readying for the coming cattle drives. Joseph W. Mason, a former army scout and an early resident, was appointed policeman. Joe, known as the "Apollo of Dodge," was a favorite with the "ladies." Joe's "glittering police star" and "immaculate topboots" were seen in action two days later when he stopped a cruel and bloody game of "lap jacket." Two colored men toed a mark and whipped each other with bullwhips "for the championship and fifty cents prize money. They took heavy new whips from the harness shop and poured in the strokes pretty lively. Blood flowed and dust flew and the crowd cheered until Policeman Joe Mason came along and suspended the cheerful exercise."[3]

On June 2, 1877, the Dodge City *Times* reported that "Texas steers are pouring in by the thousands." On the following week Kelley and the city councilmen appointed Bat Masterson's older brother, Ed, assistant marshal, and set the city lawmen's monthly salaries at $75.00 each for Deger, Masterson, and Mason. A week later the *Times* announced: "The new policemen, Ed Masterson and Joe Mason, are covering themselves with glory, and their prompt and efficient action cannot be too highly commended."

Wyatt Earp returned in July, 1877, the day after Dodge City's first Independence Day celebration. Some claim that Kelley telegraphed Earp in late June to return to Dodge City as trouble with cowboys began to increase with the arrival of the herds from the south. No records are available to explain the reason for Earp's return. The Dodge City *Times,* on July 7, 1877, had this to say: "Wyatt Earp, who was on our city police force last summer, is in town again. We hope he will accept a position on the force once more. He had a quiet way of taking the most desperate characters into custody which invariably gave one the impression that the city was able to enforce her mandates and preserve her dignity. It wasn't considered policy to draw a gun on Wyatt unless you got the drop and meant to burn powder without any preliminary talk."

Earp's biographer, Stuart Lake, claimed that "Wyatt was a shy young man with few intimates," but a man who had "absolute confidence in himself." The words, "He had a quiet way of taking the most desperate characters into custody" and "It wasn't considered policy to draw a gun on Wyatt unless you got the drop," are the most complimentary phrases made by any Dodge City newspaper about a Dodge City lawman.

Despite the *Times'* praises of Earp and his law enforcing abilities, and despite later claims that Earp was summoned to Dodge City in 1877 to "tame the town," there is no further mention of Wyatt Earp in available records of 1877, except the newspaper account of Wyatt's encounter with a drunken prostitute, Frankie Bell. Frankie's abusive language was silenced by Wyatt with a slap — resulting in a night's lodging in city jail for Frankie and a fine of one dollar for Wyatt. If Earp served as a lawman in Dodge City during 1877, it was on a part time or unofficial basis.

The rest of the summer and fall of 1877 was filled with the usual cattle town activities — horse thefts, jailbreaks, shootouts, and fights — soldiers vs. cowboys, cowboys vs. gamblers, and gamblers vs. prostitutes. A significant confrontation occurred between Marshal Deger and Mayor Kelley over the gambler, Charles Ronan, bartender and billiards expert at Kelley's saloon.

At two o'clock in the morning of July 20, 1877, Marshal Deger deposited Mr. Ronan in the city jail, a two-story wooden building built of two-by-sixes laid flat and spiked together with iron rods. One room on the ground level housed the jail, known as the "dog house" or calaboose. The one-room second story served as city offices and police court. Immediately after the arrest of Ronan, Mayor Kelley ordered the prisoner released, which Deger refused to do. Mayor Kelley's Irish temper rose, and he pronounced Deger suspended on the spot, ordering him to turn over his badge. The rotund marshal stood fast, refusing to recognize the mayor's order. Kelley then ordered the assistant marshal, Ed Masterson, and his policeman, Joe Mason, to place Deger under arrest. Deger drew his revolver and resisted, but Ed Masterson coolly avoided gunplay by suggesting to Deger that he submit in order to prevent embarrassment to his assistants. By afternoon the city council had met, overruled the mayor's decision, and reinstated Deger as marshal.[4]

By fall the cattle herds south of town had thinned, but a few herders were still in town enjoying the fruits of their summer's work. Joe Mason made six arrests the week ending September 8, 1877, but by October 6, he had resigned and was tending bar at the Long Branch. In December he left for Sweetwater, Texas, to seek his fame and fortune in the saloon business. While serving there on the police force he shot and killed Ed Ryan, a gambler. Ryan's death was deemed justifiable homicide, and Mason returned to Dodge City in January, 1878, with a gunman's reputation.

Mason returned to Dodge City at the beginning of an extremely violent period in the cattle town's history. Wyatt Earp was reported to be in Fort Clark, Texas. The largest cattle drives in the town's history were being predicted, and gamblers, confidence men, and prostitutes were pouring in, preparing for the lucrative summer months. In April, 1878, the fighting and gunplay in Dodge City culminated in the killing of Ed Masterson, who was then city marshal.

Edward John Masterson was the oldest of the famous Masterson brothers. Bat was next, followed by James, Thomas, and George. Ed, Bat, and Jim hunted buffalo south of Dodge City in 1872 and 1873. In February, 1873, Ed got a job in Dog Kelley's restaurant on Front Street. When warmer months arrived he returned to buffalo hunting.

By August, 1877, while serving as assistant marshal, Ed had earned the praises of the Dodge City *Times:* "the city was not wanting in an efficient peace officer . . . assistant marshal Edward Masterson seemed to be always on time to quell the disturbance, and to bear away to that home of the friendless (the dog house) the noisy disturbers of the peace. Mr. Masterson has made a remarkable record during the month as the docket of the Police Court will bear testimony."

In November, 1877, Ed was called upon to quell a disturbance in the Lone Star dance hall. When Masterson arrived at the scene, a cowboy, Bob Shaw, was threatening "Texas Dick" Moore with drawn revolver over an alleged robbery of forty dollars. The assistant marshal attempted to subdue Shaw with the "butt of his shooting iron, merely to convince him of the vanities of this frail world . . . The aforesaid reminder on the back of the head, however, failed to have the desired effect, and instead of dropping, as any man of fine sensibilities would have done, Shaw turned his battery upon [Masterson] and let him have it in the right breast . . ."[5] Masterson, unable to use his right arm, fired his pistol with his left hand, wounding Shaw. Texas Dick was wounded in the right groin, and a bystander caught lead in his left arm. All parties to the melee recovered. Shaw decided to quit the far West and return to his native Georgia. Ed Masterson was back on the job by the end of the month.

Ed's brother, Bat, was elected sheriff of Ford County the day after Ed's shootout with Shaw. Marshal Deger had not supported Bat for election as sheriff and was not exactly in the good graces of Mayor Kelley. It is not surprising therefore that, in December, Deger was relieved from his job as marshal. Ed Masterson was appointed in his place. Charles E. Bassett, not eligible for re-election as sheriff, was appointed assistant marshal to Ed and under sheriff to Bat.

In its fourteen years as a rough frontier town Dodge City never had a better year in the accepted Western tradition than the year that followed — 1878. In January Sheriff Bat Masterson and his posse captured two train robbers sixty-five miles south of Dodge City. Two others were arrested right in town. The shooting and death of Bat's brother, Marshal Ed Masterson, followed in April. Deputy United States Marshal H. T. McCarty was shot and killed in the Long Branch saloon on July 13, and cowboy George Hoy died at the hands of Assistant Marshal Wyatt Earp and Policeman Jim Masterson a few days later. The September flight of Dull Knife and his small band of Cheyennes across western Kansas toward their former home in the north threw Dodge City into a panic. An actress and dance hall singer, Dora Hand, was murdered while sleeping in another's bed — mistakenly shot — allegedly by a wealthy Texas cattleman's son, who fled, was captured, and then acquitted. It was a year that provided material for many exciting episodes of shoot-'em-up folklore. It was all there — plenty of cowboys, Indians, train robbers, killers, dance hall girls, sheriffs, and marshals.

In March, 1878, the *Ford County Globe,* usually critical of the police force, praised Ed Masterson and Bassett for their display of courage in "raising h-ll" at a dance hall south of the railroad tracks. Two weeks later the police force was kept jumping till 3:00 a.m. corralling disturbers of the peace — soldiers from Fort Dodge. Ed Masterson and Charlie Bassett filled the calaboose with the soldiers to await D. M. Frost's police court session later in the day. The newspaper reported that "the sports are plenty in town, at present, they are preparing for the coming cattle trade . . ." Fights were breaking out in saloons north and south of the tracks. Stockmen were estimating a drive of 300,000 cattle into Dodge City. Richard King and Miflin Kenedy, Texas cattlemen soon to be millionaires, were sending their herds of 15,000 head. Kenedy had sent his son, John, with a herd in 1877;[6] this year, son James, the ill-tempered and ill-starred scion of the Kenedy clan, would accompany the herds from south Texas. Other herds would be arriving — John T. Lytle's, D. R. Fant's, John Blocker's and Shanghai Pierce's. The prominent trail drivers of Texas would soon be gathering in Dodge City.

Things were humming by election day, April 2, 1878. The unopposed Gang slate was re-elected: James H. Kelley, mayor; James Anderson, John Newton, D. D. Colley, C. M. Beeson, and Walter Straeter, councilmen; and Samuel Marshall, police judge. N. L. (Nat) Haywood was appointed assistant to serve under the marshal. Exactly one week later at ten o'clock in the evening Marshal Edward J. Masterson was shot and killed by two cowboys in front of A. J. Peacock's saloon, next door to the Lady Gay.

Jack Wagner and Alf Walker and four other cowboys, having just arrived in town, were enjoying themselves with dancing and drinking in a dance hall and saloon south of the railroad tracks and east of Second Avenue. When the party became too rantankerous, Marshal Masterson and Policeman Haywood were called. The cowboys were carrying pistols contrary to city ordinance, and Wagner, the most intoxicated was disarmed by Marshal Masterson. The dancing and drinking commenced again and Masterson and Haywood stepped out of the dance hall onto the wooden sidewalk. Wagner ran out after the officers, pulling another pistol. Masterson saw him coming and turned to grab hold of him. Just as Haywood stepped forward to assist the marshal, two of the cowboys drew their pistols and told him to stop. One of them, Walker, snapped the hammer of his six-shooter in Haywood's face; the pistol fortunately misfired. Wagner then shot Marshal Masterson through the abdomen at such close range that it set fire to the marshal's clothing.

Several shots followed in quick succession. The newspaper accounts say they were from Ed's revolver. Wagner was shot in the belly also; he staggered into Peacock's saloon where he fell and was carried away by his friends. He died about twenty hours later, the evening of the next day, and was buried on Boot Hill the following afternoon. Wagner's friend, Walker, was shot once in the lung, two other shots breaking his right arm. The newspapers are unclear where these shots came from. The *Times* states that the first shot killed Wagner, the second, third, and fourth shots striking Walker. This account implies that Ed

A Colt .45 caliber, Frontier Model, typical of the handguns used by Dodge City lawmen in the 1870's.

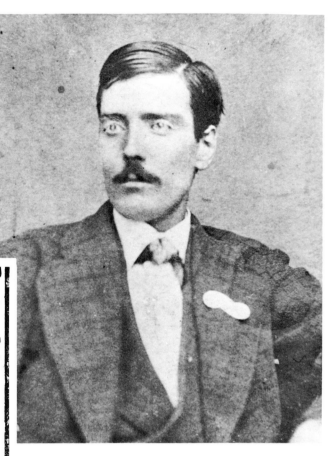

Edward J. Masterson, Bat's older brother, was marshal of Dodge City from December, 1877, until his death in April, 1878. Shot and killed by drunken cowboys, Ed Masterson was mourned as a friend and an efficient officer — but also as one who disobeyed the first rule of Western lawmen — shoot first and ask questions afterward.

Globe Extra, April 10th '78.

DODGE CITY IN MOURNING!

OUR CITY MARSHAL KILLED!

DIED IN THE DISCHARGE OF HIS DUTY.

TERRIBLE CATASTROPHE.

At 10 o'clock last night, City Marshal, Edward Masterson, discovered that a cow boy, who was working for Oburn, of Kansas City, named Jack Wagner, was carrying a six-shooter, contrary to the City Ordinance. Wagner was at the time under the influence of liquor, but quietly gave up his pistol. The Marshal gave it to some of Wagner's friends for safe keeping, and steped out into the street. No sooner had he done so than Wagner ran out after him pulling another pistol, which the Marshal had not observed. The Marshal saw him coming and turned upon Wagner and grabbed hold of him.

Wagner shot Marshal Masterson at once through the abdomen, being so close to him that the discharge set the Marshal's clothes on fire.

Marshal Masterson then shot Wagner.

About this time a man named Walker got mixed up in the fight, he it appears was boss herder for Oburn, and Wagner was working under him. He, also got shot once through the left lung, and his right arm twice broken.

Marshal Masterson walked across the street to Hoover's saloon, where after telling that he was shot, he sank to the floor. He was immediately removed to his room, where in half an hour he expired.

Walker and Wagner were, nearly all night insensible, and none thought that either of them could live through the night. However, morning has come, and neither are dead, both are in a very precarious condition, and their chances for recovery very small.

The City is in mourning; every door is draped in crape; business is entirely suspended till after the funeral of Marshal Masterson, which will take place at two o'clock P. M., and will be attended by everybody in the City.

Marshal Masterson will be buried in the Military Cemetery, at Fort Dodge.

FORD COUNTY GLOBE.

This special one-page edition of the Ford County Globe *was issued on the morning after Marshal Masterson's assassination.*

Masterson fired these four shots, but does not state so definitely. This would have been mighty good shooting for a dying man with a gaping hole in his abdomen. The *Times* does say that "the shots were fired almost simultaneously," suggesting that more than one gun was fired. "Wonder is expressed that more death and destruction did not ensue, as a large crowd surrounded the scene of the shooting. . . . The excitement was so great and the place where the shooting occurred (out on the sidewalk) being dark, no one hardly knew what was the matter until after the firing ceased. Marshal Masterson talked but very little after he was shot."

Marshal Masterson lived about forty minutes after the shooting. He staggered north from the saloon, across the railroad tracks, about 450 feet, into George Hoover's liquor store. He sank to the floor and was carried to Bat's room where he died a half an hour later surrounded by his brother and friends. Ed Masterson was well liked and respected by all of Dodge City's permanent residents. "They liked him as a boy, they liked him as a man, and they liked him as an officer."[7] Ed never learned to shoot first and ask questions afterward — a habit of caution that caused his disablement in November, 1877, and his death five months later.

By the time the sun had risen, the wounded Walker had been carried to the room over Wright, Beverley & Co.'s store on Front Street, where his friend, Wagner, lay dying. Within two hours of the murder Sheriff Bat Masterson arrested four associates of Walker and Wagner as accomplices in the murder. They were examined before a justice of the peace on the two afternoons following. The examination was conducted by Bat's close friend, County Attorney Mike Sutton, and Sutton's partner, City Attorney E. F. Colborn. Witnesses could bring forth no evidence of sufficient strength to charge any of the four with a crime. Testimony revealed that despite there being a crowd of people standing within a few feet of the shooting, no one saw the affair from beginning to end.

At ten o'clock, the morning following Masterson's murder, every business in Dodge City closed its doors. The business houses, draped with crepe, stayed closed until six o'clock in the evening following the Masterson funeral — the first such honor paid to a deceased in Dodge City's history. Services were held in Dodge City where a choir, which included Mr. and Mrs. Chalkley M. Beeson, sang the woeful dirge: "Lay him low, lay him low, In the clover or the snow — What cares he, he cannot know." After a sermon by the Rev. O. W. Wright, the funeral procession traveled five miles east to the military cemetery at Fort Dodge where the last rites were performed. The long, silent procession was headed by the city councilmen. Mayor Kelley, being absent on a buffalo hunt with Charlie Bassett, was still unaware of the death of his marshal. The hearse was followed by Sheriff Bat Masterson, then Ed's fellow members of the Dodge City Fire Company, and most of the townspeople of Dodge City in buggies, wagons, and on horseback.

Bat Masterson and his friend, County Attorney Sutton, left following the cowboys' hearings to spend a few days with the Mastersons' parents in Sedgwick County, near Wichita.

In later years residents of Dodge City claimed that Bat Masterson was responsible for the shots that killed the assassin, Wagner, and wounded his accomplice, Walker. Walker recovered sufficiently from his wounds, and upon his release, left Dodge City for Kansas City, accompanied by his father from Texas. Whether or not Bat Masterson avenged the death of his brother by wounding Walker or killing Jack Wagner, or both, will probably never be determined. The reputation of Bat as a Ford County sheriff and a Dodge City lawman need not rest on this single incident.

Bartholomew-William Barclay (Bat) Masterson was one of Dodge City's first residents, hunting buffalo south of the early settlement with his brothers, Ed and Jim, and a family friend, Henry H. Raymond. The origin of Masterson's nickname has been explained in many fanciful ways. It is said to have come from Batiste Brown, an early day character that Bat resembled. It also is said to have come from his practice of batting lawbreakers over the head with his cane, a cane that he used after acquiring a limp

Bat Masterson gave this pistol, a Colt .45, to Dr. Claude McCarty of Dodge City. It is now on display at the Boot Hill Museum.

Photographs (right and left) show Bat Masterson shortly after his headline-making term as sheriff of Ford County. Bat was an early resident of Dodge City, a buffalo hunter, Indian fighter, scout, gambler, sheriff, practical joker, and newspaperman. A controversial figure, his history in Dodge City contains all the ingredients for a dime novel or a TV Western.

These Winchester rifles, Model 1866 (top) and Model 1873 were used both by Indians and Indian fighters. At the right, James Hanrahan, a wagon master and frontiersman, was one of Bat's fellow Indian fighters at the Battle of Adobe Walls. A Dodge City saloonkeeper, he was also the first representative to the Kansas Legislature from Ford County.

This document shows payment to W. B. [Bat] Masterson of $35.00 for services as County Sheriff, January 24, 1879. The January term of the district court in Dodge City was busy with the trials of horse thieves gathered up by Ford County's energetic new sheriff.

Billy Dixon, Adobe Walls Indian fighter, joined up as an Army scout with Bat in 1874. In September, 1877, the Times announced a visit from Billy to Dodge City: "Billy Dixon, the famous scout to whom Congress voted a medal for bravery in an Indian fight during Gen. Miles' southern expedition, came up from below this week, on his way to the great court marshal [sic] trial at Ft. Lyon. His hair is something less than nine feet long, and his general appearance indicates his calling."

from a gunshot wound. The wound came about from an altercation in Texas with a corporal of the Fourth cavalry, over the affections of a young woman. A third theory comes from Heinie Schmidt, a Dodge City resident, who claimed that Henry H. Raymond, Bat's boyhood friend, told him that as boys on the Masterson farm in Illinois, Bat gained distinction among his brothers and friends by being the only one able to shoot down any of the bats in an old barn where they played. A fourth, and the most plausible explanation, is based on the fact that Bat Masterson was christened Bartholomew. He later changed or invented the names, William Barclay, and signed his name, W. B. Masterson, most of his adult lifetime. Bat and Bart, as he was sometimes called by Henry Raymond, are both accepted diminutive forms of Bartholomew.[8]

Bat's first encounter with gunplay was probably in 1874, as part of a group of hunters at a settlement on the Canadian River in the Texas Panhandle. The Battle of Adobe Walls, one of the most famous Indian fights in the West, has been retold in many accounts of frontier history.

Three stores at Adobe Walls were operated by Dodge Citians Charles Rath, Robert M. Wright, Fred Leonard, and A. C. Myers. James Hanrahan, a participant in the battle, operated a saloon at Adobe Walls and was half owner of the Occident saloon at Dodge City. When Hanrahan returned to Dodge City after the fight, he carried with him war bonnets, scalps, bows, arrows, and lances — booty from Indians killed at Adobe Walls. These Indian objects made up the paraphernalia used in Luke McGlue's "Indian Act," by the Front Street pranksters a few years later. The Battle of Adobe Walls was part of a general Indian outbreak which resulted in the formation of an Indian Territory expedition under the command of Col. Nelson A. Miles. Bat and another famous frontier scout, Billy Dixon, signed on with Miles' expedition which formed at Fort Dodge in 1874. Seven months later Bat was back in Dodge City, and shortly after was appointed deputy sheriff of Ford County.

In June, 1877, the cattle trade was booming with two hundred cattlemen in town. The merchants were enjoying a brisk trade and the gambling fraternity was up and about promoting their specialties. As Bat walked down the boardwalk on a Wednesday afternoon he spied Bobby Gilmore, the noted card manipulator, promoter of devious schemes, and well-known cattle town drifter. Bobby, an extremely eloquent manipulator of words as well as of playing cards, was having a noisy argument with Marshal Larry Deger. The *Times* reported that "Marshal Deger took exceptions, and started for the dog house with [Bobby]. Bobby walked very leisurely — so much so that Larry felt it necessary to administer a few paternal kicks in the rear. This act was soon interrupted by Bat Masterson, who wound his arm affectionately around the Marshal's neck and let the prisoner escape. Deger then grappled with Bat . . . Joe Mason appeared upon the scene at this critical moment and took [Masterson's] gun. Bat Masterson would not surrender yet, and came near getting hold of a pistol from among several which were strewed around over the sidewalk, but half a dozen Texas men came to [Marshal Deger's] aid and gave him a chance to draw his gun and beat Bat over the head. . . . Bat Masterson seemed possessed of extraordinary strength, and every inch of the way was closely contested, but the city dungeon was reached at last, and in he went. If he had got hold of his gun before going in there would have been a general killing."[9]

The bad blood between Bat and Larry Deger was surely made worse by orders, probably given out by Deger, to Bat's older brother, Ed, a newly appointed assistant marshal. Ed found it his duty to seek out and arrest his brother's friend, Bobby Gilmore, and deposit him in the wooden calaboose where the gambler and Bat spent the night. They were each fined the next day and released.

Bat's fine was remitted by his friend, Mayor Kelley, at the next meeting of the city council. Bat served out the year as under sheriff to Sheriff Charlie Bassett, pursuing a murderer north of Dodge City to Saw Log Creek, arresting a horse thief, and hunting unsuccessfully for the notorious train robber, Sam Bass. Bat used his influence with the sheriff to force Deger's resignation as deputy sheriff, a job Deger held along with his principal occupation as city marshal. In addition, Bat's influence with Mayor Kelley and the city councilmen succeeded in getting him appointed as a special policeman on the city force headed by Marshal

Deger. Bat was gaining in power and reputation with the Gang. In the fall of 1877, hearing that his foe, Larry Deger, was thinking of running for sheriff, Bat threw his hat in the ring. Charlie Bassett was prohibited by law from serving a third term, and Bat felt his time had come.

The Dodge City *Times* backed the twenty-four-year-old peace officer with these words: "Mr. W. B. Masterson is on the track for Sheriff, and so announces himself in this paper. 'Bat' is well known as a young man of nerve and coolness in cases of danger. He has served on the police force of this city, and also as under-sheriff, and knows just how to gather in the sinners. He is qualified to fill the office, and if elected will never shrink from danger." When the polls closed on November 6, 1877, Bat was the winner over Larry Deger by a margin of three votes.

On taking office in January, 1878, Bat appointed his former boss, Charlie Bassett, as under sheriff. Within two weeks Bat made headlines.

"THE TRAIN ROBBERS! . . . THEY ARE CAPTURED BY STRATEGY . . . W. B. MASTERSON MAKES A GOOD BEGINNING. . . . SHERIFF W. B. MASTERSON AND HIS HEROIC POSSE BAG THE GAME WITHOUT A SHOT. PERILOUS ADVENTURE WITH GRATIFYING RESULTS."[10]

The robbery took place at the Santa Fe railroad station in Kinsley, thirty-seven miles northeast of Dodge City. Five men, with faces blackened to avoid recognition, stepped into the station at four o'clock in the morning. Two thousand dollars lay in the safe. As a west bound train approached, the night operator escaped across the tracks in front of the moving engine, warning the trainmen on board. The armed robbers, foiled in their attempt, mounted and ran. Bat and a posse of four set out on a four-day hunt through a snow storm and returned from a cattle camp sixty-five miles south of Dodge City with two of the bandits. Bat's actions were described in glowing terms in the Dodge City newspapers: "W. B. Masterson, Sheriff of Ford county, and posse had returned from a four days hunt, bringing with them two of the gang that made the raid on the town of Kinsley and attempted the robbery of the railroad agent and the western bound express train. . . . After some hours waiting two horsemen cautiously approached from the north east. . . . After some talk they came within shooting distance when Masterson springing out with leveled rifle sang out his well known 'throw up your hands.' . . . Both surrendered and were disarmed. The programme for this successful capture was well laid. . . . The nerve, skill and energy of Sheriff Masterson and gallant posse is recorded as a brilliant achievement and is receiving just tribute for so daring a venture accomplished so adroitly and maneuvered with the skill of a warrior."

A week later, Bat, Charlie Bassett, and three others rode south in search of more of the train robbers. They lost the trail in the breaks of the Canadian River in Texas and returned home thirteen days later, having traveled over five hundred miles. In March, hearing that the suspected train robbers still at large had been seen in a dance hall south of Front Street, Sheriff Bat Masterson, Under Sheriff Bassett, and Marshal Ed Masterson chased the suspects west of town and captured two of them.

Bat Masterson distinguished himself as a hardworking sheriff of Ford County the rest of the spring and summer of 1878. Capturing horse thieves and returning stolen horses were his specialty. In April the *Times* announced: "We are glad to observe the interest manifested by both the County Attorney and Sheriff in bringing horse thieves to justice." In May the *Times* reported: "Horse thieves find hospitable reception at the hands of Sheriff Masterson. He is an excellent 'catch' and is earning a State reputation."

The first cattle herds of 1878 arrived in Dodge City the middle of May, just a few weeks after the arrival of Bobby Gilmore, the cattle town sport, bunko steerer, and dead beat. Charlie Bassett had just been appointed marshal after the death of Bat's brother. Police court was "getting lively." Front Street businesses were "jammed full" of goods. On May 8, 1878, Wyatt Earp arrived in town.

The following Saturday, the *Times* reported: "Mr. Wyatt Earp, who has during the past served with credit on the police arrived in this city from Texas last Wednesday. We predict that his services as an

H. T. McCarty,
County Surveyor.

County Surveyor's Office,

FORD COUNTY, KANSAS.

Dodge City Kan. 187

Harry T. McCarty, a painter, draftsman, and surveyor, served as county surveyor for two years (letterhead above) and was appointed deputy United States Marshal in 1878. Less than three months later he was shot and killed in the Long Branch saloon by a cattle camp cook.

James P. Masterson (left), Bat's younger brother, served as deputy sheriff under Bat, and as policeman alongside Assistant Marshal Wyatt Earp. In 1879 he was appointed marshal and served as the city's chief law officer until the defeat of Mayor Kelley in 1881. Shortly after, Jim Masterson called his brother, Bat, to aid in a quarrel, resulting in the Front Street shootout between Bat Masterson and Jim's enemies, A. J. Peacock and Al Updegraph.

officer will again be required this Summer." Three days later the *Globe* announced: "Wyatt Earp, one of the most efficient officers Dodge ever had, has just returned from Fort Worth, Texas. He was immediately appointed Asst. Marshal, by our City dads, much to their credit." Two other policemen, John Brown and Charles Trask, were appointed under Bassett and Earp.

On May 20, 1878, Henry Sturm unloaded a boxcar of beer into his ice house. The same evening the *Globe* reported, "Numerous 'cow boys' [are] under the 'influence' in town . . ." Marshal Bassett and Assistant Marshal Earp were kept busy making the rounds of the saloons and dance halls collecting taxes for city licenses. Over $1,500 was collected in the month of May. Prominent Texas cattlemen were "drinking coffee" with Deacon Cox at the Dodge House, making plans for driving their herds on to Nebraska, Wyoming, or Montana. In June, according to the *Globe,* "Thousands of cattle can be seen south of the river, and dozens of cow boys perambulate our streets daily." Three dance halls were in "full blast" south of the railroad tracks. John H. (Doc) Holliday, tubercular dentist, roving gambler, and picturesque Western character, was settled in Room No. 24 at the Dodge House.[11] The May salaries for the city police force were approved: Bassett $100.00; Earp $75.00; Brown $75.00; Trask $52.50 — good money for lawmen at a time when a Texas trail driver was paid $30.00 a month for his long days and arduous work "going up the trail."

During the first week of June, 1878, Jim Masterson, Bat's younger brother and buffalo hunting companion, replaced Charles Trask as policeman under Bassett and Earp. On June 18, the *Globe* reported: "Wyatt Earp is doing his duty as Ass't Marshal in a very creditable manner. — Adding new laurels to his splendid record every day."

Less than a month later, on July 13, 1878, shots rang out from the Long Branch saloon at four o'clock in the morning. Harry T. McCarty, a sign painter and surveyor, recently appointed deputy United States marshal, was standing at the bar in the Long Branch. The early morning's festivities were drawing to a close. A retarded hired hand, a cook for one of the cattle camps, had been started back to camp, full of whisky. He returned into the Long Branch where a group began teasing the "half-witted, rattle-brained and quarrelsome wretch."[12]   As McCarty stood at the bar talking to the bartender, the half drunken cook "snatched 'Mack's' pistol (a .45 caliber Colt) from the scabbard, and as 'Mack' turned to see who had so nimbly disarmed him, the assassin, giving the weapon a flourish or two, fired the fatal shot." McCarty died an hour later and was buried that afternoon in the newly laid out cemetery, Prairie Grove. One of the first to be buried there, H. T. McCarty had surveyed Prairie Grove Cemetery for the owners only three months earlier.

One week after the murder of Deputy U. S. Marshal H. T. McCarty, music from the festive revolver was heard at three o'clock in the morning, outside the Lady Gay dance hall and Comique theater. The Dodge City *Times* of July 27, 1878, told the story: "Yesterday morning about 3 o'clock this peaceful suburban city was thrown into unusual excitement, and the turmoil was all caused by a rantankerous cow boy who started the mischief by a too free use of his little revolver. In Dodge City, after dark, the report of a revolver generally means business and is an indication that somebody is on the war path, therefore when the noise of this shooting and the yells of excited voices rang out on the midnight breeze, the sleeping community awoke from their slumbers, listened a while to the click of the revolver, wondered who was shot this time, and then went to sleep again. . . . It seems that three or four herders were paying their respects to the city and its institutions, and as is usually their custom, remained until about 3 o'clock in the morning, when they prepared to return to their camps. They buckled on their revolvers, which they were not allowed to wear around town, and mounted their horses, when all at once one of them conceived the idea that to finish the night's revelry and give the natives due warning of his departure, he must do some shooting, and forthwith he commenced to bang away, one of the bullets whizing into a dance hall near by, causing no little commotion among the participants in the 'dreamy waltz' and quadrille. Policemen [Wyatt] Earp and [Jim] Masterson made a raid on the shootist who gave them two or three volleys, and followed the herders with the intention of arresting them. . . . The herders rode across the bridge followed by the officers. A few yards from the bridge one of the herders fell from his horse from weakness caused by a wound in the arm which he had received during the fracas. The other herder made good his escape. . . ."

Eddie Foy, who was in the Lady Gay when the Texans rode by, claimed that "everybody dropped to the floor at once, according to custom. Bat Masterson was just in the act of dealing in a game of Spanish monte with Doc Holliday, and I was impressed by the instantaneous manner in which they flattened out like pancakes on the floor. . . . I had just bought a new eleven-dollar suit, and as the night was hot, I had left the coat hanging in a dressing room. When I went back to get it after the bombardment, I found that it had been penetrated by three bullets, and one of them had started a ring of fire smoldering around the hole."[13] The *Globe,* in its account of the shooting, elaborated on Foy's story: "At the time the shooting commenced there were at least 150 people in the house all enjoying themselves immensely. Fortunately no one was, as usual, in the boxes of the Theater, everybody being down on the dancing floor, and owing to this fact no person inside the house was hurt, because the balls all passed too high to hit anyone on this floor. A general scamper was made by the crowd, some getting under the stage, others running out the front door, and behind the bar; in the language of the bard, 'such gittin up stairs never was seed.' "

A month later, in August, George Hoy, the Texas herder wounded by Jim Masterson and Wyatt Earp, died and was buried in Prairie Grove cemetery. The *Times* noted at his passing: "Hoy was like many other men who grow up on the Texas frontier, very bold and reckless, and we understand he was under bond before he came here for killing two men in Texas, however he had many good traits, and seemed to have many friends among the Texas boys." Although it is doubtful that Hoy's Texas friends "beat the drum slowly and played the fife lowly, And bitterly wept as they bore him along," it is sure that Hoy's death at the hands of Wyatt Earp and Jim Masterson increased the friction between Dodge City lawmen and Texas cattlemen.

Wyatt Berry Stapp Earp (right), Ford County deputy sheriff and Dodge City assistant marshal, gained a gunman's notoriety after the famous battle of the O. K. Corral in Tombstone. His reputation in Dodge City, however, was one of laconic and confident enforcer of the city ordinances. "He had a quiet way of taking the most desperate characters into custody which invariably gave one the impression that the city was able to enforce her mandates and preserve her dignity. It wasn't considered policy to draw a gun on Wyatt unless you got the drop and meant to burn powder without any preliminary talk."

A Colt single-action .45 caliber Buntline Special (above) allegedly was given to each of the Dodge City lawmen, Charlie Bassett, Bat Masterson, Neil Brown, Bill Tilghman, and Wyatt Earp by E. Z. C. Judson, better known as Ned Buntline. Buntline (right), showman and author of over 400 novels, mostly about Western heroes, gave the specially made pistols in appreciation for the stories and background material given him by these authentic Western lawmen.

This shotgun (right), left in care of Chalk Beeson by Ben Thompson and never claimed, is alleged to be the shotgun wielded by Thompson after the fatal shooting of Ellsworth's sheriff in 1873. According to Wyatt Earp, Ben Thompson held Ellsworth at bay with this murder weapon while his brother, the sheriff's killer, escaped. Though many historians protest, according to Earp, it was he who forced Ben to throw down this shotgun and submit to arrest.

The end page and title page of a Bible given to Wyatt Earp by law partners Mike Sutton and E. F. Colborn are shown above. Sutton was county attorney, and Colborn, city attorney, during Earp's terms as assistant marshal in Dodge City. The inscription reads: "To Wyatt S. Earp, as a slight recognition of his many Christian virtues, and steady following in the footsteps of the meek and lowly Jesus." Mike Sutton's love for rough humor and frontier jokes and Wyatt Earp's ability to neatly polish Texas heads with the barrel of his forty-five leads one to suspect that the motive for this gift was not a truly religious one.

John H. (Doc) Holliday (left) practiced dentistry in Room No. 24 of the Dodge House and graced the gambling tables of Dodge City saloons during the summer of 1878. A friend of the Earps, he left Dodge and gained his fame as a gunslinger in the O. K. Corral fight in Tombstone, Arizona, in 1881. Clay Allison (right), one of the legendary bad men of the West, visited Dodge City several times in 1878. Wyatt Earp claimed that Allison was commissioned by Texas cattlemen to kill him, and that he faced down the killer and ran him out of town. No other sources of this now classic Western encounter between Earp and Allison can be found.

102

Wyatt Earp must have distinguished himself with the party in power during the summer of 1878 in Dodge City. In August the Republicans of Ford County met to choose their delegates to the Kansas State Republican convention to be held in Topeka on August 28, 1878. Wyatt Earp, along with M. W. Sutton, Charles E. Bassett, A. J. Peacock, and six others, were chosen to represent Dodge City.[14]

On August 17, 1878, another shooting affair broke out at the bar in the Comique theater. Earp and Jim Masterson were having difficulties calming an intoxicated and troublesome cowboy. The bystanders, Texas cattlemen, came to the cowboy's aid and joined in the fight. Wyatt and Jim bruised a few Texas heads with their six-shooters. Several shots were fired but no one was injured. The *Globe* commented: "We however cannot help but regret the too ready use of pistols in all rows of such character and would like to see a greater spirit of harmony exist between our officers and cattle men so that snarling coyotes and killers could make their own fights without interesting or dragging good men into them."

On September 7, 1878, the *Times* reported another "shoot-'em-up" incident: "A wild 'hero' of the plains discharged his revolver Wednesday night, at about 10 o'clock, while passing through town up Bridge street [Second Avenue] and on his way north. He put spurs to his horse, and was soon out of the reach of the officers."

A week later an Indian scare had aroused citizens of Ford County. Dull Knife and his band of Cheyennes were fleeing across Western Kansas. Famished and dying of fever in Indian Territory, the Cheyennes left for a northern trek to their ancestral homes in the Black Hills of the Dakotas, a thousand miles distant. Cattle herders were reporting pillaging and killing in the camps south of Dodge City. The headlines of the Dodge City *Times* were sensational:
"THE RED DEVILS. The Wild And Hungry Cheyennes. COMMIT MURDER AND ARSON. Several Herders Murdered. A HOUSE BURNED DOWN. Wholesale Stealing of Horses. AN INDIAN FIGHT. Three Soldiers Killed And Three Wounded. THE BORDER WILD WITH EXCITEMENT. Straggling Bands Of Indians Raiding Everywhere. . . . IMMIGRANT TRAINS ROBBED. Four Companies Of Cavalry Ordered To Dodge. DODGE CITY UNDER ARMS."

The panic that resulted from the Indians' pillaging caused a few exaggerations. A locomotive was secured from the Santa Fe railroad, filled with volunteers, and dispatched four miles west of Dodge City to put out the flames in a house thought to have been attacked by the Indians. P. L. Beatty, Chalk Beeson, S. E. Isaacson, and Wyatt Earp were the brave volunteer firemen who doused the flames. The fire turned out to have started from a stove left burning when the frightened inhabitants of the house fled to Dodge City for protection from the approaching Indians.

The Indian scare caused a general excitement that resulted in shooting affairs on the streets of Dodge City. Al Manning, a barkeeper fired at former policeman, John Brown, wounding a bystander in the foot. Skunk Curley, a bullwhacker in a state of inebriation, shot a visitor from Great Bend, inflicting an ugly wound. Frank Trask, a former policeman, was wounded while crossing the railroad tracks near the water tank. The Dodge City newspapers commented during the last week of September, 1878: "No less than half a dozen shooting scrapes occurred in our city during the past week. We are glad to state, however, that no one was seriously hurt. The last one occurred night before last. There seems to be more danger of being shot in the city than there is danger of being scalped by the Red Man out on the plains. . . . The revolver was quite festive in Dodge City last week. The Indian 'scare' and bad whiskey did much to throw some of the boys off the track."

The feeling of panic changed to one of revenge when the *Ford County Globe* reported on October 1, 1878, that the Fort Dodge commander, Colonel W. H. Lewis, had been killed while in pursuit of Dull Knife and his Cheyennes.

More exciting highlights of 1878 were to come during the fall months.

Wyatt Earp claimed in his biography that the highlights of his career as the tamer of Dodge City were his confrontations with Texas cattlemen, Tobe Driskill and Bob Rachel, and his "High Noon" encounter with the legendary badman, Clay Allison. These tales have become traditions of American frontier history. Doubtless, they have some basis in fact — Tobe Driskill and A. A. Rachel (one of several Rachel brothers) and Clay Allison are all known to have been in Dodge City during the summer and fall of 1878. The only mention in the two Dodge City newspapers that even hints at Earp's famous meeting with the killer, Allison, are these in the September 10, 1878, edition of the *Ford County Globe:* "Clay Allison came down from the west on the 5th [two weeks after the death of George Hoy]," and "The 'hurrah' look which pervaded our streets a few weeks ago is gone, and we now linger in peace." Whether the "peace" referred to was caused by Wyatt Earp's pistol or by the natural slowing down of cattle trade activities in the fall of 1878, will never be known. The real story of Driskill, Rachel, Allison, and Earp died when these four characters passed from the Western scene.

Much nonsense has been written about Dodge City's Queen of the Fairy Belles, Dora Hand, but her romantic and novel history is yet to be fully unravelled.

Dora Hand came from St. Louis in the summer of 1878 to perform in Dodge City's variety theaters. Separated from her husband, Theodore Hand, the singer and actress now used her theatrical name, Fannie Keenan. Ham Bell once asked her, "Well, what is your real name?" "Well," she said, "Mr. Bell, take your pick, one's just as good as the other." Ham Bell and other early residents of Dodge City claimed that her beauty was marred only by a small scar on her forehead which she vainly kept hidden by combing her hair down over it.[15]

While performing in St. Louis she became a friend of Fannie Garrettson, who was also in Dodge City in 1878, performing at the Comique theater with Eddie Foy. Fannie Garrettson, a singer of ballads and a variety performer, made tours of the cattle towns and mining camps. In the fall of 1876, she performed in McDaniel's New Theatre in Cheyenne, Wyoming, singing "Select Ballads" and a "Bouquet of Melodies," providing a change of pace for the headliner, M'lle. Cerito, Queen of Magic Changes.

In July of 1878, the two Fannies were singing at the Comique in Dodge City, providing the variety for the headliners, Foy and Thompson. They shared quarters in a two-room cottage southeast of the theater. The Comique's competitor, the Varieties, owned by Ham Bell, had not been as successful, and by August was closing down. The manager of the Varieties, H. L. Seymour, had run up enormous debts and "silently stole away" the last of July on the east bound train. On August 14, Hattie Smith and Fannie Keenan played in a benefit at Ham Bell's Varieties. The *Times* announced, "They are general favorites and will be sure to draw a crowded house." Perhaps the benefit was to help unlucky Ham pay some of his debts.

Dora Hand left the Comique to join the Hernandez Comedy Company which toured the western Kansas communities of Kinsley and Larned and others along the Santa Fe railroad. The reviews of the Hernandez Comedy Company were not outstanding. As the cattle trade wound down in Dodge City, the Comique theater closed, and Dora Hand left for St. Louis. Sometime before September 24, 1878, she returned to ask her attorney in Dodge City, Harry E. Gryden, to file divorce proceedings against her estranged husband, Theodore. Her friend, Fannie Garrettson, was still in Dodge City, probably singing in Mayor Kelley's saloon on Front Street.

On the night of October 3, 1878, Fannie Garrettson and Dora Hand retired in the small frame building behind the Great Western hotel. The building was partitioned off into two bedrooms. Dora Hand occupied the back room. The front room was generally occupied by Mayor Kelley. Fannie Garrettson had been using the back room. Kelley was suffering from an illness, and not being on good terms with the town doctor, T. L. McCarty, he had gone to Fort Dodge to seek the services of the post surgeon, W. S. Tremaine. Fannie Garrettson had been sharing the back room with Dora Hand since her recent arrival in Dodge City.

Dora Hand, a singer in the variety theaters of the West under the name of Fannie Keenan, was the tragic victim of an assassin's bullet meant for the mayor of Dodge City, Dog Kelley. A performer in the Comique and Variety theaters in Dodge City, she was known as a "prepossessing woman [whose] artful winning ways brought many admirers within her smiles and blandishments."

Fannie Garrettson, a singer of ballads and a variety performer, like Dora Hand, Eddie Foy, and others, made the tour of cattle and mining camp theaters. In 1876 she was billed as a singer of "select Ballads" and a "Bouquet of Melodies" with McDaniel's New Theatre in Cheyenne, Wyoming. In 1878 she appeared in Dodge City with Eddie Foy at the Comique theater. A companion of Dora Hand, she narrowly escaped the bullets meant for their friend and saloonkeeper, Mayor Kelley.

Since Kelley would be recovering at Fort Dodge for a few days, Fannie Garrettson decided to use the mayor's bed and offered hers to Dora Hand.

Mayor Kelley had recently had words with a young Texan, resulting in a brawl — probably in Kelley's saloon. Kelley must have gotten the best of the fight. The whipped Texan was James W. Kenedy, son of Captain Miflin Kenedy, a wealthy Texas cattleman. The Kenedy family had marketed thousands of head of cattle in Dodge City during the summer. It is claimed by early historians of Dodge City that the police court docket of July, 1878, recorded an arrest by Wyatt Earp of one, James Kennedy [sic], for carrying a pistol — a plea of guilty, and fine and costs collected. Again, allegedly on August 17, 1878, said James W. Kenedy was arrested by Charles Bassett for being disorderly.[16] Unfortunately these police court dockets containing the evidence of Dodge City's wild and violent cattle town period have disappeared — either destroyed through the passage of time or mislaid in some nook or cranny of Dodge City's past.

105

According to Robert M. Wright, Kenedy left after his brawl with Kelley, went to Kansas City, bought an expensive horse, and brought it back to Dodge City.[17] Kenedy, a vengeful scion of the wealthy Kenedy clan, must still have held his grudge against Dodge City's mayor.

Four pistol shots were heard around four o'clock, Friday morning, October 4, 1878, arousing Assistant Marshal Wyatt Earp and Policeman Jim Masterson to investigate. The terrified Fannie Garrettson awoke to discover her companion, Fannie Keenan, alias Dora Hand, dead in bed. One forty-five calibre ball had penetrated the front door of the house, passing through the front door and ricocheting off the floor, striking the underside of the Garrettson-Kelley bed. The second bullet penetrated through Garrettson's bedclothes, through the plaster partition separating the two bedrooms, striking Dora Hand, killing her instants later. These two shots came within inches of killing Fannie Garrettson, asleep in Mayor Kelley's bed. Two shots evidently missed the building entirely. The fatal pistol ball ended the life of an innocent victim, Dora Hand, who according to the Dodge City *Times,* "was a prepossessing woman [whose] artful winning ways brought many admirers within her smiles and blandishments." "If we mistake not," commented the *Times,* Dora Hand has an eventful history.... After a varied life the unexpected death messenger cuts her down in the full bloom of gayety and womanhood." Dora was thirty-four years old.

The bullets, by their angle of destruction, had obviously been fired from horseback. Jim Masterson and Wyatt Earp guessed at the possible motive behind the shots and found a witness who had seen Kenedy and an unknown companion in a still-open saloon shortly after the shooting. Kenedy's companion was arrested and placed in jail. Kenedy had disappeared. The unknown companion pleaded innocent, but supplied information implicating Kenedy. By two o'clock that afternoon a posse was formed. The *Times* called it "as intrepid a posse as ever pulled a trigger..." It included Sheriff Bat Masterson, Marshal Charlie Bassett, Assistant Marshal Wyatt Earp, Deputy Sheriff William Duffey, and Bill Tilghman.

Guessing at what James Kenedy's escape route might be to his cattle ranch at Tascosa, Texas, the posse rode east along the Arkansas River to a point beyond Fort Dodge, then turning south they rode seventy miles and doubled back the next day through a rainstorm to a point thirty-five miles southwest of Dodge City. The posse's hard riding brought them to a ranch near the city of Meade, where they expected to intercept Kenedy. The words of the Dodge City *Times* record the capture of the alleged slayer of Dodge City's Queen of the Dance Halls:

"[The posse's] patient waiting was rewarded about 4 o'clock Saturday afternoon, when a solitary horseman appeared on the distant plain approaching the camp. The officers had apprised certain parties to give no heed of their presence, and from them it was afterwards learned that Kennedy had made diligent inquiries concerning the whereabouts of supposed horsemen. To these inquiries Kennedy received negative replies. The cautious manner in which he approached the camp led the officers to believe that he snuffed the danger from every movement forward. He halted when within a few hundred yards of the camp, apparently dreading to proceed further. Seeing that he would approach no nearer, the officers thrice commanded Kennedy to throw up his hands. He raised his arm as though to strike his horse with a quirt he held in his hand, when several shots were fired by the officers, one shot striking Kennedy in the left shoulder, making a dangerous wound; three shots struck the horse killing him instantly. Kennedy was armed with a carbine, two revolvers and a knife. He was brought in Sunday and placed in jail, where he is receiving medical treatment, though he lies in a low and critical condition."

Shortly after the killing, James W. Kenedy was branded by Dodge City residents as "a cold-blooded assassin," and "a fiend in human form." Ten days after his capture the *Globe* reported, "The wounded prisoner, Kennedy, is getting along finely." A week later, he was examined at a preliminary hearing and "the evidence being insufficient the prisoner was acquitted." His trial took place in Sheriff Masterson's office in the court house. The office being too small to admit spectators, the *Globe* reported: "We do not know what the evidence was, or upon what grounds he was acquitted. But he is free to go on his way rejoicing whenever he gets ready." Just prior to the release of James W. Kenedy, Fannie Garrettson, the frightened "operatic nightingale," flew to a safer climate.

The year 1878 had been a busy one for Dodge City lawmen, and Colonel John W. Straughn, Bat Masterson's jailer, found his bastille in the basement of the court house filled to capacity in October. Thomas O'Haran, charged with murder in the first degree in the shooting of Deputy U. S. Marshal H. T. McCarty; Henry Gould, alias Skunk Curley, assault with intent to kill; Dan Woodard, assault with intent to kill; James Skelly, robbery; James Kenedy, suspicion of murder in the first degree in the shooting of Dora Hand; and two others charged with lesser offenses, made up the choice quarters in the limestone basement of the county court house known as the "lime-kiln."

At the regular meeting of the county commissioners, saloonkeeper A. J. Peacock moved to instruct the county attorney to petition District Judge Samuel R. Peters "to hold a special term of court, at his earliest convenience, on account of too many prisoners in jail."

Three weeks later two horse thieves were brought in from Fort Elliott, Texas, and thrown in with the other desperate characters awaiting trial. Kenedy had been released and was now quartered at the Dodge House. Eight prisoners were in the small quarters designed to hold two comfortably. Shortly after, another prisoner was released, and Sheriff Bat Masterson added a horse thief to take his place.

In December, still awaiting trial, Skunk Curley and the three horse thieves sawed through an iron bar and escaped while jailer Straughn was visiting a blacksmith shop to secure help in making repairs to the jail. The four "struck out for tall timber," each taking a different route. The *Ford County Globe* reported: "On hearing the disastrous news the sheriff [Bat Masterson] and his deputy immediately mounted horses and scoured the country around town in search of the fugitives. Their prompt search proved partially fruitful in the capture of [Skunk Curley] about a mile from town, hid in a buffalo wallow on the prairie. . . . They . . . continued their search through the night and the next day, but the prisoners having taken to the prairies and hills, no trace could be found. . . . The sheriff, whose conduct in the capture and detention of horse-thieves, has been so frequently complimented of late, was greatly exercised over the news of the escape and made every effort to regain the prisoners." Within the week, two of the horse thieves were captured and returned to jail.

Judge Peters evidently did not deem an overcrowded jail reason to travel the distance from Newton to Dodge City to hold a special term of court. In January, 1879, the jail occupancy increased to twelve, including the renowned horse thief Dutch Henry Borne. Dutch Henry was known in several states and territories for a variety of crimes, such as horse stealing, mail robbery, and murder. He was arrested in Trinidad, Colorado, by Las Animas County law officers on a tip telegraphed to Trinidad by Bat Masterson. Dutch Henry was wanted in Ford County also, and Masterson, by exerting his influence, managed to extradite him to Kansas for trial in Dodge City. Mysterious Dave Mather, a Dodge City gunman, was in Trinidad with "Deutcher Heinrich" and may have been the one who tipped off Masterson.

Dutch Henry was well-known in Dodge City as a big spender during the cattle season of 1878. Henry rarely used his last name; he was a well-educated German-American, a roving plainsman who claimed that "his character as a horse-thief [was] greatly over-estimated."[18]

Henry Borne was charged and tried for stealing horses which had disappeared three years earlier. Since Mike Sutton had represented Borne in legal matters in Dodge City several years earlier, he disqualified himself from prosecuting the prisoner. Perhaps the lack of Mike's oratorical delivery to arouse the jury was a factor in Borne's acquittal after a two-day trial. The *Globe* announced the verdict with disappointment: "This will be a great surprise to many of the people of the west who received the news of his capture with manifestations of joy and gladness. His fame as a horse thief extends far and wide. He is a 'star' in his particular line. Many a tale of his reckless daring have we listened to with eager interest. How 'handy' he was with his revolver, and with what magnetic influence he governed his confederates.

Samuel R. Peters, from Newton, Kansas, was judge of the district court at Dodge City from 1875 to 1881. Judge Peters presided at the crowded criminal trials of January, 1879, relieving the crowded county jail, recently filled to overflowing by Ford County's new energetic sheriff, Bat Masterson.

The county jail was lodged in the basement of Ford County's courthouse built in 1876 of native stone and locally fired brick. The jail, with its iron cages built against the courthouse basement's limestone walls, was known by its occupants as the "lime-kiln."

Henry Borne, better known as Dutch Henry, a famous horse thief and Robin Hood of the West, was brought to Dodge City by Bat Masterson for trial in the district court. The jury's verdict (left), written on the back of a Santa Fe railroad timetable (right), recites: "The State of Kansas vs. Henry Born, Verdict. We the jury in the above entitled cause do find Def[endant] Henry Born Not Guilty. Jas. W. Skinner, Foreman."

Michael W. Sutton (right), known by some as "St. Michael of the Oily Tongue," was an eloquent and forceful prosecuting attorney during Bat Masterson's term as sheriff of Ford County. In 1879 Mike Sutton was a highly successful attorney and political supporter of Bat Masterson and Mayor Kelley's Gang. After his marriage to the niece of the reform candidate for mayor, A. B. Webster, and his appointment as attorney for the Santa Fe Railroad, "St. Michael" joined the Dodge City Temperance Society and turned his support away from his former friends.

The stoic faces of these Cheyenne warriors, survivors of the last Indian raid in Kansas, little comprehend the white man's law as they sit on the steps of the Ford County court house awaiting their trial for murder. This trial, initiated by County Attorney Sutton, ended adversely for the ambitious young attorney and his friend Bat Masterson. Sutton failed to get a conviction, and the expense of the trial was an important factor in Bat's defeat as sheriff in November, 1879. The man sitting on the bottom row with the Indians is George Reynolds, interpreter, who, with his father, P. G. Reynolds, operated a stage line from Dodge City through Indian Territory to Camp Supply.

109

How he rode on a magnificent sorrel horse at the head of his little band, with the solemnity and dignity of a general; and with what alacrity his commands were obeyed. How he had evaded the law. How desperately he had fought when hotly pursued, and how he had always escaped his captors. He was the 'Rob Roy' of the plains and his exploits were only equaled by 'Sixteen-Strin[g]-Jack' in his palmiest days. He was brought into court last Thursday looking as calm and serene as the noonday sun. . . . The defense closed, the jury retired, and were out but a few moments. The Judge received the paper upon which the verdict was written. The eager audience waited with expectant countenances. Judge Peters unfolded the paper and read 'Not Guilty.' Addressing Henry the Judge said: 'Mr. Henry Borne, the jury have found you not guilty, you are therefore released from custody.' 'I thank you, Judge, and you too, gentlemen of the jury,' said Henry, and was off like a shot. Making his way down stairs he hastened to the back door of the court house where a fleet steed, saddled and bridled, awaited him. He departed.''

The January term of the District Court opened on the 7th with the Honorable Samuel R. Peters, judge, presiding. Mike Sutton, county attorney, and Bat Masterson, sheriff, were present. Two of the robbers, one horse thief, and Skunk Curley pleaded guilty; one of the horse thieves was convicted, and Dan Woodard was found guilty of attempting to kill former policeman, Frank Trask. After their sentencing, the six prisoners were removed to the State Penitentiary in Leavenworth by Sheriff Masterson. County Attorney Sutton shook the hand of each prisoner as the eastbound train was boarded.

Michael W. (Mike) Sutton was one of the first attorneys to settle in Medicine Lodge, Kansas. A young Irishman and a recent student of law at Warrensburg, Missouri, he arrived in southern Kansas to find slim pickin's in the law business. Single, carefree, and not disposed to worry over his financial condition, he saved money on laundry bills by washing his single shirt in the clear waters of Elm Creek and resting in the shade of plum bushes while his garment dried in the sun. Mike moved to Dodge City around 1876 to seek better prospects for his legal talents. Elected county attorney shortly after his arrival, he became an early friend of Bat Masterson. He nominated Masterson for sheriff in 1877. By January, 1879, Mike's reputation in Dodge City had reached new heights. His efficient prosecution of the prisoners at the crowded term of the District Court resulted in praise by a neighboring town's newspaper, the Spearville *News:* "One of the prisoners remarked on his way . . . to the penitentiary that he believed that Mike [Sutton] could take that jury and try J. C. for his throne and put him off."

Letting his success carry away his common sense, feeling his oats as a political power in the city, county, and among Kansas Republicans, Sutton filed legal papers against Dull Knife and his entire band of one hundred and fifty Cheyenne warriors, for the murder of five persons within the jurisdiction of Ford County. He requested the governor of Kansas to return the Indians to Dodge City for trial after their apprehension. After Sutton returned from Topeka with a promise from military and civil authorities that the Indians would be returned to Dodge City, it became Bat Masterson's chore to go to Fort Leavenworth to identify the Indians who had just arrived in chains from Fort Robinson.

Bat Masterson had been appointed deputy United States marshal in January, 1879, replacing the slain H. T. McCarty, and was reaching the peak of his law-enforcing reputation in southwest Kansas. The Leavenworth *Times* commented on Bat's reputation upon his arrival in Leavenworth with more prisoners from Dodge City: "During Sheriff Masterson's term of office he has contributed liberally to the State's boarding house and has kept things as straight as a string in his county. He is one of the most noted men of the southwest, as cool, brave and daring as any one who ever drew a pistol. . . . Although he has been in many a tight place he has always managed to save his scalp."

The Indian prisoners were transferred from military to civil authorities to await inspection by Bat and his party from Dodge City. Accompanying Bat was his brother, Jim Masterson, and friend Charlie Bassett, and two men who claimed to have encountered the Indians in Ford County. An Army captain, A. J. French, and a scout, George (Kokomo) Sullivan, pointed out seven of the Cheyennes — Wild Hog, Old Crow, Big

Head, Left Hand, Blacksmith, Porcupine, and Nosey-Walker. The interpreter for the captive Indians must not have been an expert in his field for, by the time the Indians arrived in Dodge City, they were called Wild Hog, Old Crow, Tall Man, Young Man, Old Man, Frizzle Head, and Run Fast.

In February, 1879, the prisoners, some with wounds from their recent battles, were turned over to jailer Straughn who placed them in the recently emptied county jail. The braves languished there for six months awaiting preliminary trial to be conducted by County Attorney Sutton "whose recent successful prosecutions have been the admiration of a law-abiding people and a terror to evil-doers."[19] The Indians made repeated requests for their squaws and papooses. Colonel Straughn fed them well and sunned them on the front steps of the court house on pleasant spring days. A trial was not held until June, and by this time the attitude of the local newspapers had changed.

In February, just before the prisoners arrived, the Gang's paper, the *Times,* said, "the trial of the savages will add no little to the zest of an exciting life on this frontier, and will generally excite comment and interest." On July 1, 1879, shortly after the trial of the Indians which resulted in a change of venue to Lawrence, Kansas, and eventual acquittal, the anti-Gang newspaper, the *Ford County Globe,* made political hay from Sutton's failure to get a conviction: "The noble red men still live and will soon be free to return to their happy hunting grounds. Their trial and conviction . . . which was supposed to be a foregone conclusion, was a sad and lamentable failure. The Indians had been our guests for about six months, during which time we guarded them with jealous care and fed them with the choicest viands our market could afford, in order that they might be in a first-class condition for hanging as soon as court adjourned. After all these preliminaries we are not surprised that there is a feeling of indignation at the manner in which the case was disposed of. . . . The Indians have been an expensive luxury for Ford county and we hope the result of the farce will teach a valuable lesson."

The political future of Bat and Mike in Ford County and Dodge City became tainted with the "Indian Trial Farce." Bat had incurred large expenses in transporting the Indians to Dodge City, and after the anticlimax of the unsuccessful trial, he filed suit against the county to recover some of the expenses he claimed had not been reimbursed. This indiscreet act became cannon fodder in Bat's defeat and the Gang's downfall in the November election of 1879.

The spring of 1879 found the Santa Fe railroad contesting the right of way through the Grand Canyon of the Arkansas — the Royal Gorge — with the Denver & Rio Grande Western. In March, Bat Masterson received a telegram from Santa Fe officials asking his help. They needed assistance in defending their workmen from attacks by Denver & Rio Grande men. Bat recruited thirty-three men. According to the *Globe,* "they all boarded the morning train, armed to the teeth, Sheriff Masterson in command, and started for the scene of hostilities." Bat commuted back and forth from Colorado to Dodge City with his band of railroad guards during the spring and summer. The contest between the two railroads ended peacefully in June. The railroad property was turned over to the Denver & Rio Grande, and Bat and his posse returned to Dodge City.

But the noise of gunfire was by no means over. The pre-cattle trade season in Dodge City of 1879 started off with a classic western shootout in the Long Branch saloon. The *Ford County Globe* described it in nineteenth century journalistic style: "There is seldom witnessed in any civilized town or country such a scene as transpired at the Long Branch saloon, in this city, last Saturday evening [April 5], resulting in the killing of Levi Richardson, a well known freighter, of this city, by a gambler named Frank Loving."

Trouble had been brewing between the two for over a month. Richardson had tried to start a fight. After Loving refused, Richardson said in the direct manner of a frontier bullwhacker, that he would "shoot the guts out of the cock-eyed son of a bitch any way."[20]

"For several months Loving has been living with a woman toward whom Richardson seems to have cherished tender feelings," the *Globe* continued, "and on one or two occasions previous to this which resulted so fatally, they have quarreled and even come to blows. Richardson was a man who had lived for several years on the frontier, and though well liked in many respects, he had cultivated habits of bold and daring, which are always likely to get a man into trouble. . . . He was a hard working, industrious man, but young and strong and reckless."

Loving was known to the patrons of the Long Branch as "Cock-eyed Frank — one of his optics bearing in a northeast direction to the other."[21] Cock-eyed Frank was twenty-five years old, a gambler by profession, and according to the *Globe*, "of the cool and desperate order . . ."

Levi Richardson was in the Long Branch standing by the stove in the center of the long narrow front room of the saloon. As he started to leave, Loving came in the front swinging doors and sat down at the hazard table near the end of the bar. Richardson walked over and sat down. An argument started. Loving stood and said, "If you have anything to say about me why don't you come and say it to my face like a gentleman, and not to my back, you damn son of a bitch!" Richardson jumped to his feet and flung the gauntlet, saying, "I don't believe you will fight." The "cool and desperate" gambler said, "Try me and see!"[22] Cock-eyed Frank drew his Remington .44. It snapped twice, misfiring. Levi drew and fired twice over Loving's head. Loving dodged behind the stove, firing and hitting Richardson in the left breast. Richardson fell back but kept on shooting.

Richardson fell by the billiard table, fatally wounded, just as Marshal Bassett came running in from Beatty & Kelley's saloon at the other end of the block. Loving's six-shooter was empty; Richardson's had one shell left in the chambers; eleven shots had been fired. Loving was arrested and jailed. Levi Richardson, a twenty-eight-year-old buffalo hunter and freighter, died minutes later. The coroner's jury met on the following Monday and ruled that the shooting was done in self defense.

Lloyd Shinn, editor of the *Globe*, and a witness to the shooting, summed it up thusly: "It seems strange that Loving was not hit, except a slight scratch on the hand, as the two men were so close together that their pistols almost touched each other. . . . Gamblers, as a class, are desperate men. They consider it necessary in their business that they keep up their fighting reputation, and never take a bluff. On no account should they be allowed to carry weapons. Richardson was buried on Sunday in the cemetery north of town, and his death, be it said to our discredit, adds another grave to the already long list filled by those who have met death in a violent manner."

Cock-eyed Frank Loving met his fate in Trinidad, Colorado, three years later, mortally shot over a card game by another gambler.

After the Loving-Richardson battle, the Spearville *News*, a neighboring farm community's newspaper, reported: "A large amount of shooting must be contemplated in Dodge City this year, as they have made such an early start." This thought must have occurred to the city council, for during the same week, they raised the salaries of Deputy Marshal Wyatt Earp and Policeman Jim Masterson to $100.00 each, the same as the marshal's.

The influx of the cattle season was beginning to show again on the pages of Dodge City's newspapers: "A very interesting fight occurred on the boulevards yesterday." "Several shots were fired across the dead line last night by some very brave young men who wished to appear smart." The Hub, a new saloon, was opened, advertising Rosebud whisky, Festoon cigars, cogniac, benedictine, and a full line of French cordials. "The Long Branch is being repainted . . ." no doubt to cover over bullet holes. "A fresh invoice of gamblers arrived last Monday." "Messrs. Foye [sic] and Thompson, who performed in the Comique last summer, have been re-engaged, arriving here Monday last." Wright, Beverley & Co. were advertising "Pearl Handle Six-Shooters . . . and a choice lot of Spurs." F. C. Zimmermann advertised "all his firearms, and his ammunition to fit. No mistakes made, which is of great importance." Bobby Gilmore was back in town. "Some cow boys were flourishing their pistols, on their way out of town, west, Monday. One of the men was accidentally shot in the leg." The Dodge City lawmen, Bat Masterson, Charlie Bassett, Wyatt Earp, and

Jim Masterson were warning one and all to "Leave off your concealed weapons, and don't undertake 'to take the town'..."[23]

On the evening of May 5, 1879, three "unruly Missourians . . . on their way to Leadville, Colorado . . . undertook to 'take the town.' While Assistant Marshal [Wyatt] Earp was attempting to disarm [them] and [was] leading an unruly cuss off by the ear, another one of the party told his chum to 'throw lead.'" Sheriff Bat Masterson happened on the scene in the nick of time, and, using the broad side of his revolver over the head of the Missourian, he saved his friend Wyatt from possible lead poisoning. The next evening, the three Missourians, still smarting from their pistol whipping, "assembled in the rear of a store building . . . and sent word by a colored boy that a man wished to see [Sheriff Masterson]. The negro 'smelt a mouse,' and put the Sheriff on his guard." Masterson and his deputy, William Duffy, arrested one of the Missourians, and according to the *Times,* "These fellows remarked that they 'had run things in Missouri,' and believed they could 'take' Dodge City, but admitted that they were no match for Dodge City officers. Dodge City is hard 'to take!'"[24]

In June, a month later, the newspapers reported, "A party of eight men had been making some 'demonstrations' across the 'dead line,'. . . ." The *dead line* referred to was the railroad tracks. North of the tracks were respectable saloons and businesses where gunplay and carrying weapons were discouraged by the city police. South of the tracks the lawmen made little effort to enforce the ordinance against carrying weapons unless a complaint was made or unless actual fighting broke out. Many of the saloons north of the tracks installed boards with wooden pegs on which the cowboys were encouraged to hang their six-shooters while partaking. On this particular June evening, according to the *Globe,* "the police undertook to disarm [the] squad of cow boys who had neglected to lay aside their six shooters upon arriving in this city. The cow boys protested and war was declared." After some rough and tumble fighting with Dodge City's law officers, probably Earp and Jim Masterson, the cowboys fled. Later in the evening one of the eight cowboys driven off by the policemen was found lurking suspiciously around "the room of one of the officers. . . ."

Wyatt Earp claimed in later years that he was the officer whose room the cowboy was watching; that after reaching his room at the Dodge House, and before lighting his lamp, he looked out his window. The roar of a double-barreled shotgun brought the sash around his head in splinters. Earp said he saw a figure run south across the tracks, and he climbed through the window after him. Earp claimed he shot the fellow in the leg and lugged him back to the calaboose where he confessed. The wounded cowboy, according to Earp, was trying to collect the reward placed on Wyatt's head by disgruntled Texans.[25]

In May, the Dodge City *Times* testified to the ability of Wyatt Earp and Jim Masterson: "Officers [Wyatt] Earp and Jas. Masterson served a writ on a horse drover, out on Duck Creek, Wednesday, in order to obtain the claim of a darkey against the drover, for services rendered by the aforesaid colored individual. Seven brave horse herders stood against the two officers, who, showing no signs of 'weakening,' soon obtained satisfaction of the claim, the drover promptly paying the debt when resistance was no longer available."

In June, as Marshal Bassett went the rounds "stirring up all delinquents on city license," with his admonition, "Pay up or shut up," a fight broke out on the boardwalk of Front Street. The *Ford County Globe* described the ruckus in its inimitable way:

"Slugging On The Public Streets. . . . Last Saturday evening about half past seven o'clock on Front street in the city of Dodge City, noted for its churches and numerous worshippers of the Divine, as well as a few who bow the knee to Mammon, was fought one of the most desperate yet bloodless battles that the Globe has ever had the honor of recording in the annals of Dodge City. . . . One of the principals of this awful tragedy . . ." was R. G. Cook, justice of the peace, "a man of mighty prowess and great personal strength. . . . A tyrant grim o'er kine and swain. And never until this eventful day had he met a foeman

113

worthy of his steel." The other participant was an unknown visitor from Garden City, "also of giant frame and proud and noble bearing. It was not until late in the afternoon that the two powerful men met face to face. A few words of insult were exchanged, the gage of battle was thrown, each measured his antagonist for one supreme moment, and then like the collision of two planets they closed in deadly combat. The sky at this moment seemed to darken as tufts of hair, distracted articles of clothing and other et ceteras filled the air. How the struggle might have ended no one knows for just as the decisive round was being fought, the crowd separated and Mr. P. L. Beatty, Foreman of the Dodge City Fire Company rushed to the scene of battle, seized the two contestants by the napes of the neck and held them out suspended at arm's length until the Kansas zephyrs cooled their boyish passions and they promised to fight no more." Cook's assailant "was then hauled up before the police court and mulcted to the tune of three dollars and costs, amounting in all to about eleven dollars."

A month after Justice Cook's altercation with the visitor from the neighboring town to the west, "several bullwhackers, employed in a train camping near town, anxious for sport, emptied their revolvers by mistaking one of Mayor Kelly's hogs for a target and succeeded in killing the animal. . . . Mayor Kelley had eight or ten men arrested. . . . The hog was paid for and the shootists discharged."[26]

The same week a visitor to Dodge City wrote home to Topeka with "Gushing Compliments. . . . Dodge City must be seen and understood to be appreciated. While she may not be one of the highest toned cities in the State, and while her people may not dress in the height of fashion, yet she does more cash business to the square inch, and has more whole-soul[ed], liberal men in her corporation than any town in Kansas. The drouth in the early part of the season, hurt; but she is now in her glory. She sits upon her hills, rules with a royal will. J. H. Kelley, the Mayor, . . . knows how to treat a man, whether a friend . . . or an enemy. . . . With Charley Basset[t] for Marshal, Wyatt Earp for deputy, and Jas. Masterson as an officer, . . . an offender might as well be beneath the nether mill stone. . . . W. B. Masterson, Sheriff, a young man who makes a splendid officer, and who will be re-elected, showed me over the city. . . . Dodge is improving rapidly. . . . Its business is good and its future well assured. Where there is as much money as there is at Dodge, and liberal hearted men controlling it, things must move."[27]

Cattle season activities were still in full swing, when, according to the Globe, "An exhibition of fast riding took place on Front street last Sunday, stimulated by an overdose of booze." Although the cattle trade had not been as good in 1879 as the year before, Dodge City still held forth as the Cowboy Capital. Over one hundred cars of cattle were shipped from Dodge City the last week of August. In September, 1879, the Kansas City Times reported: " 'The end of the trail,' though not so lively as of yore, is still the booming metropolis of Western Kansas. The lime-punches of 'Chalk's' [Chalk Beeson's Long Branch saloon] and the cock-tails of Hoover's [George Hoover's liquor store] are the same as of auld lang syne, and the last of the through drive, about 4,500 beeves, are browsing on the green velvet south of the Arkansas . . ."

Compared to the summer of 1878, Dodge City was becoming a peaceful hamlet of the plains. As the season drew to a close in September, 1879, the Globe commented on the relative state of law and order: "There have been only two men killed in Dodge this summer, for which we deserve due credit. The police, under Marshal Bassett, are compelled to practice on cold oyster cans in order to keep their hands in. The morals of our city are rapidly improving. There are only 14 saloons, 2 dance halls, and 47 cyprians [prostitutes] in our metropolis of 700 inhabitants."

Wyatt Earp evidently was growing tired of practicing on cold oyster cans. He turned in his resignation the first week of September and together with some of his friends took part in a grand going-away party. The Globe entitled the celebration, "A Day Of Carnival" and claimed it brought back memories of earlier, less lethargic days. "Dodge City was redeeming herself. . . . [We were] extricating ourselves from that stupid lethargy which had fallen upon us of late, and were giving vent to our uncurbed hilarity —

'getting to the booze joint,' as it were, in good shape, and 'making a rankiboo play for ourselves.' . . . A large portion of our community were 'to the joint.' . . . The signal for the tournament to begin was given by a slender young man of handsome external appearance who regaled his friends with a pail of water. The water racket was kept up until it merged into the slop racket, then the potato and cucumber racket, and finally the rotten egg racket, with all its magnificent odors. This was continued until the faces, eyes, noses, mouths and shirt bosoms of several of the boys were comfortably filled with the juicy substance of the choicest rotten eggs, compelling them to retire from the field, which they did in a very warlike manner. As the evening shades began to appear the skirmishers were soon actively engaged, and at a little before the usual hours slugging commenced all along the line. One or two 'gun plays' were made, but by reason of a lack of execution, were not effective. . . . [They] wrestled with each other like butchered whales on harpooning day. The 'finest work' and neatest polishes were said to have been executed by Mr. Wyatt Earp, who has been our efficient assistant marshal for the past year. . . . It was not until towards morning that the smoke cleared away, the din of battle subsided and the bibulous city found a little repose. And such is life in the far, far west." Wyatt Earp departed the next day for Las Vegas, New Mexico.

The Independent Party of Ford County met in October and unanimously nominated Bat Masterson for a second term as sheriff. The *Times* announced that "Bat is acknowledged to be the best Sheriff in Kansas. He is the most successful officer in the State. He is immensely popular and generally well liked. Horse thieves have a terror for the name of Masterson. . . . Every hater of horse thieves will rejoice over Bat's triumphant election; and the friends of good order and peace will contribute to his success." The bad publicity caused by Bat's suit against the county was countered by the *Times'* reminder that "Bat Masterson is Sheriff of thirteen unorganized counties. Of course it costs something to run so much territory."

The *Globe* responded angrily: "Just think of Ford county having to pay $4000 for the simple arrest of seven lousy Cheyenne Indians and that without even an effort to convict them. . . . Masterson and Sutton made it hot for the Nations Wards whom they so cunningly conspired against, and brought to Ford county for the people to look at. They now desire to make it hot for the poor tax payers of the county, by getting them to pay the bills incurred in their innocent amusement." The Spearville *News* joined the fight: "We understand that 'Bat Masterson' is going to shoot his way into the office of sheriff." Even the Kansas City *Times* commented: "Politics are as everything else at Dodge City, 'red hot and still heating.' Our old Sheriff, 'Bat' Masterson has a foeman worthy of his steel in Mr. Geo. T. Hinkle. . . . That [Dodge City is] not retrograting as a lively town may be evinced by the fact that on yesterday six men were thrown in the cooler, while five free and easy fights occurred at the saloon of Messrs. Beatty & Kelley."

George T. Hinkle was a bartender and saloonkeeper, but unlike many of his kind, he was also a property owner and a conservative member of the anti-Gang group. Before branching out into the saloon business on his own, he tended bar at George M. Hoover's wholesale liquor store and saloon. The *Globe* reported with glee the election results on the first Tuesday in November, 1879.

Masterson was defeated for sheriff by Hinkle, 268 to 404; F. C. Zimmermann was elected county treasurer, and George M. Hoover, commissioner, both anti-Gang candidates. "The election in this county last Tuesday was characterized with about the usual activity, but the polls closed with only a few fights on record for the day, although a vigorous skirmish was kept up all along the line, and considerable ammunition expended on both sides. . . . It is the defeat of the Independent ticket, representing the influences that have controlled the politics of Ford county since its organization, and the triumph of a new element, the successful candidates running on what was known as the 'Peoples' ticket. . . . The 'Gang' is no more in existence. It failed to 'get to the joint' last Tuesday, and has lost its grip forever."

Bat did not take his defeat philosophically. The Spearville *News* wrote: "We hear that Bat. Masterson said he was going to whip every s__ of a b____, that worked and voted against him in the county." Bat answered this slander with a letter to the editor: "In answer to the publication made by Bob Fry of the Spearville News, asserting that I made threats that I would lick any s__ of a b____ that voted or worked against me at the last election, I will say it is as false and as flagrant a lie as was ever uttered; but I did say this: that I would lick him the s__ of a b____ if he made any more dirty talk about me; and the words s__ of a b____ I strictly confined to the Speareville editor. . . . W. B. Masterson." Editor Fry was reported to have been in a very nervous condition for several weeks after Masterson's letter appeared in the *Times*.

Marshal Charles Bassett resigned as city marshal shortly after the county election. Jim Masterson was appointed in his place, and Neil Brown as Masterson's assistant. D. M. Frost, editor of the *Globe,* who campaigned so outspokenly against Bat's re-election, found himself in hot water within the month. Bat, acting in his position as deputy United States marshal, with the help of his friend, R. G. Cook, a local justice of the peace and United States commissioner, swore out a warrant for Frost's arrest on the charge of buying stolen property. The property was allegedly purchased a year and a half earlier from the quarter-master's department at Fort Elliott, Texas. The value of the goods were alleged to be $140; Cook set bond at $5,000. After some inconvenience, expense, and embarrassment to Frost, the case was dropped.

The frontier finances of Ford County were not always such that employees could be paid with cash. The county used a common early day device known as scrip to make payments when the county treasury was depleted. The scrip was used as legal tender among Dodge City merchants at less than par and was redeemed after tax collections filled up the county coffers again. Just before Christmas, 1879, the county treasurer, John B. Means, was accused of forging county scrip. The discovery was explained in the *Globe:*

"On Monday night Means was pretty well 'boozed,' as the saying is, and was bantered to make a bet on a game of billiards; and not having the 'needful' he drew forth [a] . . . piece of scrip and called the game. This was a grand mistake — undoubtedly the wrong piece of scrip was put up as a wager. Some cunning eye noticed the large amount for which the scrip was drawn, and the name of W. B. Masterson being thereon, suggested the fact that [Means] was dealing in 'crooked' county indebtedness. Sheriff Masterson was immediately apprised of the circumstances . . . Masterson then demanded the piece of scrip bearing his name, saying it was a forgery. Upon further investigation it was found that Means had [a] second piece of scrip . . . which also proved to be a forgery."

The forgery was noticed by the billiard players because Means had very unprofessionally written on the piece of scrip, "$256.60, in favor of W. B. Masterson, Sheriff, for services in conveying prisoners to the penitentiary." The state of Kansas, not the county of Ford, pays the sheriff for conveying prisoners to the penitentiary. Means confessed his guilt and "wended his way westward." His term as county treasurer had only a week to run, and, despite the fact that over $1,700 of scrip had been forged, no one tried to stop his departure. As the *Times* explained, "He is broken down physically; is subject to epilepsy and boozeism. The man's deplorable physical condition excites sympathy, and for this reason no prosecution will probably be made. . . ."

Bat's last act as sheriff was to escort two horse thieves to prison at Leavenworth — a fitting end to his career as a Dodge City lawman. His legend was already preceding him before his departure from Ford County. Like his friend, Wyatt Earp, he must have kicked up his heels in Dodge City after leaving office. In February he joined his cronies to perpetrate a grand "practical joke" on a visiting "gentleman of distinction who bore the unassuming name and title of Meredith, M. D. He was what the boys would call a 'daisy.' The general outlines of his outward appearance did not indicate that he had ever finished his education with foreign travel, or that he had at any time during his earthly career peregrinated with a circus — therefore he was not thoroughly posted on the modes and costumes that prevail in chaste and civilized cities with advanced ideas, such as Dodge City possesses, and to all appearances is wonderfully proud."

The early Dodge City merchants shown above were attracted to the business of cattle raising, and by 1880 were investing in herds ranged on the lush prairie grasses south of Dodge City. Richard W. Evans (left) came to Dodge City in 1872 from Hays City and opened his grocery and dry goods store on Front Street west of the Dodge House. John Mueller (center) came in 1874 and opened his highly successful boot shop three doors east of Evans. Jacob Collar (right) born in Hungary, came to Dodge City in 1872 from Hays City. He and his brother, Morris, were successful and industrious merchants. Jake Collar's sales of groceries, furniture, and undertaking supplies enabled him to invest in real estate and cattle herds.

Col. Richard J. (Jack) Hardesty left his Kentucky home for the gold fields of Colorado and Montana. After some success he invested his new wealth in land and cattle. He came to live in Dodge City in 1880 to oversee his cattle investments nearby. Hardesty (left) and his dog, Tick, sit with Frank Chapman, a cattleman, former buffalo hunter, and Indian fighter.

These cattle brands were used by Dodge City cattle men. The brands of Robert M. Wright and George Reighard were used on cattle near the townsite of Dodge City before its founding in 1872. Chalk Beeson and W. H. Harris invested the profits of their successful operation of the Long Branch saloon in cattle marked with their COD brand.

The "doctor's" specialty was advertised as the treatment of "private diseases." Having made the mistake of writing to Dodge City to inquire if there was any interest in a lecture on this subject, he was encouraged to come by the jokesters who recommended him to a local citizen, *Luke McGlue,* a prominent citizen who would be likely to take a deep interest in his cause. "Immediately after his arrival he determined to deliver a lecture defining his particular sphere that the public might understand his great mission and come unto him to be cured and to have their organs examined.

"The old Lady Gay dance hall was engaged for the occasion and thither at early candle-lighting a large concourse assembled. Mr. W. B. Masterson, Esq. was chosen to act as chairman and introduced the speaker in a few neat and well chosen remarks."

As Dr. Meredith made his opening remarks, a plant in the audience yelled out, "You lie!" "Chairman Masterson rebuked the insult, and when order was restored the doctor began again. Proceeding further in a like manner, he was again interrupted by an insulting remark from one of the audience, and it was only by stern commands and threats of annihilation that the chairman brought the house to order.

"Again the Doctor proceeded and was just wading deep into a scientific problem when a loud, profane and fiendish yell from Luke McGlue turned the house into an uproar of excitement, and all efforts to restore order were in vain.

"Just at this critical moment a southside exhorter with one eye in a sling made an effort to drag the orator from the stand, whereupon Chairman Masterson drew from beneath his coat-tails a Colt's improved, nickel plated, size 44 shooting instrument and formed himself in a hollow square in front of the horrified Doctor, determined to defend or die! A crash was heard — the lamps went out instantaneously, windows were smashed, missiles flew through the darkness, the air was filled with demoniac yells and shooting commenced in rapid succession. . . .

"It was only after all the ammunition in the house was expended that the murderous carnival ceased and a lamp was lighted by which to remove the dead and wounded. But the dead and wounded had ere this time escaped and even the Doctor was nowhere to be found. Search was made, and at last he was discovered coiled up under the speaker's stand with his hands over his marble features and a ghastly bullet hole through the crown of his hat.

"The meeting adjourned sine die."[28]

The city elections of April, 1880, proved that the Gang had not "lost its grip forever," as reported after the November, 1879, election. Dr. T. L. McCarty, an educated and respected member of the community was nominated to run for mayor against Dog Kelley, the friend of Dodge City's sportsmen, gamblers, saloonkeepers, and dance hall girls. It looked like a shoo-in for McCarty after the defeat of Bat Masterson in November. McCarty's backer, D. M. Frost of the *Globe,* reported the election results with surprise.

"The re-election of James H. Kelley as Mayor of Dodge City, is a surprise to nearly every inhabitant of the city. . . . The general public had settled down to the conviction that McCarty would have a walkover, and his friends thought it unnecessary to organize or prepare to meet opposition. . . . The old gang element was apparently discouraged and demoralized from its defeat of last fall, and its most sagacious advisors and leaders, Messrs. Sutton, Klaine and others, endeavored, as a dernier resort, to make a compromise with McCarty's friends . . . A meeting was called at Kelley's the day before election and a love-feast and communion was indulged in. . . . 'Put up our old leader, James H. Kelley and, if die we must, let us die game!' . . . was the general response, and the silent warrior, St. Michael [Mike Sutton], he of the smoothe and oily tongue, wrote out the ticket as follows: For Mayor, James H. Kelley . . . The 'communion of the saints' broke up, each with a decided knowledge of the work he had to do; and they went forth seeking scalps. From that hour until the polls were opened the Kelley men were everywhere.

"The volcano smouldered, only to burst on the morning with unbounded fury. McCarty's friends slept the sweet sleep of the innocent, and 'woke to find their birthright stolen.' The polls were opened with twenty Kelley men on hand, each with blood in his eye, and only two or three to represent McCarty. . . . The Kelley men formed an almost solid phalanx around the polls, and it was only by a herculean effort that Christians could vote."

The *Globe,* in addition to implying that all who voted for Kelley were not Christians, also intimated that there may have been some voters who were not residents of Dodge City. The paper left no doubt as to its opposition to Kelley, but gave due credit to his advisors, Mike Sutton, Bat Masterson, and Nicholas B. (Deacon) Klaine, editor of the *Times,* for "winning a victory with odds against them." This was to be the last victory of Dog Kelley as the declining years of his political and financial success were beginning.

The spring of 1880 brought to Dodge City the same exciting preparations for the coming successful cattle season as past years. A new front was built on the Dodge House and improvements made on the inside. A pair of expensive oil paintings and a handsome buffalo head were installed in the Long Branch saloon — "fitted up in elegant style, in anticipation of the Texas Cattle trade. . . . The Long Branch presents a brilliant appearance by gas-light. The walls are handsomely decorated, papered, and in the glare of the dazzling light the spectacle is alluring. The favorite resort is thronged day and night, by liquidators, pasteboard-manipulators, stock speculators, id genus omne.

"The shure thing man beginneth to make his appearance. . . . Two dance halls in full blast and old Dodge begins to feel herself again. . . . The variety troope will commence playing in Dodge City immediately after the 4th of July. . . . The midnight air rings with the music of the violin and the festive tread of the cow boy. . . . Thieves, robbers and cutthroats seem to be running things pretty high-handed in our city at the present time. . . . Sir Robert Gilmore, an old timer, has been sauntering about our streets in his sly easy way keeping his eye peeled to business.

"Cattle men and cattle dealers are beginning to come in and are selecting their hotel quarters for the summer. They come to stay, to participate in the largest cattle drive ever brought from Texas. Dodge City will be general headquarters for the drive for 1880. . . . Since the arrival of the first through herds of Texas cattle the city is beginning to present that business aspect which usually follows the trade of the Texas stock man. Wherever you find him quartered there you find energy and enterprise and a city that can boast of doing more business in a few brief months than any other town of its size in the state during an entire year. The cattle men are arriving in Dodge City on every train. . . . Thousands of cattle are already at hand with thousands to follow."

The cattle season of 1880 proved so successful that before the summer ended many Dodge City merchants decided to venture into the cattle business. Chalk Beeson, Jacob Collar, and John Mueller were among those who tried their hand at this new occupation. Mueller sold his boot and shoe shop to devote full time to his stock. Chalk Beeson joined with his partner, W. H. Harris, to range large herds with their COD brand along Sand Creek, south of Dodge City. Other merchants, George M. Hoover, Herman J. Fringer, and Morris Collar were soon to join the ranks of cattle entrepreneurs.

The new marshal, Jim Masterson, and the sheriff, George Hinkle, were having the same problems as their predecessors — horse thefts, robberies, shootings, fights, and con-men. Violent headlines appeared once more in Dodge City newspapers at the end of the cattle season in November, 1880.

"MURDER IN DODGE CITY." The murder referred to was strangely parallel to the Loving-Richardson affair a year and a half earlier. Like Cock-eyed Frank Loving, the killer was a gambler, a quiet man, John (Concho) Gill. Like Levi Richardson, the deceased was a rustic frontiersman, Henry Heck, a rancher and former employee at Ham Bell's livery stable.

According to the newspaper reports: "Henry Heck and . . . 'Concho' bestowed their affections upon the same 'soiled dove' . . . a woman of easy virtue called Callie Moore. . . . This woman has been [Heck's] apparently faithful companion, according to the approved method of this class of Dodge City lotus eaters. She went with him to [his] ranch, and for nearly a year performed the duties which usually fall to the lot of a rural housewife. Concho has been in Dodge some months, probably a year, plying his profession as a gambler.

"Some time during last September, while Callie Moore was in the city on a shopping expedition, she met the festive Concho, and it was a dead mash at first sight. His dark brown eyes, classic features, and complexion bronzed by a southern sun, together with the indolent life of a gambler's paramour, were too dazzling to be resisted, when compared with kitchen drudgery, and the society of her more homely lover. As for Concho, the violet eyes and flaxen curls of Callie fired his warm southern blood at once into a fierce flame, and he vowed she should be his.

"Heck was left out in the cold. . . . When in the city on business he would naturally gravitate into the haunts of his lost love, which did not comprise the most puritanical orders of society. The flowing bowl was applied to in vain to quench the persistent fervency of his passion. At last he informed Callie that he could no longer endure to have her live in Ford county while another man reveled in her caresses — 'so near, and yet so far.' He told her she might have three days in which to make up her mind to either return to his wigwam or leave town. . . . Last Tuesday night the three days expired, and Mr. Heck called at the domicile of Concho (which was also the abiding place of the seductive Callie) about the hour when grave-yards yawn, and from thence he carried a bullet wound which ended his life in a short time."

The coroner's jury found that Heck came to the room where Concho and Callie were and kicked at the door. Concho got out of bed, went toward the door with pistol in hand. Heck's second kick knocked the door open. Concho fired from the middle of the room, and according to the newspapers, "[Heck], while standing at the door of the room received a pistol shot, the ball striking him on the right side below the nipple and entering the lung. Heck walked to the saloon near by, and calling for a drink, remarked to the barkeeper, that he had been shot. He walked out of the bar-room, returning in a few minutes, fell down and expired without a groan. . . . Gill, alias Concho, was arrested and placed in jail." Concho was convicted and sentenced to fifteen years in the state penitentiary.

The *Times*' postscript to its account of the killing bragged: "Dodge had still some of the bloody instinct for which she was so famous in the lawless days of her infancy, when money was as dross and whisky four bits a drink."

The winter of 1880-1881 brought financial woes to Mayor Kelley. His partnership with P. L. Beatty broke up. Beatty had been the talent behind the operation of the Beatty & Kelley saloon and restaurant and the principal working partner of the new Kelley opera house, saloon, restaurant, and barber shop. Kelley spent most of his time hunting with his pack of fine greyhounds and talking politics over the bar of his saloon. After Beatty left, Kelley found it necessary to rent his new two story hall and restaurant and move his saloon into one of the older buildings next door.

In March, a correspondent from an Oskaloosa, Iowa, newspaper visited Dodge City and sent a sensational report back to the home paper. The *Ford County Globe* reprinted the slanderous article which enraged many of the city's officials. The reporter claimed that the city attorney, Harry Gryden, bragged that he could bribe any jury in town for one hundred dollars; that he accepted fifty dollars a week for not prosecuting certain "gamblers and cutthroats"; that Mayor Kelley was "a flannel mouthed Irishman" who kept a saloon, a gambling house, and a mistress; that Marshal James Masterson and Policeman Neil Brown were also gamblers and kept mistresses; and that County Commissioner A. J. Peacock ran a saloon and dance hall "where the unwary are enticed, made drunk and robbed."

The article so incensed Kelley, Jim Masterson, and Brown that they caught the reporter and drenched him under the railroad water tank.

An era in Dodge City's history was ending.

Chapter V

SALOON WARS AND DRUG STORES

In April, 1881, Dog Kelley ended his reign as mayor of Dodge City. He was defeated by Alonzo B. Webster, Dodge City's "fighting mayor," whose first official act was to publish the following notice: "To all whom it may concern: All thieves, thugs, confidence men, and persons without visible means of support, will take notice that the ordinance enacted for their especial benefit will be rigorously enforced on and after tomorrow, April 7th, 1881. A. B. Webster, Mayor. Dodge City, Kansas."[29]

A. B. Webster, a native of Pembroke, New York, enlisted in the New York cavalry as a young boy. At the end of the Civil War he followed his fortune west to Fort Hays where he served as a dispatch scout between various frontier forts. He entered into business in Hays City where he met Larry Deger who later became Dodge City's first city marshal. While in Hays, Webster was known as "a distinguished character against the lawless element of the town."[1] He was visited one time by a committee of toughs and told to leave Hays or suffer a violent end. Refusing to knuckle under, Webster drew a revolver from under his dry goods counter and shot the leader, putting the gang to rout.

In 1872 Webster became one of Dodge City's first citizens when he opened a dry goods store on the corner of Front Street and First Avenue, opposite Beatty & Kelley's saloon and restaurant. A month before the city elections of 1881, Webster was appointed acting sheriff during the absence of the ailing George Hinkle. Webster took office as mayor the first week of April, 1881, and in less than two weeks his determination to enforce city ordinances was put to the test.

During Dog Kelley's last term as mayor, saloonkeeper A. J. Peacock joined in partnership with Marshal James Masterson, as proprietors of the old Lady Gay dance hall and saloon south of the railroad tracks. The front of the old building blew out in a March windstorm "and the entire edifice soon afterward went into a staggering condition."[2] The building was repaired and leased to the marshal and his partner. Al Updegraph, a strong friend of Peacock's, was employed as a bartender in the dance hall.

After taking office, Webster removed James Masterson as marshal and appointed Hinkle's under sheriff, Fred Singer. Singer, a Welshman, was a bartender in the Old House saloon. The Old House

Alonzo B. Webster (left above), a gun-toting mayor of Dodge City, was one of its earliest residents. Owner of the Old House saloon and proprietor of the Stock Exchange saloon, he was a leader of the faction that opposed Luke Short in the saloon war of 1883.

A. B. Webster started his dry goods, clothing, and grocery store on Front Street (called Main Street in his advertisement, right above) in 1872. In 1878 he leased it to bootmaker John Mueller and Walter Straeter for use as the Old House saloon.

Frederick Singer (right) was twice marshal of Dodge City, a deputy U.S. marshal, and under sheriff of Ford County. A bartender in the Old House, he was appointed marshal after Webster's election as mayor in April, 1881.

property was the original site of Webster's dry goods store in 1872 and was still owned by Webster. Tom Nixon, one of Dodge City's early day buffalo hunters was appointed assistant marshal under Singer.

Just after Webster's appointment of Singer and Nixon, Masterson and Updegraph quarreled. The quarrel, according to Updegraph, started when "a friend of Masterson's robbed a woman of $80 by entering her room while she was absent. I advised her to have the party arrested . . ." Updegraph continued. "Masterson thereupon came to me and insisted that I should make the woman withdraw the complaint, which I refused positively to do. He, Masterson, thereupon informed me that my services as bar-keeper was no longer needed, and I must quit. Mr. Peacock . . . insisted that I should stay, as I was right. Masterson having claimed to be a killer, then undertook the job of killing me, and attempted it on the following evening by coming into the saloon and cocking his revolver in my face."[3] The argument was miraculously broken up before blood was shed, but the next morning Updegraph filed a complaint for Jim Masterson's arrest.

At the time of Jim's encounter with Updegraph, Bat Masterson was residing in Tombstone, Arizona. Jim, fearing reprisals from Peacock and Updegraph, wired his brother in Tombstone, asking him to come to Dodge City to help settle accounts.

After Bat's defeat for sheriff in 1879, he was in and out of Dodge City. He spent a month in Leadville, Colorado, came back to Dodge City to attend the county Republican convention in Topeka, and went back to Colorado to seek his fortune. Bat returned to Dodge City during the summer of 1880, where according to the census taker, he was living with one Annie Ladue, a nineteen-year-old concubine.[4] There were many *Annie's* living in Dodge City at that time; their last names changed at regular intervals depending on whose bed they were sharing. When Bat sold his home a year later it was purchased by an *Annie* — perhaps the former Annie Ladue using a different name, perhaps not. This *Annie* lived in Dodge City to a ripe old age, well known and respected in the community, leaving two children and ten grandchildren.

After receiving his brother's telegram, Bat arrived in Dodge City from Tombstone on a Friday morning in April, 1881. On Saturday, while taking a drink with friends, he spotted Peacock and Updegraph crossing the railroad tracks. At high noon, in the classical Western tradition, Bat Masterson walked through the swinging doors, stepped down off the Front Street boardwalk, and started across the tracks toward Al Updegraph and A. J. Peacock. According to a reporter for the Caldwell *Commercial,* as Bat came within twenty feet he said, "I have come over a thousand miles to settle this. I know you are heeled; now fight."[5]

"All three immediately commenced firing, Masterson having the advantage of a slight embankment at the railroad track, while Peacock and Updegraph retreated to the corners of the city jail and fired from there. Two other parties [Charles Ronan and Tom O'Brien] opened fire from the saloon on the north side, while Masterson, thinking he was fired on from behind, laid down to reload, when he again commenced firing. . . . While lying down . . . a bullet threw the dirt into Masterson's mouth. . . ."

The *Ford County Globe* whimsically entitled the shootout, the "Musical Voice of The Festive Revolver," and described it as "one of the most daring and dangerous shooting scrapes . . . that Dodge City has ever experienced."

The *Globe* continued the account: "Both sides continued to shoot for about three or four minutes, during which time the excitement along the street was rather lively, as the shots from the calaboose party [Updegraph and Peacock] were in direct range with the stores and business houses. One bullet passed through the front of Dr. McCarty's drug store, one through the Long Branch, and one through the front of G. M. Hoover's wholesale liquor store." According to the Caldwell *Commercial,* "Updegraph, who was shot through the right lung, retreated, and Mayor Webster, with [acting] Sheriff Singer, coming up with shotguns, compelled Masterson to give up his pistols. . . . The Mastersons were arrested, pleaded guilty, fined $10 and costs, paid their fines and left on last night's train for the West. Fifteen extra police were on duty last night, but now all is quiet. It was the most determined fight made since the days of 'Wild Bill' [Hickock]. . . ."

Webster's action in assisting the sheriff, shotgun in hand, earned him the title of Dodge City's "fighting mayor." Four months later Peacock and Masterson sold their interests in the Lady Gay dance hall and saloon to Assistant Marshal Tom Nixon and an early day Dodge City buffalo hunter, Brick Bond.

Dodge City's fighting mayor had cleverly manipulated the saloon situation in Dodge City. He was the owner of the Old House saloon, now under the marshal's management. The only dance hall left in town was now under the management of the assistant marshal. In November, seven months after taking office, Webster leased the narrow building between Wright, Beverley & Co. and the Long Branch saloon. This building had once been the Alamo saloon and had recently been the location of Dr. T. L. McCarty's City Drug store. Webster dubbed his new saloon the *Stock Exchange* and advertised that "stockmen and travelers will find the choicest commodities that will slake their thirst, exhilarate a languish[ed] mind, and 'brace up' a weak constitution."[6]

Mayor Webster initiated a few revolutionary changes to the frontier community. One that was probably difficult for old timers to accept was the appearance of the marshal and assistant marshal in blue regulation uniforms. "Who says Dodge City isn't 'tony?'" asked Nic Klaine of the *Times* with tongue in cheek. Webster strictly enforced the city's occupation licenses. The license fees from saloons, gamblers, and prostitutes amounted to nearly twice the fees collected from all other businesses in town. However, by the end of Webster's first year as mayor, one saloonkeeper, Dog Kelley, remained firmly unreformed. The city treasurer's report showed Kelley's saloon license two years past due in the amount of $500.00.

The *Times* editorialized its approval of Webster's moderate, but firm stand in regard to saloons, gambling, and prostitution. "The power of the Governor [John P. St. John, a Prohibitionist] is not strong enough to suppress whisky selling, gambling and the dance hall. These things would continue in some manner, no matter who were Mayor and Councilmen. . . . We are satisfied and contended if these things are conducted properly, orderly and decently." Nic Klaine of the *Times* predicted that the passage of time, not radical change, would "purify the moral atmosphere of Dodge City." Webster was content to continue the existence of the saloons, gambling, and prostitution — as long as he was getting a piece of the action.

As the spring cattle trade began in 1882, Dodge City was showing signs of encroaching civilization. The frontier characteristics of "the wickedest city in the West" were passing. There was talk of grading and macadamizing the principal streets; three passenger trains stopped daily each way through Dodge City; the Santa Fe railroad was discussing plans for new facilities, new yards with side tracks, a round house, shops, and a new passenger depot; the saloon merchant, George Hoover, was selling drug supplies to bolster the argument that his liquor was for medicinal purposes; many new residences were being constructed about town — five rooms at a cost of $1,500 made palatial quarters for successful merchants and cattle dealers moving into the area; Henry Sturm's liquor store offered lemon, strawberry, vanilla, raspberry and ginger ale flavored soda water; and much to the horror of gamblers, saloonkeepers, and former buffalo hunters, a temperance society was organized in the Union Church on gospel hill.

The patience, toil, energy, and true grit of Dodge City's plainsmen had brought financial success to the Far West. But even more important, according to Deacon Klaine of the *Times,* as to "the great comparison of today and five years ago . . ." was the "great improvement in Dodge City moral and social customs." Klaine, the wordy and pious editor of the Dodge City *Times,* addressing of all things, the opening session of a newly formed Literary Union Society of Dodge City, used the wearing of a top hat as an example of Dodge City's moral improvement. "It is true," he said, "the 'plug hat' is not a popular head gear in this windy country, for the reason that the fashion has not yet arrived. But the 'plug hat' is not tabooed. A few years ago a 'plug hat' would have been the mark for sundry potatoes, cabbage heads, &c. . . . Like an embryo city stands Dodge — an oasis on the broad plains — marking the spot where the weary traveler, after miles of marching, can find refreshments. . . . The dignified and stately church spires are other evidences of the march of civilization. The city's rude and uncouth character is the indication of a polished and established future. As the homely child becomes a handsome man, so will Dodge, born of ugliness and roughness, mature in brightness and smoothness."

The Texas cattle drives were still pouring into Dodge City. Very few, if any, of the cowboys in charge of these herds were interested in Deacon Klaine's literary society. By June, 1882, over 100,000 cattle and 7,000 horses had arrived and been sold. Over 17,000 were grazing within a day's drive of the city. Yearling heifers were selling for $14.50; two year olds at $17.00. The cattle trails were not as free as formerly, a large portion of the land in the Texas Panhandle, Indian Territory, and southwest Kansas having been fenced. But Dodge City still reigned as the Queen of the Cowtowns.

The *Times* complained that the cowboys arriving with the herds were still giving Dodge City an undeserved bad name. "The gambling table or the dance hall takes his fancy at once — the latter institution is his favorite resort. At home, perhaps, the stranger can't feast his eyes or gratify his passions, and he is a remarkably fine young man — a model and examplary [sic] youth, a teacher in the Sunday School, perhaps, and a leader in high-toned society. Once in Dodge his weak moral nature is overcome, and straightway he is dazzled by the glare of the lights in the dance hall and enraptured by the charms and beauty of the frail feminines that hold court at the shrine of revelry, and soon the moral examplar has been fully captivated — drunken with whisky and exhilerated with the enthusiasm of the orgies. The next day comes the remorse from the night's dissipation — money all gone, a headache to remind him of his frailty. To show his home folks that he withstood the temptation in Dodge — the red glare of the dance hall, the sickly smile of the courtezan, and the 'tiger' [the faro table] — he writes an exaggerated account of the city's vices, thus attempting to show a moral courage he does not possess."

To aid and abet Klaine's campaign for morality and civilized customs, Mayor Webster passed strict police regulations which called for full-time policemen, orderly decorum, mandatory wearing of a star or shield on the left breast, abstention from intoxicating liquor while on duty, and other rules and restrictions. One of Webster's rules required, "Each and every member of the Police force shall devote his whole time and attention to the business of the department, and is hereby prohibited from following any other calling."[7] Webster's bartender-marshal, Fred Singer, resigned to devote full time to the operation of Webster's Old House saloon.

In June, 1882, Jack Bridges, a former deputy U. S. marshal from Hays, was called to Dodge City to take the position of city marshal. Bridges was well-known by old timers, and thought by some to be an indiscriminate gunman. Webster's strict police regulations, passed just before Bridges took office, probably helped reassure those who thought the pistol regime was returning to Dodge City.

In October the *Globe* commented favorably on the recent activities of Dodge City's lawmen, Sheriff George Hinkle and Marshal Jack Bridges. "Notwithstanding the fact that the merchants of our city keep constantly on hand a well assorted stock of arms, ammunition and ready made coffins, Dodge has proved to be, under the present municipal administration, not only a law-abiding but a law preserving community. Her officers are ever ready to protect the lives and property of citizens or corporations, which fact is fully appreciated. . . . "

The year 1883 brought more forms of advancement and civilization to Dodge City. A new telephone was connected between Dr. T. L. McCarty's home and his City Drug Store on Front Street. Robert M. Wright had been the first to use the new fangled device, connecting his home and Wright, Beverley & Co. in 1880. George and John Gilbert, brothers from Spearville, were beginning to take right-of-way for a new irrigating canal to be built through Ford County. Robert M. Wright was ordering a carload of box elder, cottonwood, ash, and locust trees. He planned to plant over 2,000 of these trees on his twenty-acre tract in the bottom land near the river southwest of town. There were few trees in Dodge City and the prospect for a grove within the city limits was eagerly awaited.

Another highlight of the year 1883 was the much publicized "saloon war" of Dodge City. Luke Short, a small, dandified Texan, with a background of gambling and a reputation for gunplay, came to Dodge City in August, 1882. Short was the personification of a Western gambler — under medium height but well built, clean shaven except for a natty moustache, a fashionable dresser — he sported a large diamond tie pin, twirled an elegant black walking stick with a gold head, and was not a stranger to the workings of a six-gun.

Saloons were still a profitable business in the thriving cattle town of Dodge City. Short became associated with the Long Branch shortly after his arrival, and in February, 1883, bought out Chalk Beeson's interest. W. H. Harris stayed on as Short's partner. Beeson moved next door in March, buying out Webster's interest in the Stock Exchange saloon. Webster moved to the corner of the block to the east where

Lawrence E. Deger (left), an early marshal of Dodge City, was defeated by Bat Masterson for the office of sheriff in November, 1877, by the slim margin of three votes. Less than a month later he was ousted from his job as city marshal by the mayor, Dog Kelley, a political friend of Bat's. Bat's older brother, Ed, was appointed in Deger's place. In 1883 Deger succeeded A. B. Webster as mayor, continuing his reform policies which resulted in the explosive but bloodless saloon war.

Louis C. Hartman (right), city clerk in 1883, was appointed special policeman at the outbreak of the saloon fracas in Dodge City. His exchange of shots with Luke Short marked the opening of a contest between saloonkeepers that gained Dodge City additional notoriety and resulted in an alert of state militia to keep the peace.

Luke Short (left), part owner of the Long Branch saloon, was declared persona non grata by Mayor Deger after Short's arrest in 1883. Short's anger prompted him to import his gunfighting friends and threaten to shoot his way back into Dodge City.

W. H. Harris (right), defeated by Deger in the election for mayor of 1883, was a partner with Short in the operation of the Long Branch saloon and part owner with Chalk Beeson of extensive cattle ranching operations. A gambler and saloonkeeper, Harris was easily defeated by Deger and the reformers who characterized Harris as a protector of confidence men, thieves, and gamblers.

he took over the operation of his Old House saloon. Walter Straeter who had leased the Old House from Webster since 1878 moved to the bar and restaurant in the Dodge House.

Short's partner, W. H. Harris, was a gambler, a dabbler in the cattle business, and an organizer of Dodge City's first bank. He had been Chalk Beeson's partner in the Saratoga and Long Branch saloons since 1877, and was still associated with him in the cattle business. In April, 1883, Harris was persuaded by friends to run for mayor against Webster's picked candidate, Larry Deger. Those who backed Deger felt that Harris represented gamblers and saloonkeepers and that his candidacy menaced the reign of law and order initiated by Webster.

The *Times* joined the Deger crowd and outdid itself in a smear campaign against Harris. "Three-fourths of the people of Dodge City are in favor of decency and order. They are for Larry E. Deger for Mayor, and city officers that will stamp out the serpent that hangs with a seductive smile, biting whoever may chance within the reach of his poisonous and deathly fangs." After the election, Harris and Short's enemies asserted that the Long Branch was "a refuge and resort for all confidence men, thieves and gamblers that visit the town . . ."

Deger, the weighty German-American ex-marshal, had been working for a freight company in Dodge City since his ouster as marshal by Mayor Kelley and his three-vote defeat by Bat Masterson for sheriff in 1877. An enemy of Dog Kelley's Gang element, he was a perfect candidate to carry out the moderate reform policies of A. B. Webster. Deger won by a sound majority of 214 to 143 brought about, according to some, by a large number of illegal voters — railroad employees — rounded up by Mike Sutton. Sutton had been quick to see the balance of power change in Dodge City politics. A former friend of the gamblers and saloonkeepers, he made an abrupt about face. Sutton was attorney for the Santa Fe railroad in Ford County and quite possibly was instructed by the railroad to do all in his power to tone down Dodge City, now an important division point on the A. T. & S. F. route.

Deger and his city council passed two new city ordinances two weeks after taking office. One was entitled, "An Ordinance For The Suppressing Of Vice And Immorality Within The City Of Dodge City." It prescribed fines against "any person or persons who shall keep or maintain in this city a brothel, bawdy house, house of ill-fame, or of assignation. . . . Any person whether male or female, being an inmate or resident of any brothel, bawdy house, or house of ill-fame. . . ." The other was called, "An Ordinance To Define And Punish Vagrancy," and provided for fines against "any person who may be found loitering around houses of ill-fame, gambling houses or places where liquors are sold or drank, without any visible means of support or lawful vocation, or shall be the keeper or inmate of any house of ill-fame or gambling house, or engaged in any unlawful calling whatever. . . ."[8]

A mere two days after the publication of these ordinances, extra police were put on and enforcement began. For many years piano and band music and singing were featured in the Long Branch saloon. Since Chalk Beeson's leaving, Harris and Short featured three female "singers" who many claimed were prostitutes, plain and simple. Luke Short was a popular man with the "ladies" and freely admitted that it was a common practice for saloons in Dodge City to provide facilities for prostitution.

On the Saturday evening of April 28, 1883, Luke Short's "singers" were hauled off to the calaboose. They put up no resistance, and no one denied their scarlet tinged reputations. Luke Short and W. H. Harris, however, were much put out, according to the *Globe,* "that partiality was shown in arresting women in their house when two were allowed to remain in A. B. Webster's [Old House] saloon, one at Heinz & Kramer's [Lone Star saloon], two at Nelson Cary's [Opera House saloon], and a whole herd of them at [Brick] Bond & [Tom] Nixon's [Lady Gay] dance hall. . . ."

City Clerk Louis C. Hartman was one of the special policemen put on the force under Marshal Bridges to enforce the new city ordinances. Hartman incurred the wrath of Luke Short by carrying out the arrest of his three soiled doves. "Short assumed a defiant attitude," according to the *Times,* and stormed off to

City Attorney Fred Wenie's house. At the point of his pistol Short roused the city attorney from his bed to obtain bonds for the release of the Long Branch "singers" now residing in the city jail.

Later that Saturday night, according to the *Times,* a conspiracy was organized by Luke Short and his friends for making an armed resistance to the marshal and his deputies. According to the *Globe,* "Luke Short and L. C. Hartman met upon the street and paid their respective compliments to each other by exchanging shots . . ." Neither was hit; Hartman retreating, tripped and fell. Luke, thinking he had scored a hit, retired to a friend's saloon. Hartman and Short both filed complaints against each other for the shooting. Shortly after the shooting Marshal Bridges arrested Luke Short in the Long Branch saloon. He was released later on $2,000 bond.

Rumours began flying concerning the shooting incident. Short's reputation and that of his friends aroused feelings of fear and extreme dislike among many of the supporters of ex-Mayor Webster and his protege, the newly elected Mayor Deger. Webster still smarted from financial losses while owner of the Stock Exchange saloon next door to the Long Branch. He had been unable to compete with the efficient W. H. Harris and the dapper Luke Short's female "singers." Deger, though the winner, still had not healed from the no-holds-barred mayoral campaign against W. H. Harris.

A self-styled vigilante group formed around the leadership of Webster, Deger, and Tom Nixon. Short began seeking help in his resistance to Mayor Deger's armed "Vigilanters," and Deger got word of the armed resistance that Short was threatening. On Monday, using his new ordinances as a device for removing the opposition, Deger had warrants issued for the arrest of Luke Short and six of his friends. The newspapers described Short's friends as a saloonkeeper, four gamblers, and "a former New Mexico desperado." All were placed in the calaboose to await their choice of the east- or westbound trains or the southbound stage.

Deger's and Webster's actions were later justified with frontier rationalization by the oily-tongued Mike Sutton: "[The exile of Short and his friends by the vigilantes] is only a repetition of what is found to be necessary about every two years in Dodge City; that is, a clearing out of an element composed of bold, daring men of illegal profession who, from toleration by the respectable portion of the community, are allowed to gain a prestige found difficult to unseat. This element has to be banished, or else the respectable people have to be bulldozed and browbeat by a class of men without any vested interest or visible means of support. . . ."[9]

Luke Short went east to Kansas City. A week later two of Short's exiled gambling fraternity tried to return to Dodge City. As they stepped down from the train on the south side of the tracks where they would not be noticed as readily, they were met by a dozen of Mayor Deger's special deputies with pistols in hand. The two gamblers deemed it the better part of valor to step back aboard and continue on west, at least as far as Cimarron to await further developments.

Meanwhile, Short was in Kansas City keeping in touch with the situation by letters from his friends in Dodge City. George M. Hoover wrote and advised him to sell his interest in the Long Branch or find someone to look after it. Hoover felt that under the present administration it would not be possible for Luke Short to return. Short was still determined to try all avenues of redress. He sought legal advice from an attorney in Larned who informed him that a "Shot Gun brigade" was still boarding all trains to insure that neither Short nor his friends returned. The attorney advised him to "wait for a week or 10 days yet & let matters die down a little."[10]

Luke Short then decided to travel to Topeka to lay the matter before the new governor of Kansas, George W. Glick, an anti-Prohibitionist. Luke presented the governor with a petition which alleged that he had been driven out of Dodge City by "a band of armed men" led by Mayor Deger; that "he was put in fear of his life, and . . . that had he remained in said city, he would have been murdered"; that the "leading parties" of the "band of armed men" were Mayor Deger, Under Sheriff Fred Singer, Marshal

Jack Bridges, Assistant Marshal Clark Chipman, Special Policeman L. C. Hartman, Special Policeman Bob Vanderburg, Thomas Nixon, "a proprietor of a Dance Hall," Brick Bond, "a proprietor of a dance hall," and A. B. Webster, "proprietor of a saloon & gambling house"; and further that the whole incident "arose from political differences and Business rivalry. . . ." Wherefore, Short beseeched the Governor to protect him "from the unlawful violence of the above mentioned parties — to the end that he may return and remain in safety — and prosecute his business. . . ."[11]

W. F. Petillon, clerk of the district court in Dodge City and a fellow Democrat, came to Topeka at the request of Governor Glick to testify as to the state of affairs in Dodge City. Petillon was a friend of Short's and affirmed Short's petition as the true state of affairs. Governor Glick alerted two companies of the Kansas National Guard at Sterling and Newton to await further word in case affairs in Dodge City became violent. The governor wired Sheriff George Hinkle to learn more about the situation in Dodge City. Hinkle wired back admitting that Luke Short and his friends were forced to leave. A Dodge City committee of twelve wired the governor and later traveled to Topeka in an attempt to convince him that Short's statement was not true and that there was no need for interference in Dodge City's affairs.

Luke Short saw the battle lines forming and began to assemble his troops. Bat Masterson arrived in Kansas City, and the next day Wyatt Earp, Doc Holliday, and two other Western gunslingers, Rowdy Joe Lowe and Shotgun Collins showed up. The news got back to Dodge City quickly, and Sheriff Hinkle enlisted a posse of forty-five men to await the incoming trains from the east. George M. Hoover, Robert M. Wright, and Chalk Beeson, all cattlemen, promoters of Dodge City's Texas trade, and influential businessmen, made a quick trip to Kansas City to confer with Luke Short, Masterson, and Earp in an effort to hold off any violence that they might be contemplating.

The governor, becoming more and more perplexed as to the true state of affairs in Dodge City, sent his emissary, Adjutant General Thomas Moonlight, to report on conditions in the "wicked city." Moonlight talked to the various factions in Dodge City and was successful in arranging a promise from city and county officials to allow Luke Short to return for ten days to settle his financial affairs.

For a short time anyway, it appeared that a reconciliation had been made, and that Luke Short would return to Dodge City peacefully, settle his affairs, and move on. Dodge City's saloon war would then be over. Luke Short had other plans, however. Moonlight returned to Topeka; Bat Masterson, Wyatt Earp and company headed west to Silverton, Colorado, and Luke Short traveled to Caldwell, a cattle town in south-central Kansas. Ten days passed, leaving Marshal Bridges, Sheriff Hinkle, and Mayor Deger in a state of puzzled expectation.

On May 31, 1883, Luke's emissaries, Wyatt Earp and Doc Holliday arrived in Dodge City. The fearful sheriff, George Hinkle, promptly telegraphed the governor: "Can you send Col. Moonlight here tomorrow with power to organize company of militia?"[12] An unidentified spy for the Topeka *Daily Commonwealth* wrote the newspaper of the plans for the impending battle: "Masterson, Wyatt Earp, and all the sports in the country, held a meeting at Silverton and decided to take Dodge City by storm. Short is at Caldwell but will meet the party at Cimarron, 18 miles west of Dodge, perhaps Sunday night or soon after. Horses will be taken at Cimarron and the whole party will rendezvous at Mr. Oliver's, two miles west of Dodge. Doc Holliday and Wyatt Earp are now secretly in Dodge City, watching matters. When the time for action comes a telegram will reach them worded as follows: 'Your tools will be there at _____,' giving the time agreed upon. The plan is to drive all of Short's enemies out of Dodge at the mouth of the revolvers."

On June 3, Luke Short, Bat Masterson, and W. F. Petillon met thirty-two miles east of Dodge City in Kinsley instead of Cimarron. Earp joined them to report on his efforts to smooth the way for Luke Short's entry into Dodge City. Luke and Wyatt traveled on to Dodge City on the afternoon train. No records exist telling of the reception for Luke Short and Wyatt Earp as they arrived. It must have been a stand-off for no records of violence exist, either.

Luke Short's recruited army of assorted gunslingers equalized the political power of Mayor Deger and his allies during the saloon war; a detente was reached, and Short was allowed to return and settle his financial affairs. Luke and friends gathered for this picture (left) in June, 1883. Self-proclaimed "the Dodge City Peace Commission," the group consisted of (back row, from left) W. H. Harris, Luke Short, Bat Masterson, and W. F. Petillon; (front row, from left) Charlie Bassett, Wyatt Earp, Frank McLain, and Neil Brown.

Governor John P. St. John, a Prohibitionist, singled out Dodge City as a target for enforcement of Kansas prohibition law in 1881. His efforts met with little success because the sheriff and his deputies were openly and avowedly against its enforcement.

Governor George W. Glick, an anti-Prohibitionist, successor to St. John, sided with Luke Short, and sent his adjutant general, Thomas Moonlight, to negotiate Short's troubles with local authorities.

Luke Short and W. H. Harris sold their interest in the Long Branch saloon to Roy Drake and Frank Warren and announced the sale publicly on November 19, 1883. The receipt at the right, dated the same day, accounts for gambling equipment owned by the partnership of Chalk Beeson and W. H. Harris, purchased by the new owners, Drake and Warren.

On Monday, the day after Short's arrival, Mayor Deger issued a proclamation ordering all gambling places closed. On Tuesday Bat Masterson arrived. Bat's ex-friend, the Irish opportunist, Mike Sutton, now the friend of the temperance society and anti-Short faction, promptly went into hiding.

Early Wednesday morning Sheriff Hinkle, N. B. Klaine, editor of the *Times,* F. C. Zimmermann, Mayor Deger, George S. Emerson, a merchant and city councilman, and Robert M. Wright wired Adjutant General Moonlight: "Our city is overrun with desperate characters from Colorado, New Mexico, Arizona and California. We cannot preserve the peace or enforce the laws. Will you send in two companies of militia at once to assist us in preserving the peace between all parties and enforcing the laws." Moonlight boarded the first train for Dodge City to see how bad the situation really was. By the time he arrived, Wyatt Earp, Bat Masterson, Luke Short, and W. H. Harris had met with their opposition. The anti-Short faction, A. B. Webster and his German-American supporters, Larry Deger, F. C. Zimmermann, and Henry Sturm were persuaded to compromise.

An agreement was worked out whereby gambling could commence provided it was carried on in areas partitioned or screened off from the public bar rooms and dance halls. Women would be allowed in the saloons and dance halls, but under more rigid supervision and control, and Luke Short and his supporters promised to cooperate in seeing that some of the notorious gamblers and confidence men left town.

When Adjutant General Moonlight arrived the saloon war was settling down to a peaceful conclusion. In a day and a half Moonlight "succeeded in effecting an amicable settlement between the warring factions."[13] After his return to Topeka, he made arrangements for a unit of state militia to be organized in Dodge City, made up of pro-Short and pro-Deger men. The militia was named the "Glick Guards" in honor of Governor Glick and was captained by Pat Sughrue, later a sheriff of Ford County.

Luke Short's followers made good their promise to help rid Dodge City of certain of its undesirable visitors. A day after the armistice, in June, 1883, the *Times* announced the departure of such Western notables as Shot Gun Collins, Black Jack Bill, Cold Chuck Johnny, Dynamite Sam, Dark Alley Jim, Dirty Sock Jack, Six-toed Pete, and Three Fingered Dave. A week later the *Times* announced that "Red Nosed Johnny, Cock-eyed Joe, Hunchback Jim, Off Wheeler, Guy Jim and Red top Bill have left this gaze and are now rustling among the unsophisticated travellers in the West."

There were many former Dodge City residents, friends of Luke Short, still visiting within the city. These old timers, Dodge City lawmen from an earlier period, and their friends, decided in a spirit of camaraderie, to gather for a photograph. To celebrate their reunion and the saloon war victory they sat and posed for a now famous picture which they self-captioned, *The Dodge City Peace Commission.* The group consisted of Luke Short and his Long Branch saloon partner, W. H. Harris; former sheriff, Bat Masterson; former sheriff and marshal, Charlie Bassett; former assistant marshal, Wyatt Earp; Frank McLain, a friend of Earp's; Neil Brown, a former assisant marshal; and W. F. Petillon, a political friend of Short's, clerk of the district court, and later editor of the Dodge City *Democrat.* Except for Petillon, this photograph pictures a unique gathering of Western lawmen, gunfighters, and gamblers.

Wyatt Earp returned to Silverton, Colorado, just after posing for the famous photograph. The November 20, 1883, edition of the *Globe* announced the sale of W. H. Harris' and Luke Short's interest in the Long Branch saloon. Roy Drake and Frank Warren became the new owners. Bat Masterson and Luke Short left Dodge City together, bound for Fort Worth, Texas, as the cattle season of 1883 drew to a close.

Dodge City was far from tamed in the summer of 1883 when the saloon war ended. But radical changes were taking place. In September, for the first time in the city's history, all businesses were required to close on Sundays. The butcher shop, drug store, and post office were allowed to remain open for an hour. The *Times* claimed, "The last relic of the frontier has given up the ghost," and reported that "Front street is a blank on Sunday." An increase in church attendance was also noted.

Drunken cowboys were still shooting off their pistols in wild abandon, however. The summer of 1883 witnessed a killing by cowboys, boozing it up in Bond and Nixon's Lady Gay saloon. It had never been possible to completely enforce the old ordinance against carrying firearms. Nevertheless, the crusading *Times* cried out for the pistol's prohibition: "The daily frightful occurrences, the results of the careless use of the pistol, would suggest the abolition of the carrying of these dangerous weapons. . . . The custom of the border should be modified, and the pistol given up. . . . The carrying of firearms is a barbarous custom, and it is time the practice was broken up."

Along with the new Sunday closing ordinance, Mayor Deger passed an ordinance abolishing music and singing in saloons and dance halls.[14] The purpose of this ordinance was to drive the prostitutes out of the public gaze.

Luke Short's supporters complained during the Dodge City saloon war that Tom Nixon's dance hall was "one of the hardest dance halls that ever existed in the west. . . ."[15] It was hoped by some that the new ordinance prohibiting music in the dance halls would drive Nixon's dance hall girls, mostly prostitutes, into the back rooms to solicit their customers, just as an earlier prohibition ordinance had driven the gamblers into back rooms to play their games.

A local wag sent a poem to the *Times* commenting on the recent change in *Tom* Nixon's and *Brick* Bond's Lady Gay dance hall:

> I have wandered to the Dance Hall, Tom,
> > Where in the days gone by,
> We tripped the light fantastic toe,
> > Together, you and I.
> The same old "brick" is in the hall —
> > But the "bells" "swing" not to and fro —
> The music is not the same, dear Tom,
> > As it was a few days ago.

Prostitution was still a big business in Dodge City. Numerous "parlours" were operating about town. The police dockets showed frequent charges against the town's scarlet ladies — stabbings, fights, disorderly conduct, and indecent exposure. As late as the summer of 1885, prostitution was still a troublesome, but profitable, sideline to the Texas cattle trade. In July an outraged citizen offered his house for sale. "I am being forced to make this public announcement," he complained, "from the fact that I am being surrounded by houses of prostitution. . . . A 'coon dive' on one side of me and _____'s brothels on the other, and that gentleman now seeks to add insult to injury by building another house of prostitution between my house and barn, which is more than I can stand. . . . I have serious objections to being completely hemmed in with bagnios. I have a respectable family, daughters just budding into womanhood and I don't propose to have their very existence polluted by _____'s brothels. If this sweet-scented, humpbacked old christian has lost all self-respect and has no other object in this world than to perpetuate prostitution, I am willing to turn over my part of the neighborhood to help him in his lustful calling. My property is for sale at reduced rates."[16]

The banning of music and dancing in saloons and dance halls in the fall of 1883 was cause for rejoicing for some in Dodge City — but not for Bat Masterson. Bat was back in Dodge City, gambling, politicking, and engaging in his first attempts at journalism. He left after seeing the November county elections put his candidate, Pat Sughrue, in office as sheriff.

In order to gladden the festive hearts of his constituents, Mayor Deger allowed the dance halls to open on Christmas and New Year's eve. The mayor was soon to regret his liberal decree, for on New Year's eve, the celebration at Bond and Nixon's dance hall ended with a stabbing. The *Times* commented:

Dave St. Clair, a gambler, killed the Texas cowboy, Bing Choate, in the Old House saloon on the day after Dodge City's famous Spanish bull fight celebration in July, 1884.

"No trouble has occurred at the dance halls for a long time, but the late affray offers additional argument in favor of keeping these places closed. Whisky and women are bound to make trouble, and the only remedy is keep the dance halls closed at all times."

The children in Dodge City gathered at Kelley's Opera House on Christmas eve, 1883, just as they had done in years before and after. They suffered through singing, prayers, and an address by Mayor Deger. Larry Deger, an uneducated freighter and frontiersman, was not a master of elocution. The newspaper account kindly noted, however, that the mayor's words were "appropriate and well rendered." After more singing and recitations the highlight of the celebration came at last when "Old Santa, clothed in the conventional arctic garb, . . . made glad the hearts of the children by informing them, in song, that he had presents for 'one and all, both great and small.'" Old Santa was none other than Special Policeman Louie Hartman, the target for Luke Short's pistol at the outset of the famous saloon war of Dodge City.

When the time for city elections came around in April, 1884, the saloon owners and operators were becoming edgy about a possible new prohibitory ordinance to be enforced in Dodge City. State officials in Topeka were advocating a more strict enforcement of Kansas prohibition laws. George M. Hoover, Dodge City's wholesale liquor dealer, replaced Larry Deger as mayor in 1884, and the saloonkeepers breathed easier.

Hoover picked William M. (Bill) Tilghman, Jr. to be the new city marshal. Tom Nixon, half owner of a saloon, was picked as assistant marshal. Tilghman had kept saloons and raised cattle for several years in Dodge City. In 1877 he was half owner of the Crystal Palace saloon. In 1884 he operated the Oasis saloon. He was a deputy under the new sheriff, Pat Sughrue, and had a reputation as an efficient peace officer.

Bat Masterson was back in town since the beginning of the cattle season in May, 1884. Bat was now a promoter of sporting events and a gambler, associated with the Lone Star saloon, now located on Front Street. He reconciled his differences with ex-Mayor Webster and, together with Robert M. Wright and

Mysterious Dave Mather is pictured left above, while serving as assistant marshal in 1883. Mather attempted to turn his Front Street saloon into a dance hall to compete with Tom Nixon's Lady Gay. Bad blood between the two saloonkeepers resulted in Mysterious Dave's callous killing of Nixon (right above) in 1884.

William M. Tilghman, Jr., (right) a saloon-keeper and rancher, was marshal of Dodge City during the last two years of its cattle town period. George T. Hinkle (far right) defeated Bat Masterson for sheriff in 1879 and served two terms from 1880 to 1884. Instructed by Governor Glick to institute law and order during the saloon war of 1883, he had little success against Luke Short and his company of gunmen.

Patrick F. Sughrue (far left), a blacksmith by trade, succeeded Hinkle as sheriff in 1884. He served two terms until 1888, the last sheriff of Dodge City's cowboy era. Ben Daniels (left), Dodge City assistant marshal in 1885 and 1886, shot and killed a restaurant owner, Ed Julian, five days after leaving office. Daniels was tried and acquitted, but later his application for appointment as a deputy U. S. marshal was strongly opposed by friends of Julian and was denied.

W. H. Harris, founded a city baseball club. When Webster came up with the idea of a bull fight in Dodge City, committees were formed to take charge of the grand celebration planned for July fourth, 1884. Ham Bell and Bill Tilghman were members of the executive committee which decided that there should be racing events and shooting contests to precede the bull fight. Tom Nixon and Neil Brown were on the committee in charge of horse racing. Bat Masterson was appointed to the committee in charge of foot races. News of the Dodge City bull fight spread, drawing delegations of sporting men from Denver, Chicago, Kansas City, St. Louis, New York, and New Orleans.

The racing and bull fights, the week of the Fourth, were a big success, and Dodge City was filled with many visitors in addition to the usual crowds of cattlemen. The cattle season of 1884, a profitable one, kept Marshal Tilghman busy making the rounds collecting the license fees from prostitutes, saloonkeepers, and gamblers.

A day after the bull fights ended, Bing Choate was shot and killed in Webster's Old House saloon by Dave St. Clair, a gambler. K. B. (Bing) Choate, the son of a prominent Texas cattle raiser, drove 11,000 cattle up the trail to Dodge in 1884. At one o'clock in the morning, Choate was drinking at the bar with several other men. St. Clair was sitting at the side of the room. Choate, full of whisky, pounded his revolver on the bar and began shouting obscenities at St. Clair. The gambler arose from his chair and the cattleman approached him. Winesses testified that both pulled their pistols about the same time. St. Clair drew his gun from his right hip pocket and fired at Choate who was standing about eight feet from the front door. The shot struck home and whirled Choate, his gun half drawn from its holster, toward the front doors. Choate rose to his knees and was about to fire his cocked pistol at St. Clair when Ben Daniels, a policeman, came running up and knocked the gun from his hand. Choate fell dead. St. Clair was arrested. After a hearing of witnesses to the shooting he was released and immediately headed west.

Dave Mather was another of the many colorful characters in Dodge City's history. With a reputation as a gunman in the early frontier communities of Trinidad, Colorado; Las Vegas, New Mexico; and Dodge City, he was known as "a dangerous man to have a quarrel with."[17] Little is known of his background. Born in Connecticut, he claimed to be a direct descendant of the seventeenth century Puritan theologian, Cotton Mather.[18] He was called Mysterious Dave by friends and enemies and was equally comfortable on both sides of the law. A companion of known outlaws such as Dutch Henry, the horse thief, and Dave Rudabaugh, the train robber, he also served as a peace officer in several frontier towns. In Dodge City, Mysterious Dave was assistant marshal under Jack Bridges.

After Bridges was replaced by Bill Tilghman, Mather was removed and Tom Nixon appointed assistant marshal. Twelve days after Bing Choate's death, Assistant Marshal Nixon attempted to kill Mysterious Dave.

At the time Mather was operating a saloon on the second floor of Kelley's Opera House. In May he had tried to convert it into a dance hall for the upcoming crowds expected for the bull fight. City authorities quickly put a stop to Mather's plans, and he blamed Assistant Marshal Nixon. The two were bitter enemies. Nixon took a pot shot at Mather, missed, and was quickly disarmed by Sheriff Sughrue. Nixon claimed that he shot only after Mather drew his gun; Mather claimed otherwise. Three days later, before a trial could be held, Mysterious Dave "killed his man."

At ten o'clock in the evening Nixon was on duty patrolling Front Street. While standing at the corner of Front Street and First Avenue, just outside the Opera House, he heard someone call his name. Turning toward the entrance leading up to Mather's saloon, he was confronted by Mysterious Dave who "commenced shooting at him, firing four shots, two of them striking him in the right side, one in the left side and one passed through the left nipple, killing him instantly." After the shooting, just before his arrest, Mysterious Dave callously remarked, "I ought to have killed him six months ago."[19] Despite the testimony of several witnesses who saw Nixon make no attempt to draw his revolver, Mysterious Dave was acquitted and released.

A. B. Webster and Brick Bond operated a "Drug Store" according to the advertisement above appearing in the Globe Live Stock Journal in July, 1885. Their wines and whiskies for "medicinal, mechanical and scientific purposes" amounted to quite a stock, according to the billing (right) in George Hoover's wholesale liquor account book dated April, 1885. 1,340½ gallons of whisky plus nine cases of miscellaneous spirits were purchased by Bond and Webster for their drug store, formerly known as the Stock Exchange saloon — $2,526.90 worth of snake bite medicine!

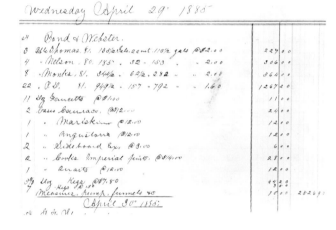

The tintype at the left shows Lo Warren (left), bartender and monte dealer, son of a buffalo hunter scalped by Indians in 1874, and Charles Heinz, saloonkeeper and Dodge City restaurateur. Heinz advertised his Lone Star saloon and restaurant on Front Street (below) until March, 1885, when the pressure of Kansas prohibition law induced him to change the name of his establishment to the Delmonico restaurant (below left). The eatery of Charles Heinz became a popular gathering place and was rebuilt as a hotel and restaurant after the disastrous fire in December, 1885.

136

The letter (left) to the Colt firearms company in Hartford. Conn., was written in 1885 on Opera House saloon stationery by Bat Masterson (below). It reads: "Gents . . . please send me one of your Nickle plated Short 45. Calibre revolvers. it is for my own use and for that reason I would like to have a little Extra paines taken with it. I am willing to pay Extra for Extra work. Make it very Easy on trigger and have the front Sight a little higher and thicker than the ordinary pistol of this Kind. put on a gutta percha handle and send it as soon as possible. have the barrel about the same length that the Ejacting rod is. . . ."

Bat Masterson returned to Dodge City in the fall of 1884 to join the Republican county convention held there in October. On November 1, 1884, he issued a small newspaper called the Vox Populi. His first and only edition was given to an abusive but well written exposé of his political enemies, especially Nicholas Klaine, editor of the Times, whom he described as a thief, liar, murderer, rapist, barn burner, and poisoner of his neighbors' horses. All of Bat's candidates won in the November election, and he ceased publication after one issue.

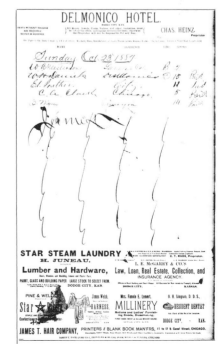

Bat Masterson returned to his old haunts in Dodge City in October, 1887, according to this page from the Delmonico Hotel register (right).

137

A year later, Mysterious Dave and his brother, Josiah Mather, engaged in a wild melee of shooting at the Junction saloon, next door to Kelley's Opera House. The Junction was formerly Beatty & Kelley's Alhambra saloon. Mysterious Dave was playing cards at the Junction with a farmer, Dave Barnes. After three games of "'seven up' at fifty cents a game . . . Mather got up and putting the money that was on the table in his pocket, walked over to the bar. Barnes followed him and claimed the money. Mather then struck him. Immediately the shooting commenced which resulted in the killing of Barnes. . . ." Two innocent bystanders were wounded. "Dave Mather [was] cut across the forehead, the ball passing out through his hat."[20]

"Sheriff [Pat] Sughrue happened to be there at the time, and no doubt saved two [or] three more from getting killed, as every body who had a pistol was firing. After the shooting was over the sheriff arrested Dave and Josiah Mather and lodged them in jail."[21] Dave and Josiah jumped their $3,000 bail bonds and faded into the western sunset.

Intoxicating liquor, the cause of most of the gunfire in Dodge City since its founding in 1872, was banned in Kansas in 1880 — "except for medical, scientific and mechanical purposes." Dodge City saloons ignored the ban for five years until the fall of 1885. For over twenty years more, liquor and beer were served in "blind tigers," private clubs, in basement rooms under Front Street.

By 1885 the temperance movement was at its height in Kansas. Attorney General S. B. Bradford came to Dodge City to initiate suits in the district court against the open saloon. Anticipating the attorney general's arrival, some of the saloons closed their doors — to open again after his departure. The Dodge City *Democrat* quipped, "The saloons have gone. 'Gone where the woodbine twineth.'"

Some Dodge City saloons made magical transformations into drug stores where wine, whisky, and various spirits could be purchased for "medicinal purposes." One saloon erected a sign, "Drug Store, Lager Beer on Ice, for Medical Purposes only."[22] A. B. Webster was back at his old stand, the Stock Exchange saloon between Robert M. Wright's general merchandise store and the Long Branch saloon. Webster and his partner, Brick Bond, announced that on the first day of May their business would be officially known as a drug store.[23]

The Long Branch decided to stick it out with only a thin disguise. Its announcement in June read: "The Long Branch Temperance Hall was opened up about a week ago by Messrs. Harris & Drake, proprietors, with such old-time lemonade and temperance drink mixers as Edward Cooley and Moses Barber, who are both gentlemenly fellows and know how to entertain their numerous customers. The Long Branch has at all times been a popular resort, being a veritable art gallery as well as a billiard hall."[24] Some of the saloons merely changed their signs, painting over *Saloon,* and writing in *Restaurant.* The *Globe* observed: "From the number of saloons that are being turned into restaurants, it would appear like the eating business was pretty good in this city."

The "art galleries," "billiard halls," "drug stores," and "restaurants" up and down Front Street now specialized in "Methodist cocktails and hard-shell Baptist lemonades." Ten years as a cattle railhead had brought success and growth to the community. Plans were developing to renew and rebuild. Since earliest days, Chestnut Street behind the Front Street stores, was a narrow passage called Tin Pot Alley where refuse, empty whisky barrels, bottles, and drunks were thrown to clutter the narrow paths to the outhouses which lined its way. Plans were now afoot to widen Tin Pot Alley into a respectable street to accommodate new brick buildings proposed to replace some of the original frame structures. The new "bricks" would extend to both streets, one door on Chestnut and the other on Front.

In 1885 the Topeka *Capital* made a keen observance about the Cowboy Capital: "There are silent but irresistible forces at work to regenerate Dodge City. The passage of the Texas cattle bill, the defeat of the trail bill and the rapid settlement of the country south and southwest of Dodge, have destroyed that place as a cattle town. The cowboy must go, and with him will go the gamblers, the courtesans, the desperadoes and the saloons."

Early in 1885 the Kansas legislature passed a quarantine law barring from the state all cattle originating in central and southern Texas, where splenic fever was rampant. Even healthy Texas longhorns could infect domestic cattle as they were driven to the northern railheads and pastures. The traditional trail drive from Texas breeding grounds to Kansas markets ended. Cattlemen appealed to Congress for a National Cattle Trail that would enable them to drive their herds north, free of embargoes and barbed wire. The bill, however, failed to pass out of committee.

In the years, 1883 to 1885, Ford County's population doubled with rural immigration that rapidly overspread the cattle ranges south of Dodge City. Local stockmen found it harder and harder to find open ranges to pasture their herds. Stock prices were at a low, and cattlemen, eager to sell, found a buyer's market in Dodge City.

Dodge City's economic fate was hastened by the conspiracy of fire and ice, soon to change the face of Front Street and bring an end to the cattle days' prosperity. In January, 1885, the *Kansas Cowboy,* one of the four newspapers then being published in Dodge City, remarked that "Dodge City is a little paradise for fire insurance companies. . . . Notwithstanding the seemingly hazardous risks which our business property affords, there has never yet been any fires in the city, involving loss to insurance companies. This is attributable to the peculiar character of Dodge City. Many of its business houses are never closed; its saloons are frequented by people at all hours, and at no time, day or night, are the streets destitute of pedestrians. Fires have broken out, but they are always discovered in their incipiency and squelched before harm is done." This statement was soon to haunt the *Cowboy.*

One day after this comment reached the *Cowboy's* readers, a fire broke out in a grocery store on Front Street between Second and Third Avenues. The *Cowboy* offices, two doors west of the burning grocery, burned, destroying its power press, leaving a large portion of its type "pied" and its quarters burned out. The fire destroyed the west half of the block and ignited several warehouses south of the railroad tracks. The fire stopped at Jake Collar's recently erected brick building. The wooden building west of it, McCarty's drug store and the post office, were saved.

At seven o'clock on a Friday evening, the following November, smoke issued from the Junction saloon on Front Street between First and Second Avenues. According to the *Globe,* the cry of fire sent "a thrill of horror through the minds of all as they rushed from their places of business, their homes and the hotels, each with a dread feeling of the terrible disaster fire brings to a frame town." A coal oil lamp exploded or broke from a fall in a room over the Junction saloon. It was believed to have been extinguished, but the smoldering menace started up again, and soon there were crowds helping to carry out the goods and moveable items from the buildings on Front Street. Men started bucket brigades to wet down the roofs of nearby buildings. Lacking water some poured salt on their roofs.

The fire spread rapidly, destroying the whole block from R. M. Wright's brick building at the west end to Dog Kelley's frame Opera House building at the east end. The buildings destroyed were the heart of Dodge City's business district — R. M. Wright & Co., formerly Wright, Beverley & Co.; Webster & Bond's drug store, formerly the Alamo and Stock Exchange saloons; the Long Branch saloon; the St. James saloon, formerly Hoover's wholesale liquor store and saloon; Adolphus Gluck's jewelry store; George Hinkle's newly opened saloon on Chestnut Street; F. C. Zimmermann's hardware store; E. R. Garland's drug store; Charles Heinz' Delmonico restaurant, formerly the Lone Star saloon; the York, Parker, Draper Mercantile Co., formerly the Saratoga saloon; Kirkpatrick & Dunn furniture store, formerly Jacob Collar's furniture and undertaking goods; the Junction saloon; and Kelley's Opera House building, housing a barber shop, saloon, and offices on the first floor, and a meeting hall and theater on the second.

For a time it was thought that the fire would spread to the block north of the burning buildings where several residences were located. With the help of friends, Mrs. Loren Warren, widow of a buffalo hunter slain by Indians in 1874, managed to move all of her household goods out while volunteer firemen soaked her house with water. The absence of wind, an unusual condition at any time of the year in western Kansas, and the efforts of many volunteers kept the fire isolated to the one block, known as the Central Block of Front Street.

After moving all that could safely be taken out of R. M. Wright & Co.'s brick building, Mr. Wright told the bystanders to help themselves. Several parties got in and out safely with goods before the building collapsed. Before the ashes cooled, temporary buildings were going up to house the burned out businesses until they could rebuild in brick. The *Globe* reported that "by an over sight some awful good whiskey was allowed to burn up." Twenty men were deputized to stand guard over merchandise roped off and stacked south of the railroad tracks. Several looters were arrested and the *Times* expressed its disgust thusly: "A man who would steal under such circumstances ought to be stretched in stocks and slowly kicked to death by grasshoppers."

The Delmonico restaurant re-opened the next day in the old vacated school house building on the corner of Walnut [Gunsmoke] Street and First Avenue. The roofs of the buildings east and west of the burned block were so covered with salt the morning after the fire it looked as if there had been a snow storm.

The *Kansas Cowboy* estimated the total loss at $150,000. "The opera house block went heavenwards in a hurry and the wooden buildings on the west were licked up with as keen a relish and with as much ease as a cow lapping salt. . . . The very business heart of Dodge City was destroyed by this fire." The *Cowboy* had a new opinion regarding the fire risk on Front Street. "The destruction of this property is a surprise to nobody acquainted with Dodge City. The fire has been anticipated for years. . . . With the exception of Kelly's opera house and Wright's store building the houses destroyed were old rookeries and allured annihilation. . . . The old Dodge, with its world-wide celebrity, has disappeared. The old rookeries and break-neck sidewalks that used to front the railroad have gone. Only a portion of the old Dodge House block remains. That portion is all that is left of old Dodge."

Before the fire had died, Robert M. Wright contracted for the erection of a temporary building on Second Avenue alongside his brick ruins which was finished five days later. York, Parker, Draper Mercantile Co. erected a temporary building south of the railroad tracks. The St. James saloon was back in business in temporary quarters at the north end of their lot three days after the fire. The Long Branch erected a temporary building at its old location.

The *Kansas Cowboy* summed up Dodge City's frontier spirit: "Not a single murmur has been heard to escape from the lips of any of the sufferers of the late fire. One hundred and fifty thousand dollars went to glory at that time and yet nobody cares a cuspidor about it." F. C. Zimmermann's losses were estimated at $8,000 with no insurance — a sizeable sum in 1885. The *Times,* however, reported that he "takes his loss with his usual good grace."

Ten days after the second fire, at midnight, according to the *Globe,* "our people were startled from their slumber by the dread cry of fire, and on emerging from their homes, saw a bright light in the center of the town, where it was known to all that blocks of frame buildings stood, that would surely go should the fire get a start."

The center of the block north of Chestnut Street between First and Second Avenues, directly north of the Central Block of Front Street, was filled with several rooming houses for the local demimonde. The fire started in one of these buildings, in the room of a "fair young lady," known about town as "Sawed-off." She was busy plying her trade in the old dance hall south of the railroad. About eleven o'clock she sent a boot black to her room to build a fire and warm up her room. According to the *Globe's* account, "The boy says he filled the stove with kindling and coal and poured on coal oil, lighting it and left the house."

The three views on this page show a snowbound Santa Fe train a few miles east of Dodge City after the devastating blizzard of 1886. This westbound passenger train with eighty passengers, was snowed in for five days.

141

A passerby "noticed the fire coming out the roof alongside the chimney; he knocked on the door, and received no response, kicked the door in, to find the room all around the stove, on the floor, side and ceiling in flames, and so hot that it was impossible to enter the house."

An attempt was made to tear down a small frame house east of where the fire started in order to save the *Globe Live Stock Journal* offices on the east corner of the block. Ropes were attached to the house in an effort to pull it into the street. This proved unsuccessful. One hundred and fifty pounds of powder were placed inside, in hopes it would be blown to pieces before it spread the fire. This proved exciting, but also a failure.

The Bee Hive dry goods store and the *Kansas Cowboy* offices at the west end of the block were destroyed — the second loss by fire to this newspaper within a year. The *Globe Live Stock Journal* offices at the east end of the block and the Odd Fellows hall on the second floor, a shoe shop, paint shop, and all the dwellings in the south half of the block were destroyed within an hour, also W. H. Harris' residence on Second Avenue north of the Bee Hive.

While the fires of 1885 burned, a signal banner flew from the court house flag staff. It was placed there on the advice of the U. S. Signal Office in Dodge City. Storms were gathering and the cold wave warning flag was placed in this prominent place where it could be seen by stockmen south of the river. New Year's eve brought the first storm.

The coming of the new year, 1886, was celebrated in a traditional way for Dodge City. As the new year arrived, a pistol shot rang out, "and then as if that had been the signal, a solid line on Front street and a not much less number across the dead line [railroad tracks] let loose with guns, pistols, fire crackers and everything that would make a noise . . . representing the report of a fair sized battle, and waking everybody within the city limits, who realized that the glad new year had come without cause of a reasonable doubt. The hilarity of the occasion lasted until late in the night, or rather early in the morning; . . ."[25]

The hilarity of the occasion changed to dread as the revelers awoke that New Year's Day to find temperatures ten to twenty degrees below zero and the north Kansas wind whipping a fine, dry snow. By the fourth morning everyone knew the weather would change, but it did not. The freezing temperatures remained and the drifting winds brought the most severe and damaging winter storms to Dodge City since its founding in 1872. The loss of range cattle was estimated at one-half to three-fourths in some herds. The Dodge City *Democrat* described the severity of this winter of 1885-'86:

"Some most pitiable cases of suffering and deaths have been reported.

"Hundreds of new-comers, living on claims in little, thin board shanties, either ignorant of our climate and misled by the beautiful and open winter until the first of the year, or careless of the kind of weather likely to come, were overtaken by these severe storms with little or no fuel and scanty supply of provisions. . . .

"The first storm commenced here on New Year's night and continued during the 2d and 3d, blockading the road so trains could not run until the afternoon of the 5th. The trains had not yet got to running regularly when the second storm and by far the most severe storm came. It commenced on the evening of the 13th and lasted during the following day and evening. . . . A west bound passenger train only a few miles east of the city has been snowed in for five or six days. Some of the passengers have walked in and provisions and fuel have been taken out by wagons to the balance. . . ."

The *Globe* reported: "Last Wednesday . . . fifty men . . . two coaches, a caboose, and four . . . locomotives, started out to the blockaded train. . . . For five days the work [shoveling snow] was kept up without gaining a car length. Thursday morning the train was snowed out of sight, and the entrance with coal and provisions to the eighty passengers, was made by going down a hole between two cars." Two hundred and forty men, women, and children, on five trains were stranded in Dodge City. Charitable citizens attempted to entertain the stranded travelers with a grand ball. Only six couples showed up for the dancing. The other snowbound excursionists had been warned of the danger of venturing on the

The ticket (left) and the invitation to an annual masquerade ball just below it, refer to the Opera House built by James H. Kelley in 1879, and rebuilt in brick after it burned in 1885. It was a popular gathering place for traveling variety companies, entertainments, dances, and political meetings.

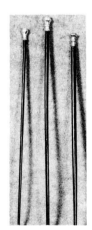

James H. (Dog) Kelley, shown (above) in 1900, gained his nickname from his fondness for greyhounds. Kelley raced his dogs and hunted the swift antelope which once ran free on the open ranges of western Kansas. The gold-headed cane (left) was given to Kelley by the Ford County Republican party in 1886 in appreciation of his services and the use of his hall for their convention.

Adolphus Gluck (right), watchmaker and jeweler, came to Dodge City in 1879. This lively Jewish merchant made friends quickly in the notorious Western town and was elected mayor in 1891. In 1898 he bought Kelley's Opera House and it was known as Gluck's Opera House until it burned in 1912.

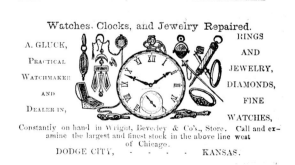

Morris Collar, a dealer in farmers' supplies, advertised this "Iron Turbine Wind Engine" (above) in the 1879 Dodge City Times. By 1885 the farm population south of Dodge City had overspread the open cattle ranges and helped bring about an end to Dodge City's cattle trail history.

These three unidentified tenderfeet with cigars slantindicular posed unrealistically in their cowboy garb around 1885. The adventurous trail drives from Texas to Kansas markets were ending; stock raising and cattle trading was a business for merchants and eastern investors; life in the far, far West was soon to be a memory recounted in dime novels and Buffalo Bill's Wild West performances.

The pioneer granger brought his horses, mules, and wagons to the fertile land of the Arkansas Valley to break the sod. By 1885 the farmers immigrating into the area provided the economic support needed to offset the end of the cattle trade.

streets of the "wicked little city" after dark, and were quick to believe that their lives might be in jeopardy in the notorious city of Dodge.

Dodge City in 1885 was on the certain road to prosperity. In one fell swoop, fire, ice, and a lingering period of depression reduced its dreams and extravagant plans for growth, quickly changing its face, its lusty habits, and its population of rough frontiersmen, gunmen, gamblers, and Western characters.

The quarantine dead line moved west, ending the Texas cattle trade; the blizzard of 1886 and the disappearance of open range broke the backs of local stockmen; the extensive freight business conducted out of Dodge City into Indian Territory was lost to the new railroads building up to the south; wheat prices dropped to forty cents a bushel, land to as low as fifty cents an acre.

Robert M. Wright lost 7,000 acres of land under the sheriff's hammer at tax sale. John Mueller, successful boot shop owner turned cattleman, lost his three ranch herds in the blizzard of 1886, and returned to boot making. By 1890 he was convinced that the new farm population did not have use for his custom made cowboy boots, and he returned to St. Louis. Adam Schmidt, a local blacksmith, successfully adapted to the changing economy of Dodge City, and purchased Mueller's fine home, the earliest stone home in Ford County.

After the fire in November, 1885, Dog Kelley rebuilt his Opera House in brick at the same site. Built at a cost of $20,000, the second floor was designed with an eighteen foot ceiling, stage, ticket office, lobby, and seating for one thousand. The first floor had five rooms rented to various stores and offices. In 1898 the building was purchased by Adolphus Gluck, a jeweler and mayor of Dodge City from 1891 to 1894. Gluck came to Dodge City from the western Kansas settlement of Ravanna, now a ghost town in Finney County. A shrewd businessman, he had a reputation in Dodge City of having "never from infancy been asleep with more than one eye at a time."[26] Dog Kelley, a pioneer founder of Dodge City, saloonkeeper, mayor, and political leader during the height of the cattle years, sold his Opera House to Gluck for $3,800. The *Globe-Republican* commented on the sale: "The mutation of fortune is one of those things that confounds philosophy. The former owner [of the Opera House, James H. Kelley] was last week employed on the streets as a day laborer."

Dodge City started as a buffalo hunting camp. With its railroad facilities, it soon became a shipping center for hides and meat and a terminus for government freight to the forts southwest into Indian Territory. Texas cattlemen made it their shipping and trading point from 1875 to 1885, the Cowboy Capital of the World. During its first fourteen years it was known for its lawlessness — "the wickedest little city in America." Its uniqueness, however, came from its efforts to establish law and order.

Dodge City's lawmen were controversial, sometimes reckless, often politically partisan, but all were strong in the face of violence. Men like Bat Masterson, Ed Masterson, Wyatt Earp, Charlie Bassett, and Larry Deger were a match for the early violence of the rough frontiersmen — buffalo hunters, soldiers, cowboys, drifters, and escaped criminals — men who had forgotten or never known the civilized ways of society. Later lawmen of Dodge, George Hinkle, Fred Singer, Bill Tilghman, and Pat Sughrue were less reckless and controversial but equally adept at enforcing law and order. They tamed the saloons, gambling, confidence rackets, and prostitution — forces that were condoned and supported by some of the earlier lawmen of old Dodge. The "mutation of fortune," the mysterious workings of nature and economics, brought about the final cracking of the whip, changing Dodge City from a town that "called that day lost whose low descending sun saw no man killed or other mischief done," to a center of wheat farming and feeder cattle.

While passing through its cattle town period, Dodge City experienced an agricultural development that carried it through the changing economics of 1886 to 1897. These years were ones of railroad speculation. Six roads had plans to build into Dodge City; only one, the Rock Island and Pacific Railroad, completed its contract and remained solvent through the depression of 1893-1897. Utility developments began in 1886 as electric lights, sewers, water works, streetcars, and telephone systems were developed to serve Dodge City. The city's expansion in these fields brought a financial crisis after 1891 when it failed to meet its bond obligations. For the next six years city warrants were settled at less than par, some at fifty cents on the dollar.

After 1901 Dodge City entered a new period of growth and prosperity, commercial and agricultural development, isolationism, and strict prohibition. Then came the dust storms and depression of the 1930's and another period of recovery and rebuilding. Dodge City is today a modern midwestern city with shaded streets, shopping centers, fine schools and churches, and active civic organizations. Still retaining its individuality, it has preserved the uniqueness of its past in museums and a replica of its early-day Front Street and Boot Hill cemetery.

For many years until the end of World War Two, some residents of Dodge City were hesitant to talk about its lurid past. When Jess C. Denious, a young newspaperman from Wichita, arrived in Dodge City in 1910 and purchased the *Globe,* he discovered a wealth of fascinating history in his old newspaper files. Thinking it would be interesting to republish the paper's articles about the days of Wyatt Earp and Bat Masterson, he proceeded to reprint some of these lusty accounts. Soon after the first article appeared, several local citizens called on Mr. Denious and informed him that this sort of thing just wasn't done in Dodge City.

Today Dodge City is proud of its Western heritage. There were no carbon copies of its Mysterious Dave, Off Wheeler, Horse Thief Ben, Dirty Ike, Blue Pete, Cock-eyed Frank, Concho, Dutch Kate, Little Dot, Eat-'em-up Jake, Stuttering Kid, Hop Fiend Nel, Emporia Belle, Scar-faced Lillie, Skunk Curley, and Big Eph. Dodge City boasts of more original characters among its pioneer population than any other city of the West. Its heroes, Wyatt Earp, Doc Holliday, Bat Masterson, Dog Kelley, Mike Sutton, Charlie Bassett, Jim Masterson, Larry Deger, Ed Masterson, Neil Brown, Luke Short, A. B. Webster, and Bill Tilghman, have grown bigger than life. Their history involves not only the facts about them but what the public has taken to be the facts.

"Braggin' saves advertisin'," said Sam Slick. As the nineteenth century ended the tendency of the Western pioneer to brag a bit furnished an abundance of material for dime novels, nickelodeons, Hollywood films, radio, and television. The history of the West has been a mother lode of entertainment riches, and the name, *Dodge City,* is its touchstone.

Wyatt Earp and Bat Masterson have evolved into brave and honest gunfighters who with courage and pure hearts bring law and civic order to their Western community like the modern folk hero, Marshal Matt Dillon, the fictional composite of Dodge's real characters. Indelibly impressed on the memory of the frontier spirit, Dodge City is part of the new folk literature of frontier conflict — the simple duel between right and wrong, white hat and black hat. From Yokohama to Frankfurt it conjures up the romanticized West — the courage of troopers, the dignity of the Indian, the stamina of cowboys, and the freedom of the lordly prairie — symbols that appeal to restless, dissatisfied, and searching people the world over.

Chapter VI
THE NEW DODGE CITY

The "New Dodge City," as the Globe-Republican called it in 1899, was no longer the city of "high carnival" where "rapturous lewdness and bawdiness held sway . . ." "Times have changed," said the Globe. " 'Clothed in her right mind,' Dodge City . . . took her departure from sin and lewdness and the city is now a paragon of virtue, sobriety and industry."

Front Street (above) around 1890, looking northeast from the newly erected city hall building south of the railroad tracks, shows brick buildings replacing the wooden structures after the fires in 1885. At left, on the corner, is the City Drug Store, an original wooden structure dating from 1872. The same view (right) from ground level shows the corner brick store of R. M. Wright & Co. The chimney of the new electric power plant can be seen in both pictures.

Clara Zimmermann (left) poses on her wedding day in 1889. Daughter of Frederick C. Zimmermann, Dodge City's gunsmith, she was born in Kit Carson, Colorado, and came to Dodge City with her family in the spring of 1872 on a flat car piled with ties for the new railroad building west. At age two months, she was the first baby to reside in the newly founded city.

Claude McCarty (right above) born in December of 1873, was one of the first births recorded in Dodge City. He was the son of Dr. Thomas L. McCarty who came to Dodge City with Mrs. McCarty in 1872.

Frederick C. Zimmermann and family standing behind their home, Fountain Grove, west of Dodge City, are seen harvesting ice from the Zimmermann fish pond and irrigation ditch in 1897. Zimmermann irrigated a large orchard and plantings of shade trees, seen at the left, a rarity in the early history of treeless western Kansas.

John Mueller, bootmaker and rancher, built this fine home of locally quarried stone in 1880. This picture, taken in 1889, shows Mueller and his son, Henry, on the porch balcony, and Mrs. Mueller and neighbors on the front steps. Mueller's house, later the residence of Adam Schmidt, a pioneer blacksmith, is now owned by the Ford County Historical Society, and is one of the few remaining from Dodge City's cattle town history.

Chalkley M. (Chalk) Beeson (below), owner of the Long Branch saloon, stockman, and farmer, sits with his sons, Otero and Merritt, and wife, Ida, around 1890.

An unidentified cowboy (above) poses on Merritt Beeson's pony, Jimmie, in front of Henry L. Sitler's house at the corner of First Avenue and Walnut Street (Gunsmoke) around 1890. In the background, at left, are the Methodist and Union churches, and at right, the court house.

Military Street east of Railroad Avenue (now Central Avenue) was a residential area in 1887 when the picture below was taken, looking southeast from the top of the Ford County Court House. The treeless prairie stretches to an unbroken horizon beyond the growing rail yard of the Atchison, Topeka & Santa Fe railroad.

149

Chalk Beeson (front row, center) in the picture at the left, used his musical ability to good advantage at his Saratoga and Long Branch saloons in the 1870's and '80's. Later his orchestra with son Merritt (second from left, seated) and Otero (with drum), played at the fashionable gatherings of the '90's and early 1900's.

Money was raised in June, 1878, to purchase musical instruments for a "Dodge City Silver Cornet Band," and the Times bragged that "Dodge City can toot her own horn." The Silver Cornet Band, later called the "Dodge City Brass Band," led parades on the Glorious Fourth, played in muted, minor key for funeral processions, entertained at openings of saloons and flour mills, and serenaded on election day. In 1880 it began calling itself the "Cowboy Band" (right). Dressed in leather chaps, boots, spurs, bandannas, and cowboy hats, each member carried an ivory-handled six-shooter and wore a cowboy hat decorated with an outline of a longhorn steer and a prominent cattle brand. Their audiences in Kansas City, Chicago, St. Louis, and other points east were fascinated with real cowboys playing music with skill and gusto. The highlight of the Cowboy Band history was its appearance at the inauguration

of President Benjamin Harrison in Washington, D.C., on March 4, 1889. The original Cowboy Band instruments shown below include a side drum owned by W. G. Viquesney, dating from the Civil War. The leather chaps are those of Chalk Beeson, manager and organizer of the band.

The Dodge City Cowboy Band in 1886 is shown at the left. D. M. Frost, vice-president (front row left) was editor and publisher of the Dodge City Globe-Republican. S. S. Prouty, press agent (front row right), was editor and publisher of the Kansas Cowboy, another Dodge City newspaper. Manager Chalk Beeson sits next to Prouty, and Musical Director Roy Drake is on the second row behind the drums.

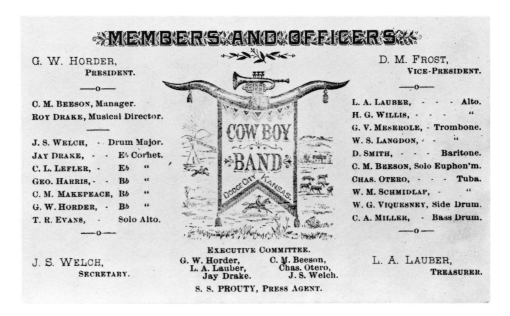

MEMBERS AND OFFICERS

G. W. HORDER,
PRESIDENT.

—o—

C. M. BEESON, Manager.
ROY DRAKE, Musical Director.

———

J. S. WELCH, - Drum Major.
JAY DRAKE, - Eb Cornet.
C. L. LEFLER, - Eb "
GEO. HARRIS, - Bb "
C. M. MAKEPEACE, Bb "
G. W. HORDER, - Bb "
T. R. EVANS, - Solo Alto.

—o—

D. M. FROST,
VICE-PRESIDENT.

—o—

L. A. LAUBER, - - Alto.
H. G. WILLIS, - - - "
G. V. MESEROLE, - Trombone.
W. S. LANGDON, - - "
D. SMITH, - - Baritone.
C. M. BEESON, Solo Euphon'm.
CHAS. OTERO, - - Tuba.
W. M. SCHMIDLAP, - "
W. G. VIQUESNEY, Side Drum.
C. A. MILLER, - Bass Drum.

—o—

COW BOY BAND
DODGE CITY KANSAS

EXECUTIVE COMMITTEE.
G. W. Horder,   C. M. Beeson,
L. A. Lauber,   Chas. Otero,
Jay Drake,   J. S. Welch.

S. S. PROUTY, PRESS AGENT.

J. S. WELCH,
SECRETARY.

L. A. LAUBER,
TREASURER.

In 1890 Dodge City's Cowboy Band disbanded and sold its uniforms, musical instruments, and equipment to a group which reorganized the band in Pueblo, Colorado, but retained the name, Dodge City Cowboy Band (below). In 1905 the band was transferred to Idaho Springs, Colorado. A new Dodge City Cowboy Band was organized in Dodge City in the spring of 1911 (above), but the young, clean-shaven faces were of another generation that remembered little of the rip-roaring cattle days.

P. G. Reynolds' tame buffalo got wind of a visiting band parading the streets in February 1886, and took exception. With head down and tail up (left) he charged, the music ceased, and the band did some excellent running. The Globe described it as "the worst broke up parade you ever saw."

Around 1890, Dodge City's hose cart team (above) could run 200 yards from a standing start, stretch 100 feet of hose, and put water on a blaze in 31 and 4/5ths seconds. The team, dubbed "prairie grass-eaters" and "bow-legged grangers" by the oldtimers, paraded and competed with other fire company teams, but they are not known to have put out any real fires while in "uniform." Their hose company building (left) was Dodge City's first fire station.

Gluck's Opera House, formerly Kelley's Opera House, west of First Avenue between Front and Chestnut Streets (above), burned in March, 1912. One of the city's earliest fire trucks (left), is filling up at Ham Bell's auto company on Chestnut Street.

Asa T. Soule (right above), patent medicine magnate from Rochester, New York, came to south-west Kansas in 1883 to found the city of Ingalls and make various investments — a national bank in Dodge City, private banks in Ingalls and Spearville, and a new railroad, the Dodge City, Montezuma, and Trinidad, completed but later abandoned. He donated land at the north edge of Dodge City and $50,000 to build a Presbyterian college (above left). Soule College opened in 1888, but because of financial difficulties, it was sold to the Methodist Church in 1893. In 1912 it became a girls' school, Saint Mary of the Plains (below), operated by Sisters of Saint Joseph of Wichita, Kansas.

In May, 1942, a tornado destroyed Soule's buildings and Saint Mary of the Plains closed until 1952 when it was reopened at a new site — now a co-educational four-year college.

Asa T. Soule organized the Eureka Irrigation Canal Company in 1883 to draw water from the Arkansas River at Ingalls, 96 miles across Gray and Ford counties, into Coon Creek in Edwards County. Work began near Dodge in 1884, and water reached Spearville in July, 1888. An ambitious and expensive engineering project, the canal eventually went dry when similar schemes upstream and periods of drought lowered the river's water level. This construction camp (above) was northeast of Dodge City near Spearville. The scenes below show the canal under construction with horse-drawn equipment, an ambitious four-year project. Shortly before Soule's death in 1890, the canal company stock was sold to English investors for $1,100,000.

Water flows through the Soule ditch in 1911 six miles west of Dodge City, in pictures at the left and below.

The two pictures at the bottom of the page show early-day wheat harvesting. On the left is a threshing scene on the Chalk Beeson farm around 1894. At the right is another scene showing headers cutting in the field around 1890.

This flour mill at Santa Fe Trail Street and Seventh Avenue was destroyed by fire in April of 1890.

The Dodge City Mill and Elevator Company (left) at the northeast corner of Second Avenue and Trail Street.

A well-known old threshing machine (below).

Wheat harvest crew in July, 1918.

Harvest crew, around 1905.

157

John T. Riney (left), former member of the Confederate Congress, came to Dodge City in August, 1872, with a crew building the grade for the approaching Santa Fe railroad. Riney was tollkeeper for the first bridge across the Arkansas River at Dodge City. This bridge (right, in high water) at the south end of Second Avenue, then called Bridge Street, was completed by the Dodge City Bridge Company in 1874 at a cost of $8,000.

A Bridge Company toll ticket good for a return trip with a two-horse team, signed by John Riney, tollkeeper in 1874.

In 1885 Dodge City's toll bridge was purchased by the county and became a free bridge. Repairing the old wooden bridge (above) became a burden, and in 1906 it was replaced with a steel structure.

Dodge City looked prosperous as seen from south of the bridge in 1888. Prominent landmarks are the first school on Boot Hill at the left, Bell's Elephant stable straight ahead, and the court house at the far right. George Reighard and William States, early Dodge City merchants, operated their stable and hotel (ad at right) at the south end of the bridge in 1880 before the toll was removed.

The unusual "bird's eye view" above shows Dodge City in the spring of 1887 at the end of its wild cattle trail history. Below, left, Dodge City's steel bridge was built in 1906 to replace the wooden toll bridge (above) across the Arkansas River. The cyclist, out for a Sunday ride, stops on the new bridge, probably around 1914 when Dodge City was widely known for its Fourth of July motorcycle races.

The concrete bridge (left below) across the Arkansas replaced the steel bridge in 1935. It was officially named Riney Bridge in June, 1967, (right below) to honor John T. Riney, pioneer of Dodge City and tollkeeper of the first bridge across the Arkansas at Dodge City.

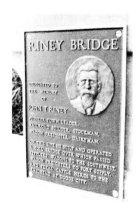

The Rev. Ormond W. Wright (right), Dodge City's first full-time minister, conducted the funerals of many early victims of the festive revolver and preached in the non-denominational Union Church (above) built in 1876. The butt of many cowboy pranks, he persevered, and in 1879 was the organizer and first minister of the Presbyterian Church in Dodge City.

The Presbyterian Church (left), the first denominational church building in Dodge City, was built in 1880 on Central Avenue. The Methodist Church (center), built in 1883 on First Avenue, was organized in 1874, the first religious society founded in Dodge City. The Catholic Church (right), built in 1882 on Central Avenue, held services earlier in the court house and the Union Church.

The Christian Church (left) was built in 1893 on the southwest corner of Second Avenue and Spruce Street. Third Ward School on Boot Hill can be seen in the background. The Baptist Church was organized in 1879 and built its church (center) at Sixth Avenue and Cedar Street in 1885. The Episcopal Church was organized in 1888. Its building (right) at First Avenue and Spruce Street was completed in 1898, and remains the oldest church building still in use in Dodge City.

Alice Wright (Mrs. Robert M.) came to western Kansas with her husband in 1859.

Calvina Anthony (Mrs. A. J.), mother of eleven children, came to Dodge City after her marriage in 1872, and found few families with the courage to stay.

Carrie Rath (Mrs. Charles) came to Dodge City in 1872 with her husband, a dealer in buffalo hides and an Indian trader.

Amanda Webster came from Hays City with her husband, Alonzo B., in 1872.

Matilda Zimmermann (Mrs. Frederick C.) came to Dodge City with two babies in 1872 to join her husband, Dodge City's gunsmith.

Sally McCarty (Mrs. T. L.), wife of the first doctor to settle in Dodge City, set up housekeeping in a lean-to behind Fringer's drug store in 1872.

Sara Evans (Mrs. Richard W.) came from Hays City in 1872 and settled in a plain wooden building behind her husband's store on Front Street.

Jennie Collar came from Hays City in 1872 with her husband, Jacob, Front Street dealer in furniture and coffins.

The monument, left, above, was erected in 1927 to mark the location of the first school house in Dodge City, built in 1873, at the northwest corner of First Avenue and Gunsmoke (Walnut) Street. Dodge City's first school was replaced by the brick schoolhouse on Boot Hill (above) in September, 1880. Construction began in 1879 soon after the bodies on Boot Hill were removed and placed in the first official cemetery east of town.

Left, above, is shown Mrs. Margaret A. Walker, the first woman school teacher in Dodge City. Directly below is the bell placed in the tower of the Boot Hill school in August, 1880, by Col. J. W. Straughn, the county coroner, who moved Boot Hill bodies to their new resting place in Prairie Grove Cemetery. Right, above, is Dodge City's Second Ward school, built around 1886 on Central Avenue.

A first grade class (left) in 1887.

A stage production by an unidentified Dodge City school group (above) in the 1880's. The Third Ward School (right) replaced the original Boot Hill School in 1890 at the same site. It remained on Dodge City's Boot Hill until 1927 when it was razed for the location of a new city hall.

Home talent (below) in the cast of "Mrs. Jarley's Waxworks," the latest hit in 1910.

These ladies and one studious gentleman (above) posed for their grammar school commencement exercises in Gluck's Opera House in May, 1900.

Dr. T. L. McCarty (at left) participates with members of the Dodge City Bicycle Club around 1890.

163

Dr. McCarty's City Drug Store on Front Street at Second Avenue is seen from the front around 1882 above; the inside of the drug store is seen below around 1889.

Dr. Thomas L. McCarty, a pioneer physician of Dodge City, established his practice here in 1872. At the right is Dr. McCarty's Chinese houseboy, Sing Lee.

Dr. W. F. Pine (left), a founder of the Ford County Medical Society, started as a clerk in the City Drug Store. Dr. C. A. Milton (right) came to Dodge City in 1882 and associated with its pioneer physician, Dr. T. L. McCarty.

McCarty Hospital (below) was opened in 1905 by Drs. T. L. McCarty and his son, Claude. The building, originally built in 1885 for a hotel, was converted into Dodge City's first hospital.

Dr. Samuel J. Crumbine (left) settled in Dodge City in 1885. He became secretary of the State Board of Health in 1904, and won national recognition for his "Swat the Fly" and "Don't Spit on the Sidewalk" campaigns and for his crusades against the common drinking cup and roller towel.

DODGE CITY MESSENGER.
VOLUME 1.   DODGE CITY, KANSAS, THURSDAY, FEBRUARY 26, 1874.   NUMBER 1.

DODGE CITY TIMES.
VOL. IV.   DODGE CITY, KANSAS, APRIL 13, 1878.   NO. 22.

Ford County Globe.
VOL. IV.   DODGE CITY, KANSAS, JANUARY 1, 1881.   NO. 3.

The Dodge City Democrat.

Volume 1.   DODGE CITY, KANSAS JULY 5, 1884   Number 44

D. M. FROST

LLOYD SHINN

N. B. KLAINE

The newspapers whose nameplates are shown above were the recorders of Dodge City's early wild and woolly history. The Messenger was brought to Dodge City by A. W. Moore who moved his equipment from Holton, Kansas, in February, 1874, and established the first newspaper. He suspended in the spring of 1875, just prior to the booming of the cattle business. The Times was first published in May, 1876, by brothers Lloyd and Walter C. Shinn. Lloyd Shinn (center left) left the newspaper in 1878 to run a buffalo hide tannery in Dodge City. Nicholas B. Klaine (lower left) purchased Shinn's interest in the Times and was its editor and publisher until its suspension in 1893. The Ford County Globe was first printed in December, 1877, by Daniel M. Frost (upper left) and W. N. Morphy. Shortly after, Lloyd Shinn, unsuccessful at buffalo tanning, joined Frost in publication of the Globe. It became the Globe Live Stock Journal, the Globe-Republican, the Dodge City Globe, and finally the Daily Globe in 1911. The Dodge City Democrat, founded in 1884, became the Journal-Democrat, later the Dodge City Journal, now the High Plains Journal, a five-state agricultural publication. The Kansas Cowboy was a short-lived newspaper brought to Dodge City in 1884 from Ness County by Col. Samuel S. Prouty. At that time all of the newspapers pictured above except the Messenger were publishing weekly in Dodge City. Prouty's paper was twice burned out in the fires of 1885, and never revived. Below is shown the interior of the Dodge City Globe-Republican in 1906.

The town's first city hall (left) was dedicated in September, 1888. Located south of the railroad tracks and west of Second Avenue, it replaced the two-story wooden shack used for thirteen years as a city jail and city clerk's office. The new city hall housed a United States land office, the fire department, and other city offices. Below, Ham Bell (far left) stands with his horses and livery crew in front of the city hall around 1893.

The wagons (below) are loading seed barley from a Rock Island car in the spring of 1918. Ham Bell's building, originally the Elephant Stable, is in the background (at right) west of the city hall. In the picture at the right a circus parades north across the railroad tracks in 1912.

F. C. Zimmermann's hardware store on Front Street (above) in 1890 could supply nearly every need from buggies to bullwhips.

Front Street (above) around 1890, between First and Second Avenues contained (from left) Wright's general merchandise store, the Palace drug store, the Long Branch and St. James saloons, Adolph Gluck's jewelry store, F. C. Zimmermann's hardware store, the Delmonico hotel and restaurant, the York-Draper Mercantile Co., Kirkpatrick & Dunn's furniture store, and James H. Kelley's Opera House at the east corner. R. M. Wright rebuilt his store (left) at the same location after his original brick building burned with the rest of the wooden structures in this block in 1885.

In 1900 the York-Draper Mercantile Co. (right) placed more emphasis on women's apparel than it did during the booming business of the earlier cattle trade.

The store (left) was formerly the ornate Delmonico hotel and restaurant. In 1898 it was the jewelry store of Philip H. Young who shared his quarters with druggist W. S. Amos. Young (far left) started as a cowhand, ranching twenty-five miles east of Dodge City in 1878, but turned to his original trade of jeweler and watchmaker when the cattle boom ended in 1885.

The building (left), its pyramid-shaped cupola an early landmark, was built in 1885 to house the town's first bank, The Bank of Dodge City, founded in 1882. It was built on the corner of Front Street and First Avenue, the original location of Webster's Old House saloon. The Bank of Dodge City closed its doors in 1889, other banks formed and failed, and in 1904 the First National Bank in Dodge City, known then as the National Bank of Commerce, opened here.

Looking north up First Avenue from Front Street around 1910 (above), the Kelley-Gluck Opera House is at the left. The view changed (below) after the Opera House fire of 1912, as seen here around 1920.

Front Street west of Second Avenue around 1912.

A Fourth of July parade (left above) passes by the City Drug Store on Front Street in 1899. Right, above, the Robinson hardware store east of the City Drug Store is shown around 1890. Below, the City Hardware Store around 1910 at the northwest corner of Front Street and Second Avenue was formerly the City Drug Store. Built in 1872, it was the last original Front Street building to be razed.

A Fourth of July parade in 1899 (left above) passes the Merchants State Bank and post office at the corner of Chestnut Street (Wyatt Earp Blvd.) and Second Avenue. Right, above, is shown Billy Baeder's "Joint" on Front Street between First and Central Avenues.

A lady with baby and carriage, at the left, pauses in front of the post office, cater-cornered from the Bee Hive dry goods store, Chestnut and Second Avenue around 1894. The Bee Hive dry goods is shown at the right.

Chestnut Street looking east, the main business thoroughfare, around 1902.

170

The Stars and Stripes fly from the Army recruiting office in the Rath and Bainbridge drug store building (left) at Chestnut Street and First Avenue around 1916.

A popular spot around 1900 was the soda fountain in this drug store (above) on Second Avenue.

The old U.S. Signal Service Station, built in 1875, stands dilapidated (above) at the corner of Walnut Street (Gunsmoke) and Second Avenue around 1914.

This crowd stands (left) in front of Dr. T. L. McCarty's roller skating rink in 1909. McCarty's building, originally a theater, was built in 1885.

The party shown at the right was held at the McCarty rink in 1891.

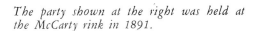

171

The entrance to the National Bank of Commerce (above), seen here in 1912, is at the north end of its original location, the corner of First Avenue and Chestnut Street. At the right, the short and jaunty Adolph Gluck, a director, stands, hat atilt, second from left, with the cashiers and bookkeepers of the National Bank of Commerce. At the upper right is the State Bank of Dodge City, chartered in 1898. Its entrance in 1918 was the white door at left on Second Avenue. This bank consolidated with another in 1933 and became the present Fidelity State Bank of Dodge City.

Rural mail carrier J. B. Shumard (above) stops in front of the city hall around 1909. To the left, this view of Dodge City around 1910 looks west to the Third Ward School on Boot Hill. The City Furniture Store, a new location for the post office, is one door south (left) of a frame house once owned by Bat Masterson from July 1879 to October 1881.

172

The Greensburg Commercial Club tours through Dodge City past the Bee Hive dry goods in June, 1912.

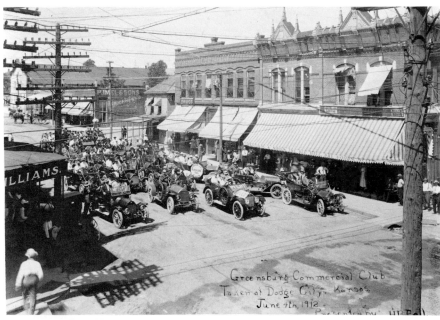

The spire of the Catholic Church can be seen in the background (below) of this growing residential district, looking south on Central Avenue past Division Street around 1910.

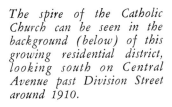

The "Ol' Swimmin' Hole" was at the foot of Boot Hill as seen above around 1916, with Third Ward School in the background.

Frank Cox (at left) does a thriving business in 1910 at his Pioneer Barber Shop, formerly the Long Branch saloon on Front Street. Chalk Beeson, owner of the building, keeps mementoes of the Long Branch hanging over the mirror.

The salesman above has just landed a big order with Stubbs meat market on Second Avenue south of Walnut Street in 1915.

173

Looking east on Spruce Street from the bell tower of the Third Ward school on Boot Hill in 1909. In the center-background, at left, is the McCarty hospital, at right the court house. The newly erected Carnegie public library is at the northwest corner of Spruce Street and Second Avenue (center left), the First Baptist Church at the northeast corner. Below, is shown Third Avenue at Walnut Street. flooding after a hard rain in July, 1911.

In 1886 the population of Dodge City was a little less than 4,000. By 1888 it was over 7,500. McCarty hospital and the court house are seen in this picture showing construction in progress on the one hundred foot chimney of the Electric Light & Steam Heat Co. building in 1887.

The Electric Light & Steam Heat Co., facing north on Walnut Street, supplied power for the first electric lights in Dodge City.

In the background of the picture below, from left to right, is the Dodge City Mill & Elevator Co., the Great Western hotel, and the city hall. seen looking southeast from the Third Ward school in 1909.

VIEW OF BRICK GANG SHOWING SAND CUSHION,
BRICK SETTERS AND ASPHALT KETTLE IN BACKGROUND.
W. E. BALDRY, CITY ENG'R.

These brick streets were laid in Dodge City in 1914 — here we are looking south on First Avenue (above), and looking north (below).

VIEW OF VERTICLE FIBER BRICK PAVING AT DODGE CITY
SHOWING SETTERS AT WORK.

Dodge City was a railroad town from its founding in 1872. This view from the city hall tower around 1900 shows the east end of Front Street and the Santa Fe's new depot, Harvey House restaurant, and hotel.

The first rail was spiked May 11, 1912, on the Dodge City and Cimarron Valley Railroad, a short line absorbed later by the A. T. & S. F.

An A. T. & S. F. pile driver works above on a washout at the foot of Third Avenue.

A locomotive's view of Dodge City around 1900 would be this picture to the left, approaching Dodge City from the west.

*Old No. 314 toots its whistle for two Dodge City railroad buffs standing on its running board —
Mike Sutton's son, Stuart, and his friend, pioneer physician, Dr. T. L. McCarty.*

*The Rock Island depot at Dodge City (left) was built in 1897. A Rock Island locomotive (right
above) stops for its photo alongside the city hall in Dodge City.*

*An Atchison, Topeka and Santa Fe locomotive poses, decked out for the Fourth of July in 1891 (left
above). The A. T. & S. F. modern reproduction (right above) of a similar locomotive is dubbed the
"Cyrus K. Holliday," named for the builder and first president of the Santa Fe railroad.*

The Santa Fe freight and passenger depots around 1909 are shown right.

The Atchison, Topeka and Santa Fe depot was completed in January, 1898. It housed a Fred Harvey hotel and dining room, and was "fire proofed" with a tile and copper roof and iron awnings. The Harvey House dining room, an institution of local pride for fifty years, was named El Vaquero (The Cowboy). An early view of the Harvey House lobby is seen below.

The Harvey Girls in their standard uniforms of black shoes and stockings and plain black dress (above) had to have their hair plainly done and ornamented with a white ribbon, only, neatly tied. Adept in culinary niceties and social poise that distinguished Harvey House staffs, their starting wage was $17.50 a month plus tips, board, and sleeping quarters.

Robert M. Wright, standing here with his son, Connor (above), planted these trees which are now part of the city park named for him. Wright was a freighter, stage line operator, Indian fighter, wood and hay contractor, Army post trader, townsite proprietor, shipper of buffalo hides, and an outfitter of hunters, cow hands, cattle drovers, and stockmen. He was a state legislator, mayor of Dodge City, and an influential leader during Dodge City's formative years.

George M. Hoover and wife, Margaret,(above) here give little hint of Dodge City's early rough and tumble days. Custom and tradition have it that the city began when Hoover (above) pitched his tent on the townsite and began selling whisky from a barrel and tin cup. Hoover left a large part of his estate at death in 1914 to the city of Dodge City, partly to build the Hoover Pavilion (left), a popular public meeting hall in Wright Park.

Four of Dodge City's patriarchs (right) at the dedication of a Santa Fe Trail marker at the corner of Santa Fe Trail Street and Second Avenue in 1906. From left are A. J. Anthony, post trader and rancher, John Riney, first tollkeeper of Dodge City's bridge across the Arkansas, Robert M. Wright, and Michael W. Sutton.

Ham Bell, early day liveryman, shows off his new 1926 Chalmers roadster to three of his pioneer friends: (from left) Dr. T. L. McCarty, first doctor to reside in Dodge City; Bell; Brick Bond, buffalo hunter, saloonkeeper, and druggist; and George W. Reighard, freighter, buffalo hunter and rancher. All witnessed the founding of Dodge City except Bell, who arrived in 1874, remained an active merchant for seventy years, and left the Western scene at the age of ninety-four.

Chapter VII
THE NOW DODGE CITY

A view of Front Street (above) around 1930 shows that R. M. Wright & Co. is now F. W. Woolworth Co., the City Drug store corner is a filling station, and a new five-story "skyscraper" has risen in the background.

The Front Street buildings, built after the fires of 1885, were razed in 1970 to make way for downtown improvements. Boot Hill Museum's Front Street Replica, a reproduction of the original wooden buildings, can be seen in the upper left background, a reminder of Dodge City's history and legend.

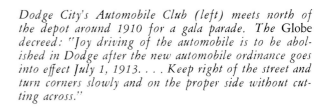

Dodge City's Automobile Club (left) meets north of the depot around 1910 for a gala parade. The Globe decreed: "Joy driving of the automobile is to be abolished in Dodge after the new automobile ordinance goes into effect July 1, 1913. . . . Keep right of the street and turn corners slowly and on the proper side without cutting across."

Cornerstone laying ceremonies (right) were held in 1912 for the new Ford County court house.

The new court house, shown at the left under construction, was completed in May, 1913, at a cost of $100,000.

Footings are being laid (above) for a new five-story hotel in Dodge City. The completed court house is in the background. The new hotel (left) completed in 1928, was named the Lora-Locke for Lora Howell, wife of the hotel's president, and Harriet Locke Theis, wife of its secretary-treasurer.

182

Ham Bell displays his Chalmers touring car (right) and hearse in front of his Land and Auto Company around 1916. Ham owned the first horse-drawn hearse and the first motor-driven hearse in Dodge City.

These Dodge City matrons helped with the American Red Cross canteen at the Santa Fe depot in 1917.

A welcome arch was built in the summer of 1919 and placed at the intersection of Second Avenue and Walnut Street to welcome home the soldiers and sailors of World War I.

Ham Bell, age ninety-one, (left) viewing the fourth war in his lifetime, christens a Marauder B-26 at the Dodge City Army Air Field in 1942.

Uncle Sam and his cow pony (right) lead the parade celebrating the Dodge City Army Air Field's open house in 1944.

The Globe *in December, 1911, noted: "Greatest snow fall ever recorded, 14.5 inches during the past 36 hours. There is joy in the Western Kansas Camp today and 1912 wheat crop is going up several points per hour." Pictures above show 1911-1912 snow storms. Below, a winter storm in the early 1930's brought Dodge City traffic to a standstill, with a blanket of deep snow.*

Five years of drought brought dust storms that climaxed in one of the area's worst (left above) in April, 1935. This tornado (right above) struck north of Dodge City in May, 1949. Dodge City was paralyzed with an early spring blizzard (left below) in 1956. The Arkansas River rampaged (right below) in this disastrous flood of 1942, and again in 1965.

184

Ham Bell, Dodge City pioneer, and Ann Sheridan (left) say howdy on the Hollywood set of Dodge City. Bell was a member of the committee in Hollywood to invite Jack Warner to hold the premiere of his film in the Cowboy Capital.

A Kansas delegation stands on the Dodge City set at Warner Brothers studio with Ann Sheridan and executive producers Jack L. Warner and Hal B. Wallis. From the left: Dodge City old timer Dr. Claude E. McCarty, Wallis, Kansas Lieutenant Governor C. E. Friend, Warner, Kansas Senator Jess C. Denious, Sheridan, Chamber of Commerce president Harry M. Starks, and Ham Bell.

"Oomph" girl, Ann Sheridan (right), plays Ruby, a saloon girl in the "Gay Lady" dance hall.

Two scenes from Dodge City (above), directed by Academy Award winner, Michael Curtiz, were part of the story that made this Warner Brothers big budget film the beginning of a new trend of historical Westerns. . . . The Dodge City premiere became an extravagant publicity trip for Warner Brothers. Their stars posed for pictures (below) at each stop of the chartered Santa Fe special from Los Angeles to Dodge City. Front row, from left: Hoot Gibson, Buck Jones, Guinn (Big Boy) Williams, Humphrey Bogart, Jean Parker, and Lola Lane. Back row, from left: Frank McHugh, Slapsie Maxie Rosenbloom, Priscilla Lane, Errol Flynn, John Garfield, Rosemary Lane, Wayne Morris, John Payne, and Alan Hale.

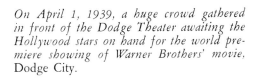

On April 1, 1939, a huge crowd gathered in front of the Dodge Theater awaiting the Hollywood stars on hand for the world premiere showing of Warner Brothers' movie, Dodge City.

Fifty Thousand fans waited three hours at the Santa Fe depot (below) to greet two dozen stars — some from the cast of Dodge City, some Hollywood window dressing.

Errol Flynn arrives in Dodge City appropriately surrounded by Hollywood beauties (from left) Priscilla Lane, Rosemary Lane, and Jean Parker.

Errol Flynn makes his appearance (below) on the stage of the Dodge Theater, one of three where the premiere festivities were held simultaneously through the night.

Errol Flynn accepts the key to Dodge City. From left, standing: Lola Lane, Frank McHugh, Flynn, Rosemary Lane, Priscilla Lane, and Jean Parker. In front of Flynn squat Humphrey Bogart (left) and John Garfield.

Humphrey Bogart sits with wife number three, Mayo Methot, and John Payne at a dinner honoring the dignitaries in Dodge City. Bogart had yet to gain his stardom in the 1941 hit, The Maltese Falcon, and Casablanca in 1942.

This ad appeared in a German-language news-paper in 1939, three months after Germany's invasion of Poland. It announced the latest hit from America, Der Draufganger von Dodge City (The Daredevil of Dodge City) mit Errol Flynn. According to this movie advertisement, Dodge City was "the city of adventure and women of ill repute; the city of the famous dancer from the Red Lantern cabaret; the meeting place of the sons of Buffalo Bill; and the city of robbers, bandits, and pimps." The appearance of TV's Gunsmoke in European cities since World War II has done little to change this conception of the now-peaceful western Kansas community.

Gunsmoke, America's favorite TV Western, is familiar to viewers in Japan, distributed by Fuji Television Company with dubbed voices of Japanese actors and actresses. A page (right) from a Fuji news release for Japanese newspapers and magazines says: "Introducing the cast of the program — James Arness is Marshal Matt Dillon, with a physique of six feet six inches, making him ideal for the character of Dillon, the sole upholder of law and order in Dodge City." Note the characters sidelined with dashes, Japanese phonetics for Dodge City, a name now familiar to television fans the world around.

この映画の主人公であるディロンというのは硝煙けむる西部の荒野をガンを片手に粗末な服を着て大股に歩み去る長身の男。

六フィート六インチ、二二五ポンドの見事な体格のスターヂェイムス・アーネスは、もはやマーシャル・ディロンその人である。

この六尺豊かなディロンはいわば〝男がほれる男〟の理想像であろう。ガンの早さはもとより、その反面の冷静さ、人間味、優しさなどにむしろスポットがあてられている。

マーシャル・ディロンはアメリカの開拓の歴史に一頁を加えたダッヂ・シティーのみすぼらしい、しかも英雄である一保安官のほろしの姿なのだ。

∧出演者紹介∨

ヂェイムス・アーネス…マーシャル・マット・ディロン

六呎六吋のその巨体だけでも、アーネスはディロンその人になり切つていた、ダッヂ・シティーの法を守る唯一の人物と思えるから

— 159 —

In 1970, Front Street fell under demolition crews, (above) clearing the now blighted area for off-street parking and downtown beautification (left below). The Bank of Dodge City (right below), a private banking corporation, built this building in 1885 at the Front Street and First Avenue corner location of the Old House saloon. The home of Dodge City's first bank fell to the wrecker's hammer in 1970.

Front Street (below), a part of Dodge City's legend, has been accurately reproduced in a picturesque replica, drawing thousands to Dodge City each year.

Dr. O. H. Simpson (center above), a pioneer dentist of the Southwest, came to Dodge City in 1885. His top hat brought jeers from Front Street loungers, but his practice prospered. Known in dentistry for his techniques of casting gold inlays, he is better known in Dodge City for his sculpture. Simpson's cowboy statue, cast in cement from a live model — Policeman Joe Sughrue — is shown here in 1928 before its placement on Boot Hill. The steer heads, upper right, also by Dr. Simpson, were erected on Boot Hill as a reminder of the Texas cattle driven to the Dodge City railhead.

Boot Hill cemetery was revived at its original location with cement death masks and boots cast by Dr. Simpson. As a joke during a 1932 Rotary convention, Simpson made some skulls and boots, and buried them on the cemetery site. The mock graves attracted so much attention they were left on Boot Hill near the city hall. Simpson's cowboy statue was unveiled in 1929 (right above) as part of the dedication ceremonies for the new city hall. Added to this statue was the inscription, "On the Ashes of My Campfire This City Is Built." The city hall (right) was dedicated in November, 1929 as part of a "Last Roundup" celebration to honor the early pioneers of Dodge City.

189

Merritt Beeson, son of Chalk Beeson, breaks the sod (right) on Boot Hill in 1947 for construction of its first museum (below). For two generations the Beeson family collected and preserved relics, artifacts, and pictures of Dodge City's history now housed in this museum.

The Fort Dodge jail (above), built at the military outpost in 1864 five miles east of Dodge City, is now located near the Boot Hill Museum. The only undisturbed portion of Boot Hill (left) is now fenced off to memorialize its former use as a cemetery from 1872 to 1879. Dr. Simpson's cement boots and death masks, carried away by vandals, have been replaced by ironic epitaphs and the remains of a hangman's tree from Horse Thief canyon northeast of Dodge City.

Hugh O'Brien, star of the Wyatt Earp *television series, stands with Mayor Nate Reese at the cornerstone dedication of Dodge City's Front Street replica in 1958.*

This replica of Front Street in the 1870's (above) contains a variety theater, restaurant, shops, and fine museum displays (below).

Col. Richard J. (Jack) Hardesty, Dodge City cattleman and rancher, and his wife, Maggie (above) came to Dodge City in 1880 to make their home, which now (below) restored, with original furnishings, is relocated near the Front Street replica.

General Store.

Frontier Bank.

Gunsmoke's *Miss Kitty* views relics from the Long Branch saloon.

A skeleton uncovered in 1950 is on display in the Boot Hill Museum.

In July, 1966, The Texas Longhorn Breeders Association, commemorating the one hundredth anniversary of the beginning of the great trail drives of Texas cattle, ended its modern longhorn cattle drive in Dodge City.

The marshal and his posse meet the incoming stage, re-enacting Dodge City's exciting past.

Visitors to Dodge City's Boot Hill and Front Street

Hugh O'Brien, television's Wyatt Earp.

Smiley Burnett examining the festive revolvers of old Dodge.

Joel McCrea, lawman in the movie, Gunfighter in Dodge City.

Kansas Governor Fred Hall and Miss Kitty (Amanda Blake).

Senator John F. Kennedy, speaking in Dodge City during his primary campaigns of 1959, accepted a cowboy hat and traditional welcome from Marshal Ramon K. House. Rarely photographed in a hat, he posed stiffly for this picture. Later, President-elect Kennedy invited the marshal and his colorful posse to ride in the 1960 inaugural parade.

Kansas Governor Robert Docking and Ramon K. House, Marshal of Dodge City.

Victor Borge, the Danish Luke McGlue, at work in the Long Branch saloon.

Matt Dillon (James Arness), "upholder of law and order in Dodge City," renames Walnut Street, Gunsmoke, after his television series, at these ceremonies in 1958.

James King, Wagnerian tenor — home town boy returns.

Vice President Hubert Humphrey becomes an honorary marshal.

Chill Wills, dry as a buffalo chip, warmly accepts Miss Kitty's invitation to step into the Long Branch for a dust of grog.

Spiro Agnew joins the exclusive group of vice presidents who are honorary marshals of Dodge City.

Scenes from Gunsmoke, *a TV Western adapted from radio that has used Dodge City's uproarious reputation for over twenty years as a plot for its unexaggerated, believable tales of the far West.*

Gunsmoke's *cast have been frequent visitors to Dodge City. From left: Amanda Blake (Kitty), James Arness (Matt), and Milburn Stone (Doc).*

A real Dodge City marshal — Ramon K. House.

193

Credits

Except as otherwise shown, all illustrations are courtesy of the Kansas State Historical Society, Topeka, and the Boot Hill Museum, Dodge City.

Special appreciation is extended to the following for permission to use the many other photographs which were courteously made available for reproduction here.

Page 4, Wooden Cross: Lola Harper, Dodge City, Kan.

Page 5, Santa Fe Trail Map: Cultural Heritage Center, Dodge City.

Page 8, Fort Dodge Dugouts: Kansas Soldiers' Home, Fort Dodge, Kansas.

Page 9, Fort Dodge Barracks: Mrs. Henry B. Douglas, Saddle River, N. J.

Page 9, Fort Dodge, 1878: Kansas Soldiers' Home.

Page 10, Gen. W. T. Sherman: Kansas Soldiers' Home.

Page 10, Gen. N. A. Miles: U. S. Signal Corps, The National Archives, Washington, D. C.

Page 11, Scalped Hunter: Western History Collections, University of Oklahoma, Norman, Okla.

Page 26, Dodge City Plat: Dodge City Abstract & Investment Co.

Page 42, F. C. Zimmermann (young man): Mrs. Beatrice McClure and Ford County Historical Society, Dodge City.

Page 47, Prairie Grove Cemetery: Violet Watson, Dodge City.

Page 47, Statue: Denver Public Library Western Collection, Denver.

Page 50, Longhorn Steer: N. H. Rose, San Antonio, Tex.

Page 56, R. M. Wright: Dodge City Public Library, W. Wayne Duree Collection, Dodge City.

Page 64, Sketch of Dodge House: Regional History Division, Kenneth Spencer Research Library, University of Kansas, Lawrence, Kan.

Page 85, Stadium and Racetrack: D. P. Young, Dodge City.

Page 89, Bat Masterson and Wyatt Earp: Carolyn Lake, 3916 Portola Place, San Diego, Calif. 92103 (not to be reproduced without specific permission of copyright owner).

Page 91, Sketch of City Jail by Ado Hunnius: Spencer Research Library.

Page 97, Billy Dixon: Spencer Research Library.

Page 105, Theater Billing: Wyoming State Archives and Historical Department, Cheyenne, Wyo.

Page 143, James H. Kelley's Cane: Trohman L. Robinson, Dodge City.

Page 153, Reo Fire Truck: Violet Watson.

Page 154, College Buildings: St. Mary of the Plains College, Dodge City.

Page 154, St. Mary of the Plains Tornado Damage: Dodge City Public Library, Duree Collection.

Page 159, Riney Bridge Plaque: Lola Harper.

Page 163, Bicycle Club: Dodge City Public Library, Duree Collection.

Page 164, Dr. Samuel J. Crumbine: High Plains Publishers, Inc., Dodge City.

Page 166, City Hall and Ham Bell: Dodge City Public Library, Duree Collection.

Page 168, National Bank of Commerce: Dean R. Young, Dodge City.

Page 172, National Bank of Commerce: D. P. Young.

Page 172, National Bank of Commerce (interior): Dean R. Young.

Page 172, City Furniture Store: Dodge City Public Library, Duree Collection.

Page 173, Automobiles on Second Avenue: Violet Watson.

Page 173, Residential District: D. P. Young.

Page 173, Swimming Hole: D. P. Young.

Page 173, Cox's Barber Shop: Frank Cox, Dodge City.

Page 174, View from Third Ward School: Jay S. Andrews, Minneola, Kan.

Page 175, View from Third Ward School: Jay S. Andrews.

Page 178, Cyrus K. Holliday Locomotive: Santa Fe Railway, R. C. Bradley.

Page 179, Depot and Harvey House: Dodge City Public Library, Duree Collection.

Page 181, Front Street Demolition: Urban Renewal Agency, Dodge City.

Page 184, Tornado: Lola Harper.

Page 186, Premiere at Dodge Theater: Dodge City Chamber of Commerce.

Page 185, Movie Stars at Rear of Santa Fe Train: Dodge City Chamber of Commerce.

Page 186, Humphrey Bogart, Mayo Methot, and John Payne: Dodge City Chamber of Commerce.

Page 187, Swiss Newspaper Ad: Mrs. Louise B. Young, Dodge City.

Page 187, Japanese Review of *Gunsmoke*: Philip L. Newman, New York.

Page 188, Front Street Demolition, Urban Renewal Agency.

Page 190, Boot Hill Museum and Cemetery (east of city hall): Dodge City Chamber of Commerce.

Page 192, John F. Kennedy: Dr. Arnold H. Baum, Dodge City.

Notes

PREFACE

1 *Ford County Globe,* October 21, 1879.
2 Dodge City *Times,* August 11, 1877.
3 *Ibid.,* August 4, 1877.
4 *Globe,* June 17, 1879.
5 *Times,* December 29, 1877.
6 *Ibid.,* April 28, 1877.
7 *Ibid.,* July 6, 1878.
8 Stanley Vestal, *Queen of Cowtowns, Dodge City* (New York: Harper & Brothers, 1952).

CHAPTER I

1 Louise Barry, "Kansas Before 1854." *Kansas Historical Collections, L* (1967).
2 *Records of the War Department,* Letters Sent, 1866-1882, Fort Dodge, Kansas, November 24, 1866, quoted in David K. Strate, *Sentinel to the Cimarron* (Dodge City: High Plains Publishers, Inc., 1970).
3 Ralph K. Andrist, *The Long Death* (New York: Macmillan, 1964).

CHAPTER II

1 Joseph W. Snell and Don W. Wilson, "The Birth of the Atchison, Topeka and Santa Fe Railroad." *Kansas Historical Collections, LI* (1968).
2 Dodge City *Globe-Republican,* June 16, 1893.
3 George W. Brown, "Life and Adventures." *Kansas Historical Collections, XVII* (1926-28).
4 J. B. Edwards, Abilene, Kansas, letter sent to O. H. Simpson, Dodge City, dated November 18, 1925. Beeson Collection, Boot Hill Museum, Dodge City, Kansas.
5 George M. Hoover, "Some Reminiscences of the Early Days of Dodge City." Dodge City *Democrat,* June 19, 1903.
6 Ida Ellen Rath, *The Rath Trail* (Wichita: McCormick-Armstrong Co., Inc., 1961).
7 Edwards, *op. cit.*
8 Helen G. Gill, "The Establishment of Counties in Kansas." *Kansas Historical Collections, VIII* (1903-04).
9 A. T. Andreas and W. G. Cutler, *History of the State of Kansas* (Chicago, 1883).
10 George W. Reighard, interview with Merritt Beeson, February 7, 1934. Beeson Collection, Boot Hill Museum, Dodge City, Kansas.
11 Andreas & Cutler, *op. cit.*
12 *Ibid.*
13 Owen D. Wiggans, "History of Dodge City, Kansas." (M.A. thesis, Colorado State College, 1938); Dodge City *Democrat,* June 19, 1903.
14 Ernest Dewey, "He Slew the White Buffalo," Hutchinson (Kan.) *News-Herald,* June 17, 1951.

CHAPTER III

1 Dodge City *Times,* May 19, 1877.
2 Leavenworth *Daily Commercial,* October 14, 1872.
3 Dodge City *Globe-Republican,* June 30, 1898.
4 Dodge City *Democrat,* June 19, 1903.
5 *Ford County Globe,* February 10, 1880.
6 *Democrat,* June 19, 1903; Robert M. Wright, *Dodge City, the Cowboy Capital* (Wichita: Wichita Eagle Press, 1913).
7 Marion County *Record,* March 29, 1873.
8 *Times,* May 18, 1878; *Globe,* September 3, 1878.
9 Source not identified, quoted in Harry E. Chrisman, *Lost Trails of the Cimarron* (Denver, Sage Books, 1961).
10 *Times,* June 16, 1877.
11 *Ibid.,* June 8, 1878.
12 *Ibid.,* July 13, 1878.
13 *Ibid.,* June 16, 1877.
14 Kinsley *Graphic,* quoted in Dodge City *Times,* July 6, 1878.
15 Myra E. Hull, "Cowboy Ballads." *Kansas Historical Collections, XXV* (1939).
16 *Times,* June 16, 1877.
17 *Globe,* December 25, 1877.
18 *Times,* July 27, 1878.
19 Joseph W. Snell, footnote to Henry H. Raymond, "Diary of a Dodge City Buffalo Hunter." *Kansas Historical Collections, XLVIII* (1965).
20 *Globe-Republican,* September 13, 1906.
21 *Ford County Globe,* February 17, 1879.
22 *Times,* August 25, 1877.
23 *Ibid.,* July 21, 1877. (This excerpt has been used quite unfairly by some authors as proof of Wyatt Earp's disreputable character. Not so. There was little dishonor involved in slapping a drunken prostitute in the Dodge City of 1877. F.Y.)
24 *Ibid.,* July 28, August 18, August

25, 1877.

25 *Globe,* September 2, 1879.
26 *Times,* June 8, 1878.
27 *Ibid.,* June 9, 1877.
28 Eddie Foy and Alvin F. Harlow, *Clowning Through Life* (New York: E. P. Dutton & Company, 1928).
29 *Globe,* January 1, 1879.

CHAPTER IV

1 J. Marvin Hunter, ed., *The Trail Drivers of Texas* (Nashville: Cokesbury Press, 1925).
2 *Ibid.*
3 Dodge City *Times,* May 12, 1877.
4 *Ibid.,* July 21, 1877.
5 *Ibid.,* November 10, 1877.
6 Hunter, *op. cit.*
7 *Ford County Globe,* April 16, 1878.
8 Snell, footnote to Raymond Diary, *op. cit.*
9 *Times,* June 9, 1877.
10 *Ibid.,* February 2, 1878; *Globe,* February 5, 1878.
11 *Times,* June 8, 1878.
12 *Ibid.,* July 13, 1878.
13 Eddie Foy and Alvin F. Harlow, *Clowning Through Life* (New York: E. P. Dutton & Company, 1928).
14 *Globe,* August 13, 1878; *Times,* August 17, 1878.
15 Heinie Schmidt, interview with James J. Mangan, tape recorded November 5, 1960. Schmidt, a friend of H. B. Bell, is the author of a collection of historical anecdotes, *Ashes of My Campfire* (Dodge City: Journal, Inc., 1952).
16 Stanley Vestal, *Queen of Cowtowns, Dodge City* (New York: Harper & Brothers, 1952).
17 Robert M. Wright, *Dodge City, the Cowboy Capital* (Wichita: Wichita Eagle Press, 1913).
18 *Globe,* January 7, 1879.
19 *Times,* February 22, 1879.
20 *Globe,* April 8, 1879.
21 *Times,* April 20, 1882.
22 *Globe,* April 8, 1879.
23 *Ibid.,* April 15, May 6, 13, 20, 1879; *Times,* May 10, 17, 31, 1879.
24 *Times,* May 10, 1879.
25 Stuart N. Lake, *Wyatt Earp, Frontier Marshal* (Boston: Houghton Mifflin Company, 1931).
26 Spearville *News,* July 26, 1879.
27 *Globe,* July 22, 1879.
28 *Ibid.,* February 17, 1880.
29 *Times,* April 14, 1881.

CHAPTER V

1 Obituary of A. B. Webster, Hays *Globe-Democrat,* n.d., Beeson Collection, Boot Hill Museum, Dodge City, Kansas.
2 *Ford County Globe,* March 30, 1880.
3 *Ibid.,* May 10, 1881.
4 Tenth United States Census, Ford County, Kansas, June 22, 1880.
5 Caldwell *Commercial,* April 21, 1881, quoted in Nyle H. Miller and Joseph W. Snell, *Why the West Was Wild* (Topeka: Kansas State Historical Society, 1963). (This quotation actually reads: "I know you are healed; now fight." An obvious typographical error, it must have been intended to read: "heeled," meaning "armed, as with a gun." F.Y.)
6 Dodge City *Times,* October 6, November 3, 1881. (Many authors claim that Luke Short's saloon war was the result of enmity between the Long Branch saloon and the Alamo next door — owned by Mayor A. B.

Webster. At the outset of the saloon fracas in April, 1883, the Long Branch's neighbor was called the Stock Exchange saloon; Webster was no longer the owner, and was not the mayor — small details, but a few of many mixups in the tales of old Dodge. F.Y.)

7 *Ibid.,* June 22, 1882.
8 *Ibid.,* April 26, 1883.
9 Topeka *Daily Capital,* May 18, 1883, quoted in Miller & Snell, *op. cit.*
10 "Governors' Correspondence," archives division, Kansas State Historical Society, quoted in Miller & Snell, *op. cit.*
11 "Governors' Correspondence," quoted in Miller & Snell, *op. cit.*
12 *Ibid.*
13 Topeka *Daily Commonwealth,* June 8, 1883, quoted in Miller & Snell, *op. cit.*
14 *Times,* September 6, 1883. (Many authorities to the contrary, this ordinance was not actually passed until after the conclusion of the saloon war. F.Y.)
15 Kansas City (Mo.) *Evening Star,* May 9, 1883, quoted in Miller & Snell, *op. cit.*
16 Dodge City *Democrat,* July 18, 1885.
17 Dodge City *Globe Live Stock Journal,* July 22, 1884.
18 Topeka *Commonwealth,* August 3, 1884, quoted in Miller & Snell, *op. cit.*
19 *Globe Live Stock Journal,* July 22, 1884.
20 *Ibid.,* May 12, 1885; *Democrat,* May 16, 1885.
21 *Democrat,* May 16, 1885.
22 *Ibid.,* July 18, 1885.
23 *Globe Live Stock Journal,* April 21, 1885.
24 *Ibid.,* June 9, 1885.
25 *Ibid.,* January 5, 1886.
26 Dodge City *Globe-Republican,* April 26, 1906.

Bibliography

BOOKS

Andreas, A. T., and W. G. Cutler. *History of the State of Kansas.* Chicago, 1883.

Botkin, B. A., ed. *A Treasury of American Folklore.* New York: Crown Publishers, 1944.

Chrisman, Harry E. *Lost Trails of the Cimarron.* Denver: Sage Books, 1961.

Dobie, J. Frank, *The Longhorns.* Boston: Little Brown and Company, 1941.

Dodge, Richard I. *The Hunting Grounds of the Great West.* London: Chatto and Windus, 1877.

Dodge, Richard I. *Plains of the Great West.* New York: Archer House, Inc., 1959.

Dykstra, Robert A. *The Cattle Towns.* New York: Alfred A. Knopf, 1968.

Foy, Eddie, and Alvin F. Harlow. *Clowning Through Life.* New York: E. P. Dutton and Company, 1928.

Haines, Francis. *The Buffalo.* New York: Thomas Y. Crowell Company, 1970.

Hunter, J. Marvin, ed. *The Trail Drivers of Texas.* Nashville: Cokesbury Press, 1925.

Kansas Historical Collections, Topeka.

Lake, Stuart N. *Wyatt Earp, Frontier Marshal.* Boston: Houghton Mifflin Company, 1931.

Miller, Nyle H., and Joseph W. Snell. *Why the West Was Wild.* Topeka: Kansas State Historical Society, 1963.

Rath, Ida Ellen. *The Rath Trail.* Wich-

ita: McCormick-Armstrong Co., Inc., 1961.

Schmidt, Heinie. *Ashes of My Campfire.* Dodge City: Journal, Inc., 1952.

Strate, David K. *Sentinel to the Cimarron.* Dodge City: High Plains Publishers, Inc., 1970.

Streeter, Floyd B. *Prairie Trails and Cow Towns.* Boston: Chapman and Grimes, Inc., 1936.

Taft, Robert. *Artists and Illustrators of the Old West.* New York: Charles Scribner's Sons, 1953.

Vestal, Stanley. *Queen of Cowtowns, Dodge City.* New York: Harper and Brothers, 1952.

Wiggans, Owen D. "History of Dodge City, Kansas." (M. A. thesis, Colorado State College, 1938).

Wright, Robert M. *Dodge City, the Cowboy Capital.* Wichita: Wichita Eagle Press, 1913.

NEWSPAPERS

Most newspapers published in Dodge City since 1874 were used for study and reference material. These include the *Messenger* (1874-1875), *Times* (1876-1893), *Ford County Globe* (1877-1884), *Globe Live Stock Journal* (1884-1889), *Democrat* (1884-1905), *Kansas Cowboy* (1884-1885), *Globe-Republican* (1889-1910), *Globe* (1910-1911), and *Daily Globe* (1911-1971).

Index

This "bird's eye view" of Dodge City, drawn by a commercial artist in 1882, corresponds accurately with photographs, maps, and title records of the same period. At left it shows the new school house on Boot Hill, at top center, four churches on Gospel Hill and John Mueller's stone house surrounded by trees, and at far right, the railroad's cattle loading pens.

Published by J. J. Stoner, Madison, Wis.

1. Court House.
2. School House.
3. U. S. Signal Service Office.
4. Odd Fellows Hall.
5. A. T. & S. F R. R. Depot.
6. Post Office, Lloyd Shinn, P. M.
7. Dodge City Grist Mill, H. F. May & Co., Prop's.
X—Methodist Episcopal Church.
A—Presbyterian   "
B—Roman Catholic   "
C—Union   "

BIRD'S

DODGE C

COUNTY SEA

POP